Suicide Assessment and Treatment Planning

A Strengths-Based Approach

John Sommers-Flanagan
Rita Sommers-Flanagan

AMERICAN COUNSELING
ASSOCIATION

6101 Stevenson Avenue, Suite 600 • Alexandria, VA 22304 • www.counseling.org

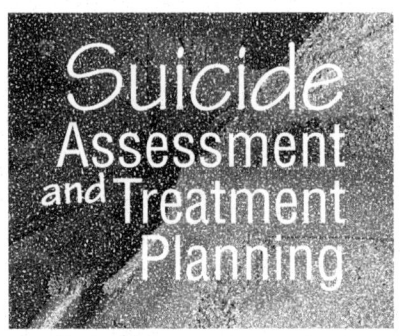

Copyright © 2021 by the American Counseling Association. All rights reserved. Printed in the United States of America. Except as permitted under the United States Copyright Act of 1976, no part of this publication may be reproduced or distributed in any form or by any means, or stored in a database or retrieval system, without the written permission of the publisher.

American Counseling Association
6101 Stevenson Avenue, Suite 600 • Alexandria, VA 22304

Associate Publisher • Carolyn C. Baker

Digital and Print Development Editor • Nancy Driver

Senior Production Manager • Bonny E. Gaston

Copy Editor • Beth Ciha

Cover and text design by Bonny E. Gaston

Library of Congress Cataloging-in-Publication Data

Names: Sommers-Flanagan, John, 1957– author. | Sommers-Flanagan, Rita, 1953– author.
Title: Suicide assessment and treatment planning : a strengths-based approach / John Sommers-Flanagan and Rita Sommers-Flanagan.
Description: Alexandria, VA : American Counseling Association, [2021] | Includes bibliographical references and index.
Identifiers: LCCN 2020041407 | ISBN 9781556204050 (paperback)
Subjects: LCSH: Suicidal behavior—Diagnosis | Suicidal behavior—Treatment
Classification: LCC RC569 .S64 2021 | DDC 616.85/8445--dc23
LC record available at https://lccn.loc.gov/2020041407

Dedication

We dedicate this book to all the school, mental health, health care professionals, and students who are so busy saving lives that they will probably skip this dedication. We see you, and we honor you and your work.

Table of Contents

Preface	vii
About the Authors	xi
Acknowledgments	xiii

Chapter 1
Emotional Preparation — 1

Chapter 2
Competence and Ethics — 21

Chapter 3
Suicide Assessment — 49

Chapter 4
The Emotional Dimension — 87

Chapter 5
The Cognitive Dimension — 111

Chapter 6
The Interpersonal Dimension — 139

Chapter 7
The Physical Dimension — 163

Chapter 8
The Cultural-Spiritual Dimension — 187

Chapter 9
   The Behavioral Dimension   213

Chapter 10
   The Contextual Dimension   235

   References   245
   Index   277

Writing a book about suicide may not have been our best idea ever. Rita made the point more than once that reading and writing about suicide at the depth necessary to write a helpful book can affect one's mood in a downward direction. She was right, of course. Her rightness inspired us to pay attention to the other side of the coin, so we decided to integrate positive psychology and the happiness literature into this book. As is often the case when grappling with matters of humanity, focusing on suicide led us to a deeper understanding of suicide's complementary dialectic—a meaningful and fully lived life—and that has been a very good thing.

Before diving into these pages, please consider the following.

Do the Self-Care Thing

In the first chapter, we strongly emphasize how important it is to practice self-care when working with clients who are suicidal. Immersing ourselves in the suicide literature required a balancing focus on positive psychology and wellness. While you are reading this book and exploring suicide, you cannot help but be impacted emotionally, and we cannot overstate the importance of you taking care of yourself throughout this process and into the future. You are the instrument through which you provide care for others, and so we highly encourage you to repeatedly do the self-care thing.

What Is a Strengths-Based Approach?

Many people have asked, "What on earth do you mean by a strengths-based approach to suicide assessment and treatment planning?" In response, we usually meander in and out of various bullet points, relational dynamics, and assessment procedures and try to emphasize that the approach is more than just strengths based—it is also wellness oriented and holistic. By "strengths based," we mean that we recognize and nurture the existing and potential strengths of our clients. By "wellness oriented," we mean that we believe in incorporating wellness activities into counseling and life. By "holistic," we mean that we focus on emotional, cognitive, interpersonal, physical, cultural-spiritual, behavioral, and contextual dimensions of living.

You will find the following strengths-based, wellness-oriented, and holistic principles woven into every chapter of this book:

1. Historically, suicidal ideation has been socially constructed as sinful, illegal, or a terribly frightening and bad illness. In contrast, we believe that suicidal ideation is a normal variation on human experience that typically stems from difficult environmental circumstances and excruciating emotional pain. Rather than fear client disclosures of suicidality, we welcome these disclosures because they offer an opportunity to connect deeply with distressed clients and provide therapeutic support.
2. Although we believe that risk factors, warning signs, protective factors, and suicide assessment instruments are important, we value relationship connections with clients over predictive formulae and technical procedures.
3. We believe that trust, empathy, collaboration, and rapport will improve the reliability, validity, and utility of data gathered during assessments. Consequently, we embrace the principles of therapeutic assessment.
4. We believe that counseling practitioners need to ask directly about and explore suicidal ideation using a normalizing frame or other sophisticated and empathic interviewing strategies.
5. We believe that traditional approaches to suicide assessment and treatment are excessively oriented toward psychopathology. To compensate for this pathology orientation, we explicitly value and ask about clients' positive experiences, personal strengths, and coping strategies.
6. We believe that the narrow pursuit of psychopathology causes clinicians to neglect a more complete assessment and case formulation of the whole person. To compensate, we use a holistic, seven-dimension model to create a broader understanding of what is hurting and what is helping in each individual client's life.

7. We value the positive emphasis of safety planning and coping skills development over the negative components of no-suicide contracts and efforts to eliminate suicidal thoughts.

The Book's Organizing Themes

This book includes 10 chapters organized to build on one another in ways that are consistent with our understanding of the research literature in suicide theory, research, and practice. We begin our discussion of the seven dimensions with the emotional dimension, because, as Edwin Shneidman (1993) wrote, psychological or emotional distress is the primary driving force at the heart of suicide. In our model, all risk factors and life dimensions contribute in some way or another to deep and excruciating emotional distress, and deep and excruciating emotional distress pushes people toward suicide.

Language Use

This book is written for counseling professionals and other professionals who work directly or indirectly with people who are suicidal. As a consequence, although we usually refer to *counselors* and *counseling*, we also use the words *clinician* or *practitioner* to recognize members of other disciplines who provide counseling or mental health services. When referring to the people who receive counseling or treatment, we usually use the word *client*, but we also use *student* or *patient* as a method of incorporating school counselors and health professionals who work in medical settings.

In all cases, we strive to use person-first language. Instead of reading the phrase *suicidal clients*, you will read the slightly more cumbersome *clients who are suicidal*. Using person-first language is essential to separating the problem from the person and is consistent with the constructionist or social constructionist theory that undergirds the strengths-based approach.

We avoid using language and phrases that have a history of offending people. For example, unless quoting others, we do not use the phrase *commit suicide*. We try to use positive language to refer to people who are suicidal. We occasionally use the language of mental disorders, but because we do not want to tightly construct suicide or mental disorders as internalized pathological states, more often we avoid negative labeling. These ways in which we are using language are foundational to our strengths-based approach.

Information in this book is broadly research based. When discussing evidentiary support, we use the following terminology:

Empirically supported is used when there is substantial and specific research support; *evidence based* is used when there is general research support, but that support may not be especially robust or specific. We avoid using *best practice* because this phrase implies direct comparisons and rank orderings of all potential practices (which have not been done) and is often used to communicate normative practice standards rather than procedures with underlying empirical support.

Incorporating Positive Psychology

Positive psychology is broadly defined as the scientific study of well-being and human experiences that contribute to a well-lived life. To balance our focus on suicide and to practice a strengths-based orientation in this book, in each chapter we include a pullout box on how to use a specific positive psychology intervention to elevate mood. We call these sidebars *Wellness Practices*. Each one is founded on research or common sense and can be applied to you—as a practitioner—or used therapeutically with your students, clients, or patients. We encourage you to try these wellness practices with a hopeful spirit of experimentation.

Case Material

Case material in this book is used to illustrate the many ways in which suicidality manifests and the many ways in which providers can work with clients and students. All cases are anonymous; they are often composites of multiple cases. Age, sex, gender, and other identifying factors were sometimes changed. Several cases are adapted from video simulations (for a three-part, 7.5 hour video training, see: https://www.psychotherapy.net/video/suicidal-clients-series.

About the Authors

John Sommers-Flanagan, PhD, is a professor of counseling at the University of Montana. He is the author or coauthor of more than 100 professional publications, including the books *Tough Kids, Cool Counseling* (2007, American Counseling Association), *Clinical Interviewing* (6th ed., 2017, Wiley), and *Counseling and Psychotherapy Theories in Context and Practice* (3rd ed., 2018, Wiley). When not immersed in writing, speaking, teaching, and researching, John keeps busy watering the zucchini, picking beans, and starring in videos along with his grandchildren. He also excels at making pancakes, waffles, and quiche. He was drawn to writing this book because of his earnest belief that effective suicide assessment and intervention simply must become more positive, skilled, and compassionate. You can find what he is up to on his blog, https://johnsommersflanagan.com/.

Rita Sommers-Flanagan, PhD, is an author, counselor, passive solar advocate, and professor emerita of counseling at the University of Montana, with many published books and articles. She enjoys collecting rocks and driftwood, jogging, blogging, and contemplating the meaning of life. Her experiences with and views about suicide have been shaped and changed by clients, colleagues, students, and friends who have had to cope with the phenomenon of suicide clinically and/or personally. She looks forward to writing further in this area, including addressing end-of-life policies and practices as they intersect with the materials in this book. In the meantime, you can follow her on her blogs: https://drbossypants.wordpress.com/author/ritasf13/ and https://godcomesby.com/.

As coauthors, the Sommers-Flanagans have stylistic differences that are distinct but usually complementary. John dives way too far down various rabbit holes, skims and reads too many journal articles and book chapters, jots notes on several hundred different small pieces of paper, and then begins a word processing version of loose associations about arcane facts. (Did you know that suicide rates among males older than 85 in the United States are 13.17 times higher than suicide rates among females older than 85 in the United States? Should we include results from that one cool study showing that trait impulsiveness is not associated with increased suicide attempts but that negative state-triggered impulsiveness is linked to suicide attempts?) At some point, Rita nudges John out of his loose associations and research reveries, takes her commonsense garden clippers to John's meandering prose, pulls a few of his worst puns, and voilà! After mostly agreeing with each other's brilliance, they send the resulting draft out to a plethora of volunteer readers, collect feedback, marvel at the diversity in perspective, integrate the input, get organizing and copyediting assistance through the publisher, and end up with pretty much what you are about to read.

Acknowledgments

This book was made possible by the amazing work of many researchers, practitioners, suicide survivors, students, clients, and suicidologists who came before us and illuminated the way. We are indebted to all of them. We are also grateful to the American Counseling Association's editorial team—Carolyn Baker, Nancy Driver, Bonny Gaston, and others—who have helped make our words clearer and our points sharper. A big thanks to Pete MacFadyen, Katie DiBerardinis, and Robin Hill of the Big Sky Youth Empowerment Program for their support of our work and their commitment to suicide prevention in Montana. Thanks also to Victor Yalom of Psychotherapy.net and Kelley Donisthorpe of the University of Montana.

We offer special thanks to Erin Binkley of Wake Forest University and Victor Chang of Southern Oregon University for their thorough reviews and detailed feedback. Thanks also to the many professionals who volunteered to read a chapter or two or the whole manuscript. Your insightful comments and feedback have resulted in a better book:

- Alexis Cancemi – Alexis Mental Health, North Miami Beach, Florida
- Amanda Tashjian – University of Arizona
- Benjamin Willis – University of Scranton
- Beronica Salazar – Northwest Nazarene University
- Cara Metz – Ashford University
- Christie Nelson – University of North Carolina–Charlotte
- Claudia Sadler-Gerhardt – Ashland Theological Seminary

Dari Tahani – University of Toledo
Devyn Savitsky – Ohio University
Diane Shea – Holy Family University
Erin M. Hopper – Liberty University
Jill Schott – Onward Behavioral Health
Jo-Ann Sanders – Heidelberg University
John Harrichand – State University of New York–Brockport
Julie Williams – Thrive Counseling & Consultation, Tampa, Florida
Kara Hurt-Avila – Montana State University
Keiko Sano – Antioch University–Seattle
Kenneth Messina – Slippery Rock University
Kristin Bruns – Youngstown State University
Kristopher K. Garza – Texas A&M University–Kingsville
Latoya S. Moss – Savannah College of Art and Design
Laura I. Hodges – Troy University Montgomery
Laura M. Schmuldt – University of the Cumberlands
Melissa Sanders-DeVillier – University of the Cumberlands
Michelle Santiago – Moravian University
Molly Stehn – Webster University
Nicholas Rudgear – Grand Canyon University
Patricia Brenner – Kutztown University of Pennsylvania
Philip Gnilka – Virginia Commonwealth University
Robin S. Archer – Mindful Paths
Sara Carpenter – University of Texas–Austin
Shalini J. Mathew – Northern State University
Tara Gray – Prescott College
Teah Moore – Spalding University
Tracie Self – Ascend Therapeutic and Wellness Services

Chapter 1

Emotional Preparation

All by itself, the word *suicide* activates anxiety for most mental health professionals. Imagine the following scenario:

> Your new Monday morning client shows up early for her 9 a.m. appointment. Her name is Alina. She is a 29-year-old lesbian woman. She lives alone, is unemployed, and complains that "life is impossible" without a partner. Alina is primarily of Croatian descent. Her family of origin lives about 500 miles away; Alina says she is glad to have distance from her family because "they're all about judging me."
>
> Alina talks about her chronic struggle with anxiety and depression and says, "I'm not sure anything can help me feel better." She discloses that she wishes she could "go to sleep and not wake up." You ask directly, "Have you had thoughts about suicide?" Alina admits to intermittent suicidality but denies an active plan. She says that even though she wants to stay alive, "thinking about suicide gives me a mental escape in case life gets worse." Alina made a suicide attempt about 6 months ago using a combination of pills and alcohol. She ended up in the emergency department of her local hospital. She was glad to survive her attempt, which gives you hope about her motivation to live. After her suicide attempt, Alina was on antidepressant medications and had three counseling sessions, but she did not find either treatment helpful. She tells you she has heard you are a good counselor but that she would rather not take any medications.
>
> Although you are worried about Alina's suicidality, you also feel positive about her openness and motivation to work in counseling.

Before the session ends, you and Alina develop a safety plan, you get a signed release of information form so you can communicate with her physician, and you make a request for her previous treatment records. As she leaves, you feel confident about her short-term safety and her commitment to treatment, but she is a client you will be sure to think about during the week.

As Alina's counselor, you might feel uncomfortable because she has described several significant suicide risk factors. She has current suicidal ideation and a recent previous attempt. She feels socially isolated. Her family has not supported her sexual identity. She has symptoms of depression combined with high personal distress. All of these factors—and more—contribute to your concerns.

Cases like Alina's naturally ignite self-doubt and anxiety in clinicians. But cases like Alina's also hold great potential. If you connect with Alina, the two of you develop a therapeutic relationship, and she responds well to your work together, you might experience immense gratification. As a mental health professional, what could feel better than helping a distressed and struggling person through an extremely difficult time? For many of us, the chance to help people like Alina is exactly why we chose this challenging professional path.

Our goals for this book are to increase your self-awareness, knowledge, and skills for working effectively with clients who are suicidal. Whether you are working with a 16-year-old version of Alina in a school setting or a grieving 70-year-old who is considering whether life is worth living, we want to help you feel more prepared, comfortable, and competent to work with people who are suicidal.

In the 21st century, counseling professionals are more likely than ever to work with youth and adults who are suicidal (Binkley & Leibert, 2015; Lund et al., 2017). This is partly because the latest data available indicate that suicide rates in the United States have increased by 42% (from 10.0 deaths per 100,000 individuals in 1999 to 14.2 deaths per 100,000 individuals in 2018; American Foundation for Suicide Prevention, 2020). Although the relative per capita increase in suicide of 42% is troubling, the raw numbers are even worse. In 1999, an estimated 29,180 Americans died by suicide. In comparison, in 2018 (the latest year for which data are available), there were 48,344 deaths by suicide. This represents a 65.7% increase in the raw number of deaths by suicide over 19 years. Suicide is the 10th leading cause of death in the United States and the second leading cause of death among youth and young adults ages 10 to 34 years (Hedegaard et al., 2020).

Although we do not currently know how recent events like the coronavirus (COVID-19) pandemic or ongoing world events like climate change will affect suicide rates, most health professionals, suicidologists, and sociologists predict that social distancing, unemployment, and economic hardships will adversely affect mental health and contribute to further increases in suicidality, suicide attempts, and death by suicide (Bryan et al., 2020). The need for providers who can conduct suicide assessments and interventions will likely only increase in the coming years (Copelan, 2020).

Not only have suicide rates increased, but suicide attempts have also increased (to approximately 1.4 million in 2018; American Foundation for Suicide Prevention, 2020), and more clients and students than ever are talking about suicide. Many different cultural and sociological phenomena have combined to make it more likely that teenagers and young adults will use the word *suicidal* when describing their emotional pain or personal distress. Media productions like the feature film *Thirteen* (Levy-Hint et al., 2003), the Netflix television series *13 Reasons Why* (Season 1 released in 2017; Incaprera, 2017), and the proliferation of publications and internet websites oriented toward self-mutilation and suicidality contribute to increased thoughts about suicide (e.g., Asher, 2007; see also Ybarra, 2015). All of these factors speak to a need to redouble our efforts to gather knowledge and develop skills for working with people struggling with suicidal thoughts and impulses.

Throughout this book, we emphasize that suicidality does not represent a deviant or pathological state. During difficult times it is not uncommon for people to consider suicide an option (J. Sommers-Flanagan, 2018a). Counseling can help clients reduce or eliminate suicidal thoughts and urges. However, although we believe deeply in suicide prevention, we also respect human autonomy and individuals' right to die by suicide. Consequently, this book does not provide guidance for working with clients who have terminal illnesses and wish for compassionate assistance to end their lives. There may be some crossover, but along with Freedenthal (2018), we believe that those circumstances represent a distinctly different clinical domain.

Getting Ready

Despite rising rates, death by suicide is a rare event (about 14 to 15 deaths per 100,000 people in the United States in 2018; American Foundation for Suicide Prevention, 2020). However, early and often throughout your career, you are likely to see many students and mental health clients who struggle with suicidality (Binkley & Leibert, 2015; Roush et al., 2018). Being ready to respond competently and calmly to suicidal thoughts and impulses is essential. As Joiner (2005) wrote, "Suicide is an urgent issue—it kills people—but urgency need not entail panic" (p. 17). Becoming and remaining competent is your best antidote to panic.

Practical Realities

Often, as in the case of Alina, concerns about suicide emerge partway into a session, even though suicidality was not the primary reason for the referral or meeting. Other times suicidality will be the immediate issue demanding your focus. In still other scenarios, your client will not mention distress or suicide until near the end of the session, leaving you with very little time to deal with a very big issue.

As you develop competence for handling suicide scenarios, at a minimum, you have your own attitudes and values to examine; assessment skills to learn, practice, and memorize; professional and ethical responsibilities to manage; intervention strategies to consider; and many other competencies to acquire and fine-tune. No wonder this is a stressful domain for most counselors. If thinking about these responsibilities causes you anxiety, you are not alone. Most health and mental health care professionals rate suicide assessment, management, and treatment planning as one of their greatest stressors (Binkley & Leibert, 2015; Maris, 2019). When clients talk about suicide, it is natural to begin worrying about a range of issues, including potential hospitalization and your responsibilities for keeping clients and students alive.

Increased suicide rates have translated into increased demand for competent professional assessment and treatment services. Unfortunately, suicide assessment and treatment competencies have not been systematically integrated into the training curricula of students in counseling, psychology, social work, nursing, and psychiatry (Cramer et al., 2013; Granello, 2010a; Morris & Minton, 2012). This lack of systematic training in suicide assessment and treatment has relevance for you and your practice. Along with most of the mental health and health care workforce, you may feel uncertain about suicide assessments, unclear about how to develop suicide-specific treatment plans, and uninformed about research-supported interventions for clients and students who are suicidal.

Before reading further, take a moment to check in with yourself. You know that this is a book about suicide assessment and treatment planning, but even that obvious fact deserves reflection. Although we are taking a positive, wellness-oriented approach, content in the following pages and chapters can and will be activating. You will find yourself reacting to the material.

In many places, we write about suicide directly, using actual and constructed suicide cases as well as composite and hypothetical suicide scenarios (note that identifying information is removed or modified to protect confidentiality). Our purpose is to prepare you to work in counseling situations in which suicidality is a concern. We write about suicide in provocative ways for several reasons:

1. You never know whether or when your next client or student will be suicidal. We believe that you can and should be prepared to address suicide and suicidality with competence and confidence.
2. Competence begins with understanding your own attitudes, beliefs, and values. Throughout this book, we will intermittently ask you to check in with yourself and to notice, accept, and manage your thoughts, emotions, and behavioral impulses.
3. Working with clients who are suicidal is emotionally activating. Becoming comfortable with suicide as an issue in counseling is a developmental process that takes time and practice. One way of looking at the content of this book is as an exposure experience that will improve your ability to self-regulate when facing crisis situations as a counseling professional.

If your goals are to become comfortable, confident, and competent when working with clients who are suicidal—and we hope these are your goals—your best route is to strengthen your professional suicide assessment and treatment competencies. Rigorous and direct exposure to suicide-related material in this book and others, along with workshop training and supervision, will get you on track toward professional competence in suicide assessment and treatment.

In the end, we want you to know—in your head and in your heart—that you have the knowledge and skills to provide effective suicide assessment and treatment. Having confidence in your knowledge and skills will be emotionally stabilizing; it will also help you develop a positive and optimistic attitude toward suicide intervention and prevention that you can then pass on to your clients and students.

Emotional Responses to the Topic of Suicide

We began facilitating workshops, lectures, and trainings on suicide assessment and intervention in the 1990s. One presentation stands out. We asked about 80 school and mental health professionals, "How many of you have worked with clients or students who are suicidal?" Nearly everyone raised their hand. We followed up with, "How many of you have worked with a client who died by suicide?" About 15 hands went up. We asked how many had faced more than one client death by suicide; a few hands hesitantly went up. After thanking the group, we shared our own experiences and then transitioned to talking about coping strategies for professionals when clients complete suicide.

While talking, we noticed activity in the back of the room. Rose, a colleague we knew well, stood up and slipped out. Rose was a licensed mental health professional, an unflappable woman with a reputation for working with the toughest teens in town. We did not make much of her exit, but later Rose contacted us. "Sorry about leaving. You got to me. When you started talking about clients dying, I had to get out. I've had too many. Maybe I haven't dealt with some of my losses."

Regardless of your experience, suicide is a difficult topic, and emotional reactions run deep. Your own reactions may link to values, religious beliefs, losses, or future fears. Maybe you have had a friend, client, or family member die by suicide. In such situations, waves of painful emotions might come up whenever suicide is mentioned. Or you may struggle with suicidal thoughts yourself. No matter your background, conversations about suicide will activate or trigger your unique emotional response. Gaining experiences can reduce the intensity of your emotional responses to suicide scenarios, but there is also a chance it might magnify them. Either way, recognizing and having a plan for coping with your emotional responses will make you a more competent, ethical professional (Corey et al., 2018).

Professional Self-Care

Rose left the suicide workshop after recognizing that her emotional bucket was full. She stopped listening and removed herself from the room. She realized that she needed to take care of herself. We recommend that as you read this book and work with people who are suicidal, you weave lifestyle strategies for managing the input of stressful information into your life.

Stop Reading

Be sure to follow Rose's example and stop reading if you need to. During suicide workshops and college classes, we tell people that to avoid being triggered, they can do what our teenage clients do: Just stop listening to us. Suicide information overload happens. One method for dealing with overload is to stop the input, step back, and take time to absorb and regroup.

If you are an avid reader, you can get swept into information about death and suicide and forget to take a break. Planning intermittent breaks from this book and other suicide-related material is wise. You can use the Pomodoro technique: Set a timer for 20 or 30 minutes, and then take a break. Consider inserting a fun, creative, social, or reflective activity into your break time.

You can use a variation on this "stop reading" approach during counseling sessions. For example, if you are feeling overwhelmed in a session, it is perfectly reasonable to take a break from information gathering and instead focus on coping in the moment. You might say something like "When we're talking about intense topics in counseling, we should also practice positive coping strategies at the same time. So let's pause, take some breaths, and then talk about how we can weave coping strategies like deep breathing and problem-solving into our session."

Taking breaks is one coping technique, but not the only one. We recommend having a variety of strategies for self-care. Based on numerous research studies, Norcross and Vandenbos (2018) identified effective strategies that professionals use to manage stress. What follows is our version of Norcross and Vandenbos's recommendations.

Recognize the Hazards

Facing and talking about death is an emotional undertaking. Do not expect to read this book without experiencing some distress. Humans are not built to continually focus on suicide and death. If you would rather avoid topics of suicide and death, join the club. You are not being weak. Recognizing and accepting that too much focus on suicide and human mortality can be hazardous to well-being is a healthy and reasonable start.

Once you have admitted that this is not easy, then you can take steps to address the dangers and make accommodations for yourself as necessary. The sections below offer suggestions, but you know yourself and what you need, so you may want to make your own list.

Intentionally Focus on Positive and Rewarding Life Experiences
Professionals who cope effectively with powerful life stressors do not wait for positive experiences to come to them—they weave health-enhancing activities into their daily lives. As a counselor, you will hear harrowing client stories and be susceptible to vicarious traumatization (Foreman, 2018; Trippany et al., 2004). To care for yourself and to be a positive role model for clients, it is essential that you integrate healthy habits into your life. To inspire you to embrace positivity, at the end of every chapter in this book we feature one activity from the positive psychology literature that you can use yourself and/or offer your clients. We call these activities *Wellness Practices* (see Wellness Practice 1.1).

Beyond the Three Good Things activity in Wellness Practice 1.1, you can explore, through journaling, discussion, or counseling, what brings you joy, laughter, and gratification. When your busy life interferes with joyful or positive activities, you may need to post sticky notes or set your personal electronic device to remind yourself to focus on the joyful and positive. As professionals, we can get so caught up in helping others that sometimes we need explicit reminders to use positive interventions with ourselves.

Use a Variety of Self-Care Strategies
A single self-care strategy will not work as the best solution for everyone; we all have our own preferred coping techniques. The best way to cope with stress and stay healthy is to develop a smorgasbord of stress management and self-care strategies (J. R. Nelson et al., 2018). If you love exercise, that is great, but you cannot exercise incessantly. You need other activities in your stress management toolbox. Try meditation; support groups; recreational pursuits; your own personal counseling; gourmet food; excellent movies or concerts; spiritual, religious, or social justice groups; or whatever alternatives appeal to you. Your self-care mantra should be to use what works for you—and then keep expanding your repertoire.

What most people find especially health enhancing is to flex their personal choice-making muscles. The exact thing you do hardly matters. What matters is that you intentionally override natural tendencies toward lethargy, inactivity, or self-destructive choices. Free online apps that promote healthy behaviors include (a) 7 Minute Workout, (b) Happy Habits: Choose Happiness,

Wellness Practice 1.1
Three Good Things (or Three Blessings)

Positive psychology researchers have identified at least a dozen evidence-based activities that increase happiness and well-being. Martin Seligman (2002) developed one of the first and most well-known happiness activities; he called it Three Good Things. Three Good Things can work for you or for your clients.

The Three Good Things assignment is implemented each night, before going to bed, and goes like this: "Write down three good things that happened and why you think they happened" (Seligman et al., 2006, p. 776). (You can find a 1-minute video of Seligman describing the activity at https://www.youtube.com/watch?v=ZOGAp9dw8Ac.)

According to Seligman, after doing this for a week, most people continue doing the Three Good Things activity because it feels so good. Intentionally focusing on good things helps orient people toward the positive, but perhaps even more important, asking individuals to reflect on why the good things happen seems to remedy the human tendency to ruminate on daily mistakes. Contemplating why good things happen initiates a process of ruminating on the positive.

Clients who are deeply depressed may reject the idea that anything good could be happening. If so, we recommend you consider shifting the language to something your client views as more possible. For example, instead of monitoring for three good things, clients can be asked to monitor for three "not so bad" things. However you frame it, we recommend that you experiment with this positive psychology activity for yourself and for your clients.

(c) Sleep Better, (d) Headspace, (e) Calm, (f) Happy Now, (g) Pzizz, and (h) Inner Balance.

Manage Your Environment

Achieving complete control of your environment is impossible, but there is solid research on stimulus control as a tool for resisting temptation and triggering healthy behaviors (Quinn et al., 2010). Stimulus control means making sure your environment prompts positive behaviors; it might mean a pair of running shoes by the door, healthy snacks in your desk, or your best friend in your

Favorites or on your speed-dial. Because you know yourself best, strive to create an environment that not only is comfortable but also will prompt you to engage in healthy behaviors.

Accept Your Distress and Engage in Self-Soothing Behaviors
If you are feeling distressed, one healthy response is to find a safe time and place to accept and explore the emotion. First, notice the distress and accept it. There is no shame in being distressed. Then, when you are ready, ask yourself, "When I'm upset, what helps me calm down?" The answer might include going for a walk, breathing deeply, coloring, or holding hands with a friend or romantic partner. Several forms of counseling require that clients find their safe space before facing difficult or traumatic memories (Shapiro, 2001; J. Sommers-Flanagan & Sommers-Flanagan, 2018). As you read this material, consider what you can do to soothe and calm yourself when the content gets intense. One caveat here: We recommend that you remove the use of mind-altering substances for self-soothing from your list. Although using substances for recreational purposes is a reasonable personal choice, relying on substances for self-comfort is a bad idea in the long run.

Practice What You Preach
Many school and mental health professionals benefit from obtaining their own personal counseling or therapy. We recall listening with great interest to a famous behavior therapist speak of his preference for the emotional focus of gestalt therapy. He used behavioral approaches in his own clinical practice, but when he went for personal therapy, he chose experientially oriented counselors and psychotherapists who helped him explore deep emotions in the here and now. We hope that like this unusual behavior therapist who liked gestalt therapy, you will be open to pursuing whatever form of counseling you believe might be helpful to you and your situation.

Counselors and other helping professionals are consistently exposed to interpersonal and emotional stressors. In addition, perhaps more than ever, emotional stability is constantly affected by the global pandemic, social distancing, disrupted social networks (including networks of family and counseling peers), heightened awareness of racial and social injustice, sociopolitical upheaval, and other sources of uncertainty. To cope with common and uncommon stressors of professional counseling, you should consider whether you might benefit from engaging in personal counseling, creating peer support groups, or obtaining supervision. If you are working regularly with clients who are suicidal, your need for counseling support is magnified.

Examining and Bracketing Attitudes and Beliefs

Ethical counselors cannot allow personal values and attitudes to interfere with the provision of professional services (American Counseling Association, 2014; Corey, 2020). For example, let us say you believe that death by suicide is a mortal sin. You may feel pressured to push clients to banish their sinful suicidal thoughts. Although in most cases, counselors are ethically mandated to help prevent suicide, suicide researchers emphasize that competent suicide assessment and interventions begin with the acceptance of suicidal impulses. If you advocate too hard and too soon against suicide, you may activate client resistance (Brehm & Brehm, 1981; J. Sommers-Flanagan & Shaw, 2017). Instead of saving lives, you may end up alienating clients, thus putting them at greater risk.

The opposite extreme can occur when professionals believe fervently in the right to die by suicide. This belief can be communicated in destructive ways. For example, if your client leaves the session thinking, "My counselor seems to be an advocate for suicide" or "I didn't get the sense that my counselor wants me to live," then you have done your client a disservice and probably engaged in malpractice.

If your personal, religious, or philosophical beliefs about suicide interfere with your ability to provide competent and nonjudgmental assessment services, develop a therapeutic relationship, establish a collaborative treatment plan, or provide ongoing management of suicidal behaviors and implement research-supported interventions, then you are engaging in unprofessional and unethical practice. Professionals must be cognizant of their sometimes less than helpful attitudes and beliefs about suicide. Awareness allows professionals to ethically bracket attitudes, beliefs, and biases that could potentially interfere with competent care.

What Is Ethical Bracketing?

Ethical bracketing is defined as "the intentional separating" or "setting aside" of personal values to "provide ethical . . . counseling to all clients" (Kocet & Herlihy, 2014, p. 182). Ethical bracketing requires that counseling practitioners honor their commitment to working in the best interests of their clients—even when doing so conflicts with their religious values or beliefs.

Staying Focused When Strong Emotions Rise Up

As a Catholic, Mateo had deep moral values and an especially strong belief that suicide was morally wrong. As a graduate student in counseling, Mateo was learning about the need to bracket his values and not impose them on his clients. In his second year of training, Mateo worked with two clients who talked a lot about suicide. Whenever the word *suicide* came up in counseling, Mateo felt himself flinch inside. He had an impulse to plead with these clients to focus on God's love as a solution to their suicidal crises. Mateo began questioning whether he could contain his moral judgments about suicide; he also began questioning whether he could continue in his training to become a professional counselor.

Mateo decided to discuss the feelings he was having with his supervisor. Mateo's supervisor listened and helped Mateo explore his feelings. Later they brainstormed and problem-solved different ways Mateo could become better at monitoring and bracketing his moral judgments. In the end, Mateo and his supervisor identified four self-statements Mateo could use to compartmentalize or bracket his moral reactions:

1. "I know the research and clinical guidelines say that I can more effectively prevent suicide if I accept my clients' suicidal ideation and remain nonjudgmental" (Jobes, 2016).
2. "I know that people who are feeling suicidal are already feeling shame; therefore, if I shame them in any way, I could increase their misery or sense of powerlessness."
3. "I want to prevent suicide for religious and professional reasons. My best chance at preventing suicide involves using evidence-based assessment and treatment strategies."
4. "When I feel triggered and judgmental, I will refocus my efforts on using nondirective paraphrases, reflections of feeling, open questions, and other motivational interviewing skills" (W. R. Miller & Rollnick, 2013).

Kocet and Herlihy (2014) offered a five-step counselor values-based conflict model to aid students and clinicians in ethical bracketing. Using Mateo's situation as an example, we walk you through the steps of the model.

1. *Determine the nature of values-based conflict.* Mateo's conflict was both personal and professional. Mateo believed that suicide was a sin, but he also knew that suicide competencies

required him to listen nonjudgmentally as his clients talked about suicide.
2. *Explore core issues and potential barriers to providing an appropriate standard of care.* When his clients talked about suicide, Mateo was emotionally activated and felt impulses to confront clients with statements like "God loves you" and "Suicide is immoral" and "If you kill yourself, you'll end up in hell." These moralizing thoughts interfered with Mateo's ability to have empathy for his clients.
3. *Seek assistance/remediation for providing an appropriate standard of care.* Mateo recognized his personal/professional conflict. He chose to meet with a supervisor he trusted to discuss the issues.
4. *Determine and evaluate possible courses of action.* Mateo and his supervisor agreed that Mateo could not avoid working with suicidality in counseling. They worked together to provide Mateo with a good rationale for using evidence-based (rather than religious-based) strategies for working with his clients. In addition, they identified internal cues that Mateo could use to alert himself to shift to using nondirective motivational interviewing skills.
5. *Ensure that proposed actions promote client welfare.* Mateo and his supervisor agreed to collaboratively and continuously monitor Mateo's values-based judgments and behaviors during counseling sessions.

As illustrated in Mateo's situation, personal values and attitudes have a complex and interactive relationship with self-care and ethical behaviors. Ethical bracketing is an important process for helping you juggle your values, attitudes, reactions, self-care, and ethical responsibilities. We return to ethical issues and counselor competence in Chapter 2 and beyond. For now, we turn to our strengths-based model for understanding and working with people who are suicidal.

Seven Dimensions of Being Human: Where Does It Hurt, and How Can I Help You?

We began this chapter by describing the case of Alina. Most likely, what you remember about Alina is that she is displaying several frightening suicide risk factors and has openly shared her suicidal thoughts. However, Alina is not just a person who is suicidal—she is a unique individual with a delightful array of idiosyncratic quirks, problems, and strengths who also happens to have suicidal thoughts.

When clients or students begin talking about suicide, it is easy to overly focus on suicidality. Suicidality is such a huge issue that it overshadows nearly everything else and consumes your attention. Nevertheless, all clients—suicidal or not—are richly complex and have a fascinating mix of strengths and weaknesses that deserve attention. To help keep focused on the whole person—and not just on weaknesses or pathology—we use a seven-dimension model for understanding people with suicidal thoughts and impulses.

Suicide Treatment Models

In the book *Brief Cognitive-Behavioral Therapy for Suicide Prevention*, Bryan and Rudd (2018) described and assessed three distinct suicide intervention models. The *risk factor model* emphasizes correlates and predictors of suicidal ideation and behavior. Practitioners who follow the risk factor model aim their treatments toward reducing known risk factors and increasing protective factors. Unfortunately, a dizzying array of risk factors exist; some are relatively unchangeable; and in a large, 50-year, meta-analytic study, researchers concluded that risk factors, protective factors, and warning signs are largely inaccurate and not useful (Franklin et al., 2017). Consequently, treatments based on the risk factor model are not in favor.

The *psychiatric model* focuses on treating psychiatric illnesses to reduce or prevent suicidality. The presumption is that clients experiencing suicidality should be treated for the symptoms linked to their diagnosis. Clients with depression should be treated for depression, clients diagnosed with posttraumatic stress disorder should be treated for trauma, and so on. Bryan and Rudd (2018) noted that "accumulating evidence has failed to support the effectiveness of this conceptual framework" (p. 4).

The final model is the *functional model*. Bryan and Rudd (2018) wrote, "According to this model, suicidal thoughts and behaviors are conceptualized as the outcome of underlying psychopathological processes that specifically precipitate and maintain suicidal thoughts and behaviors over time" (p. 4). The functional model targets suicidal thoughts and behaviors within the context of the individual's history and present circumstances. Bryan and Rudd emphasized that the superiority of the functional model is "well established" (pp. 5–6; they cited a meta-analysis showing that functional approaches are significantly superior to the psychiatric model for suicide risk reduction; Tarrier et al., 2008).

Our approach differs from the functional model in several ways. Given our wellness and strengths-based orientation, we studiously avoid presuming that suicidality is a psychopathological process. Instead, consistent with social constructionist philosophy, we believe that locating psychopathological processes within clients risks exacerbating and perpetuating psychopathology as an internalized phenomenon (Hansen, 2015; Lyddon, 1995). From a constructionist perspective, client problems (including suicidality) are not necessarily within the self but instead are viewed as constructed by individuals and social groups. In addition to our wellness, strengths-based, constructionist foundation, we rely on an integration of robust suicide theory and practice (we rely on works from Jobes, Joiner, Klonsky & May, Linehan, O'Connor, and Shneidman). We also embrace parts of the functional model, especially the emphasis on individualized contextual factors that can increase or decrease risk. Overall, our goal is to provide counseling practitioners with a practical and strengths-based model for working effectively with clients and students who are suicidal.

The Seven Dimensions

Counseling and psychotherapy theorists and practitioners have a long history of using dimensional models to formulate client problems and develop treatment plans (Ellis, 1962; Lazarus, 2006; Myers, 1991; Witmer & Sweeney, 1992). Many authorities in many disciplines have articulated life dimensions. Some argue for three, others for five, seven, or nine dimensions. We settled on seven that we believe reflect common sense, science, philosophy, and convenience. Each dimension is multifaceted, overlapping, dynamic, and interactive. Each dimension includes at least three underlying factors that have theoretical and empirical support as drivers of suicidal ideation or behavior (J. Sommers-Flanagan, 2018a). The dimensions and their underlying factors are shown in Table 1.1.

In her memoir, Judy Collins (2003) wrote, "Two questions that are at the heart of treating someone who wishes to end their life are: 'Where does it hurt?' and 'How can I help you?'" (p. 117). The "hurt" Collins refers to is not always located in a single place. Chronic pain, social isolation, lack of employment or shelter, emotional turmoil, constricted thinking, destructive habits, addictions, existential nihilism, and many more factors can trigger suicidality.

Given the immense range and complexity of human suffering and helping options, we believe that organizing our search for "where it hurts" and "how we can help" is essential. Using the

TABLE 1.1
Brief Descriptions of the Seven Dimensions

Dimension	Evidence-Based Suicide Driver	Wellness Goal
Emotional		
All human emotions	1. Excruciating emotional distress	1. Emotional peace and calm
	2. Specific disturbing emotions (guilt, shame, anger, or sadness)	2. Specific positive emotions (happiness, joy, etc.)
	3. Emotional dysregulation	3. Emotional regulation
Cognitive		
All forms of human thought, including imagery	1. Hopelessness	1. Hope
	2. Problem-solving impairments	2. Problem-solving skills
	3. Maladaptive thoughts	3. Adaptive thoughts and beliefs
	4. Negative core beliefs	4. Positive core beliefs
Interpersonal		
All human relationships	1. Social disconnection and perceived burdensomeness	1. Social connection and perceived usefulness
	2. Interpersonal loss and grief	2. Skills for coping with loss
	3. Social skill deficits	3. Positive social skills
	4. Repeating dysfunctional relationship patterns	4. Repeating functional relationship patterns
Physical		
All human biogenetics and physiology	1. Biogenetic predispositions and physical illness	1. Healthy biogenetics and wellness
	2. Sedentary lifestyle, poor nutrition	2. Active lifestyle, positive nutrition
	3. Agitation, arousal, anxiety	3. Physical calmness
	4. Trauma, nightmares, insomnia	4. Skills for coping with trauma
Cultural-spiritual		
All religious, spiritual, or cultural values that provide meaning and purpose	1. Religious or spiritual disconnection	1. Religious or spiritual connection
	2. Cultural disconnection or dislocation	2. Cultural connection
	3. Meaninglessness	3. Meaningfulness
Behavioral		
All human action and activity	1. Using substances or cutting for desensitization	1. Openness to experience
	2. Suicide planning, intent, and preparation	2. Life planning and preparation
	3. Impulsivity	3. Self-control
Contextual		
All factors outside of the individual that influence human behavior	1. No connection to place or nature	1. Connection to place or nature
	2. Chronic exposure to unhealthy environmental conditions	2. Healthy environmental conditions
	3. Socioeconomic oppression or resource scarcity (e.g., poverty)	3. Socioeconomic support, resources, and social justice

seven-dimension model for case formulation will make it easier to notice and nurture client strengths. In addition to Collins's questions of "Where does it hurt?" and "How can I help you?" we add "Where are you strong?"

Using the Seven-Dimension Model for Initial Treatment Planning

Although we have only minimal information about Alina in the opening case presentation, the seven-dimension model can contribute to a holistic understanding of her and her situation. We offer a brief description of how you might use the dimensional model to guide further assessment and treatment planning.

Emotional Dimension

Alina's previous attempt, her cutting behaviors, and her presenting affect speak to her intense distress. At a minimum, initial work with her could focus on strategies for emotional regulation and practical methods for distress tolerance.

Cognitive Dimension

Alina's statement about not being sure that anything will ever help her feel better is an indication of hopelessness. Much more assessment is needed, but beginning with questions about what gives her hope and what diminishes her hope is a reasonable place to start.

Interpersonal Dimension

Alina is isolated and lonely. Not only does she long for a romantic relationship, but she also feels estranged from her family. Gathering more information about her relationship history, patterns, hopes, and skills is essential to building a comprehensive treatment plan.

Physical Dimension

Alina is opposed to antidepressant medications. To provide a complete treatment plan, it is important to gather more information about her medical history and her exercise, sleep, and nutritional habits.

Cultural-Spiritual Dimension

Alina's sexual identity may have made her a target for micro- or macroaggressions as well as cultural oppression. In addition, it would be helpful to know more about Alina's Croatian culture and whether components of that culture contribute to her wellness or suicidality. More assessment information is needed about the role of spirituality or religion in her life.

Behavioral Dimension

Although Alina denies suicidal intent, she may be engaging in behaviors that increase her vulnerability to suicide. Within the behavioral dimension, assessing Alina's substance use and previous overdose is essential. In addition, making sure Alina does not have easy access to firearms or other lethal means is essential and can be addressed in a collaborative safety plan.

Contextual Dimension

Gathering information about Alina's living conditions and her unemployment situation is important. Helping Alina identify community supports, identify financial resources, and understand the potential role of discrimination in her life may help decrease distress and provide a sense of direction.

Concluding Comments

We would love to offer a clear and easy formula for preventing all suicides, but we cannot; no one can. Suicide rates are on the rise, and suicide is neither 100% predictable nor 100% preventable. Regardless of these discouraging realities, people struggling with suicidal thoughts and impulses need the best care available. Providing the best care requires professionals who are comfortable and skilled when working with client suicidality.

Facing the daunting professional task of providing suicide assessment and treatment services may leave you feeling overwhelmed. Feeling overwhelmed—including having self-doubt and anxiety—is part of a normal developmental process linked to learning about suicide assessment and treatment. As you progress through these chapters, your knowledge and skills will grow and your feelings of being overwhelmed will shrink.

Practitioner Guidance and Key Points to Remember

Over the course of your professional life, you are likely to have many people who are suicidal on your caseload. As you face the stress that these situations evoke, you will benefit from developing personal and professional self-care strategies. In this chapter, we recommended the following:

- Stop reading (take breaks from suicide content as needed).
- Recognize the hazards inherent to working with people who are suicidal.
- Intentionally focus on positive and rewarding life experiences.
- Use a variety of self-care strategies.
- Accept your distress and engage in self-soothing behaviors.

In addition to developing self-care strategies, you also need to manage your attitudes toward suicide, including your personal values. Ethical bracketing—or setting aside your personal values to focus on your clients—is one method of preventing your personal values and attitudes from negatively affecting clients. We recommend using Kocet and Herlihy's (2014) five-step counselor values-based conflict model to facilitate ethical bracketing.

Currently, the functional model for treating suicidality has the strongest evidence base. The functional model is used to identify psychopathological processes that underlie suicidal thoughts and behaviors and target them in treatment. Similar to the functional model, our suicide assessment and treatment model targets suicidal thoughts and behaviors within the context of the individual's history and present circumstances. However, the model used in this book is a wellness-oriented, strengths-based, and holistic model that views suicidality through the lens of seven dimensions of human functioning:

- Emotional
- Cognitive
- Interpersonal
- Physical
- Cultural-Spiritual
- Behavioral
- Contextual

The seven-dimension model is a foundation for focusing on the whole person—including personal strengths—as you develop treatment plans for clients who are suicidal. Counselors and other professionals who are working with clients contemplating suicide are encouraged to gently and collaboratively explore the questions "Where does it hurt?" "How can I be of help?" and "Where are you strong?"

Chapter 2

Competence and Ethics

Imagine you are working with Kevin, a 21-year-old college student. Kevin identifies as a White cisgender heterosexual male. He is mandated to see you for five sessions after receiving a campus citation for using alcohol in his dorm. During your first three sessions, he strikes you as affable, engaging, and relatively well adjusted. He is physically fit, gets good grades, and does not seem depressed. Kevin acknowledges that his father had problems with alcohol; he openly admits to guilt over his own use. During the second session, Kevin expresses an interest in cutting back on drinking, partly because of his father's problems and partly because his girlfriend thinks he drinks too much. Then, after his third session, out of the blue, you get a call from his girlfriend. She tells you she is breaking up with Kevin, and he is threatening suicide. She says, "Kevin needs to see you right away," and asks you to call him. Tragically, before you make contact, Kevin places the barrel of a gun in his mouth, pulls the trigger, and dies by suicide.

In the swirling aftermath of Kevin's suicide, you are emotionally devastated. You keep replaying session vignettes in your mind, wondering, "How could this have happened?" and "What did I miss?" Your confidence is shaken. You are questioning your professional competence.

Understanding Suicide Competence

Suicide competence refers to what clinicians need to know and do to provide professional services to clients at risk for suicide. In a general sense, suicide competencies encompass three parts of a symphony that includes many different notes, movements, and melodies. Like all competency models (Cramer et al., 2013), these three parts include the following:

- *Self-awareness and attitudes.* This includes developing greater awareness of your own attitudes toward suicide and how your attitudes, beliefs, and personal values might play out in specific clinical scenarios. Exploring your attitudes toward suicide helps you cope with personal and emotional reactions while maintaining a therapeutic relationship and implementing state-of-the-art suicide assessment and treatment planning procedures.
- *Knowledge acquisition.* Foundational knowledge includes information on effective assessment and treatment and an understanding of ethical and legal standards. Having greater foundational knowledge of suicide helps increase your confidence and frees you to experience and express compassion for clients struggling with suicidality.
- *Skill development.* This refers to learning and practicing specific skills and strategies, including (a) comfortably asking about suicide; (b) empathically interacting with clients who are experiencing depression, hopelessness, and irritability; (c) engaging in collaborative assessment; (d) developing collaborative treatment and safety plans; (e) implementing specific interventions; and (f) documenting clinical decision-making.

At the beginning and throughout the symphony of suicide-related self-awareness, knowledge, and skill acquisition, there is a steady drumbeat of ethical and legal standards in the background. This drumbeat will sometimes distract you; other times it will provoke anxiety. On good days, local and national practice standards will guide your work with clients who are suicidal. Practice standards include knowledge of ethical decision-making models, breaching confidentiality, documentation, and much more.

Within the counselor education discipline, there is little guidance or consensus regarding suicide assessment and treatment competence. The 2016 Council for Accreditation of Counseling and Related Educational Programs (CACREP) Standards (CACREP, 2016) include two statements pertaining to required counseling coursework in "Suicide prevention models and strategies" (Section 2.F.5.l.) and "Procedures for assessing risk of aggression or danger to others, self-inflicted harm, or suicide" (Section 2.F.7.c.). Similarly, the *ACA Code of Ethics* (American Counseling Association [ACA], 2014) mentions suicide once, but only in the context of the storage and disposal of records. Standard C.2.b. of the *Code* offers general guidance for "New Specialty Areas of Practice." It reads: "Counselors practice in specialty areas new to them only after appropriate education, training, and supervised experience . . . counselors take steps to ensure the competence of their work and protect others from possible harm." Although working with suicidality is not an identified practice specialty, counselors need specialized education, training, and supervised experience in suicide assessment and treatment.

Similar to counselor education, other professional disciplines also offer little guidance regarding suicide-related competence. The American Psychological Association (2010) does not use the words *suicide* or *suicidal* in its accreditation standards or ethics code, but it does have a helpful informational and resource-oriented website (see https://www.apa.org/topics/suicide/). Although the American Academy of Child and Adolescent Psychiatry has a practice parameter for the assessment and treatment of children and adolescents with suicidal behavior, its guidance has not been revised since 2001. Similar to ACA and the American Psychological Association, the National Association of Social Workers (2017) provides links to documents about suicide prevention and treatment but offers no formal training guidelines.

Recently, the American School Counselor Association took a step forward in this area, publishing a "Suicide Risk Assessment Position Statement" (Sara Carpenter, personal communication, July 3, 2020). This statement clarifies the role of school counselors as part of a collaborative care team that uses evidence-supported strategies and always reports students' elevated suicide risk to parents, guardians, or, in cases of caregiver abuse or neglect, child protective services (American School Counselor Association, 2020).

In contrast to the sparse mention of specific training protocols linked to professional organizations, the scientific literature on suicide assessment, treatment planning, and interventions is immense. At the time of this writing, we found more than 32,000 publications on PsycINFO with *suicide* or *suicidal* in the title. Keeping up with the professional literature on suicide could be a full-time job.

Fortunately, suicide researchers and professional organizations frequently summarize the literature. Several researchers and organizations have described essential suicide assessment and treatment competencies. Most prominently, the American Association of Suicidology (AAS; 2010), a national organization dedicated to studying suicide, identified 24 competencies organized under eight broad categories. Several additional competency guidelines and models exist. To simplify the smorgasbord of competencies available, Cramer and colleagues (2013) distilled principles from five different competency guides (including AAS) into 10 core competencies. Even simplified, the 10 core competencies constitute a wide array of attitudes, knowledge, skills, and practice standards. In this chapter, we provide an initial overview; throughout the rest of this book we offer case vignettes, extended case examples, and commentary relevant to the 10 core competencies.

Ten Suicide Assessment and Treatment Planning Competencies

Cramer and colleagues (2013) reviewed suicide competencies from several published documents, including AAS (2010), Joiner (2005), Kleespies et al. (2009), Rudd (2006), and Sullivan and Bongar (2009). Based on their review, they identified 10 suicide assessment and treatment planning competencies. Although they drew primarily from psychology, psychiatry, and the interdisciplinary AAS, Cramer et al.'s competencies are consistent with content from the counseling discipline (Granello, 2010a, 2010b). For each suicide competency, we provide a descriptive summary and commentary illuminating particular challenges that professionals face when mastering these competencies.

Competency 1: Be Aware of and Manage Your Attitude and Reactions to Suicide

Competency begins with self-awareness. Nearly every source on suicide prevention and intervention emphasizes self-reflection designed to answer the question "Can I work effectively and ethically with clients who are suicidal?" (J. Sommers-Flanagan & Sommers-Flanagan, 2017). Granello (2010b) recommended that professionals manage and balance their emotional reactions:

> Counselors may overreact to any mention of suicide and impose overly restrictive controls. The opposite risk, which can be much more serious, occurs when counselors deny the level of threat and underreact by not imposing sufficient controls. Either situation, when arising from the emotional reactions of the counselor rather than the needs of the client, is dangerous. (p. 222)

Everyone has preexisting attitudes toward suicide. Some individuals hold the belief that suicide is sinful; others believe in the individual's right to die by suicide. As a mental health or school professional, it is important for you to be aware of your preexisting attitudes and to be prepared for ways in which suicidality in clients might affect you. This includes being aware of your religious beliefs, your personal history with suicide, and any ways that you are inclined to instantly judge people who mention the word *suicide*.

Competency 2: Develop and Maintain a Collaborative, Empathic Stance With Clients

When clients disclose suicidality, conflicts between clinician goals and client goals arise (AAS, 2010). Clients who present with suicidal ideation or impulses are often expressing a desire to die; in contrast, your professional goal is to help clients stay alive. This inherent conflict makes it difficult to establish collaborative relationships (Jobes, 2016).

Clients know their pain and the nature of their suffering. If clinicians do not honor client perspectives, clients can refuse to open up; they can slide the deadbolt to their inner thoughts and feelings and block clinicians from gathering information. A collaborative attitude requires respecting client perspectives. That often means honoring your clients' desire to keep suicide as an option to life. Pushing against clients' rights to die by suicide may activate psychological reactance or resistance and end up pushing them toward, rather than away from, suicide (Brehm & Brehm, 1981; J. Sommers-Flanagan & Shaw, 2017). A collaborative relationship is central to all contemporary and evidence-based approaches to suicide assessment and management (Bryan & Rudd, 2018; Jobes, 2016; Wenzel et al., 2009).

Regardless of your clients' problems, empathy is a robust predictor of positive counseling outcomes (Elliott et al., 2018). Maintaining empathy with clients who are suicidal can mean that counselors accept and try to understand intense emotional pain. Unremitting hopelessness is common (e.g., "Nothing will ever help me feel better"). If clinicians pivot away from emotional pain and hopelessness and bring up solutions too quickly, clients may feel isolated, misunderstood, or judged. It can be uncomfortable to continue paraphrasing and resonating with your client's emotional pain, especially when your goal is to nudge your client toward a safety plan or hospitalization.

Although working with suicidality requires a specific knowledge base and skill set, many basic counseling skills transfer. Skills for working collaboratively, showing empathy and positive regard, and using problem-solving form the foundation for effective suicide assessment and treatment (Michel & Jobes, 2010). Continuing to develop your general counseling skills, obtaining specific suicide-relevant workshop training, and studying from resources like this book will help you establish competency.

Competency 3: Know and Elicit Evidence-Based Risk and Protective Factors

Cramer and colleagues (2013) wrote, "One of the clinician's primary objectives in conducting a suicide risk assessment is to elicit risk and protective factors from the client" (p. 6). As we discuss in greater detail later, this competency is problematic for at least three reasons. First, in an extensive meta-analysis covering 50 years of research, the authors concluded, "All risk (and protective factors) [for suicidal thoughts and behavior] are weak and inaccurate. This general pattern has not changed over the past 50 years" (Franklin et al., 2017, p. 217). In other words, there is no clear formula of risk and protective factors that accurately predict suicide.

Second, the number of potential risk and protective factors of which counselors should be aware is overwhelming. Granello (2010b) reported 75-plus factors, we have a list of 25 (J. Sommers-Flanagan & Sommers-Flanagan, 2017), and even Cramer and colleagues (2013) lamented, "It would be impossible for clinicians to be familiar with every risk factor" (p. 6). Jobes (2016) referred to suicidology as "a field that has been remarkably obsessed with delineating countless suicide 'risk factors' (that do little for clinically understanding acute risk)" (p. 17).

Third, prominent suicide researchers have concluded that efforts to categorize client risk are ill advised (McHugh et al., 2019; Nielssen et al., 2017). For example, even the most commonly identified symptom of suicide, suicidal ideation, is a poor predictor of suicide in clinical settings; this is because suicidal ideation occurs at a very high frequency, but death by suicide occurs at a very low frequency. In one study, 80% of patients who died by suicide denied having suicidal thoughts when asked directly by a general medical practitioner (McHugh et al., 2019). Even the oft-cited risk factor of a previous suicide attempt has only a small statistical relationship to death by suicide. In a review of 17 studies examining 64 unique suicide prediction models, Belsher and colleagues (2019) reported, "These models would result in high false-positive rates and considerable false-negative rates if implemented in isolation" (p. 642).

To summarize, this suicide competency includes a deep dialectic. Clinicians absolutely must be aware of suicide risk factors, warning signs, and protective factors. Granello (2010b) recommended that counselors keep a list of relevant risk factors and warning signs on their desks. However, as Belsher et al. (2019) noted, risk and protective factors and warning signs—or any checklist or instrument—should not be used in isolation; an overemphasis on checklists impedes development of the therapeutic relationship, and the statistical reality is that suicide is not predictable and risk categorization is typically inaccurate. This competency can be boiled down to four parts, some of which form a dialectic:

1. Competent practitioners should have knowledge of evidence-based suicide risk and protective factors.
2. Competent practitioners are aware that evidence-based suicide risk and protective factors may not confer useful information during a clinical interview.
3. Instead of relying on checklists of suicide risk and protective factors, competent practitioners collaboratively identify and explore client distress and then track client distress back to individualized factors that increase risk and enhance protection.
4. Competent practitioners use skills to collaboratively develop safety plans that address each client's unique risk and protective profile.

Although risk and protective factors do not provide an equation that tells clinicians what to do, knowing and addressing each unique individual's particular risks and strengths remains an important competency (Granello, 2010b).

Competency 4: Focus on Current Plan and Intent of Suicidal Ideation

Asking directly about suicide and collaboratively exploring suicidal ideation, suicide planning, and suicidal intent are essential to competent suicide assessment. However, as noted for the previous competency, when asked about suicide, many clients or patients who will go on to die by suicide deny suicidal ideation (McHugh et al., 2019). Simply asking directly about suicide is not enough. Competent practitioners have clinical skills for asking about suicidality in ways that make it easier for clients to be open and honest.

Several important tasks are linked to this competency (and described in Chapter 3). These tasks include the following:

1. Use effective listening skills to show empathy and develop rapport.
2. Use sophisticated clinical interviewing skills to discuss suicidality with clients in ways that make it easier for them to disclose suicidal thoughts.
3. Collaboratively explore the frequency, intensity, duration, and termination of suicidal ideation.
4. Identify what distracts clients from a preoccupation with suicide and other ways to decrease the frequency, intensity, and duration of suicidal ideation.
5. Be able to use subjective suicide rating scales with clients.
6. Ask directly—using a collaborative style—about client plans, suicide methods, previous attempts, and behaviors related to suicide preparations.

Competency 5: Determine the Level of Risk

As discussed previously, accurately determining client suicide risk is probably impossible. Nevertheless, there are situations and contexts in which employment responsibilities will require you to make your best estimate of client suicide risk. However, because your specific suicide predictions may be incorrect, avoiding overconfidence, consulting with others, and collaborating with clients is recommended.

Sometimes so-called high-risk clients (based on traditional risk and protective factors) can be managed using a detailed safety plan and close in-home monitoring. Historically, these clients were hospitalized—often involuntarily. Although sometimes it is the only option, hospitalization is not an especially effective treatment for suicide, and the period after hospitalization is a time of heightened suicide risk (Large & Kapur, 2018).

Tasks associated with this competency include the following:

1. Recognize that because your ability to accurately categorize risk is limited, no matter the risk level, you should collaboratively establish a treatment plan to maximize client safety. This will likely involve safety or crisis planning (Bryan & Rudd, 2018; Stanley & Brown, 2012).
2. Expand your knowledge of the client (Granello, 2010b). Obtain previous medical/mental health records as well as collateral information from friends, family, or other supportive contacts (Wheeler & Bertram, 2019). This will require client consent; in some circumstances, you may need to breach confidentiality (e.g., when clients are suicidal and refuse treatment, when

you have a duty to warn family about elevated risk, or when youth have suicidal ideation or make suicide gestures).
3. When clients will not collaborate on safety planning, or when you are setting mandates, categorize risk using "phraseology such as low, moderate, high, and extreme risk" (Cramer et al., 2013, p. 7). Most experts advise against using a no-risk category.

*Competency 6: Develop and Enact a
Collaborative Evidence-Based Treatment Plan*

Suicide treatment planning should be strengths based and collaborative whenever possible. However, sometimes clients are unable to collaborate. They may be agitated, impulsive, lethargic, unengaged, and/or only minimally responsive. On other occasions, clients will flat out resist your collaboration efforts. When clients are unable to contribute to safety or treatment planning, risk is likely higher, and you will need to take the lead in safety planning.

When clients report suicidal ideation, short-term safety planning is recommended. Two short-term safety planning protocols have evidentiary support. These are Stanley and Brown's (2012) safety planning intervention and Bryan and Rudd's (2018) crisis response plan.

Longer term treatment planning is an important part of this competency. As Linehan (1993; Linehan et al., 2012) has discussed, sometimes clinicians need to be bold and direct. She typically speaks frankly, saying things like "We may have to go through hell together." Her purpose is to show her commitment to the treatment process and to give clients messages of hope (e.g., "I know this therapy I'm offering you can help"). Consistent with general counseling and psychotherapy guidelines, engaging clients in an ongoing treatment plan requires you to present a clear rationale that connects counseling tasks to collaboratively generated counseling goals (J. Sommers-Flanagan, 2015b).

To have competency within this domain, you will need to do the following:

1. Invite clients to collaborate with you on short-term safety planning or longer term treatment planning.
2. Be able to implement specific steps linked to either the safety planning intervention (Stanley & Brown, 2012) or the crisis response plan (Bryan & Rudd, 2018).
3. Become directive, take the lead, and possibly initiate intensive treatment (e.g., a residential facility or psychiatric hospital) when clients are not willing or able to engage in safety planning.

4. Speak to clients about your hope for positive outcomes, your desire for them to commit to ongoing treatment, and the rationale for counseling tasks and goals.
5. Scan for and reflect strengths in your clients' presentation. This will require knowledge of protective factors and reframing skills (Cureton & Fink, 2019).

Competency 7: Notify and Involve Other Persons

Social isolation is a risk factor for suicide (Joiner, 2005). To address isolation, treatments for clients who are suicidal often involve the recruitment of supportive people, including other treatment or medical providers, friends, family, church or community members, mentors, and others. Involving other people in treatment and safety planning can be a critical component of successful treatment (Cramer et al., 2013).

Ideally you can work with your client to generate a list of people to contact and involve as supporters of treatment. However, if you are working with a client who resists your efforts to identify and establish social support networks, you will need to establish a safety plan without social connections or breach confidentiality and make the contacts. Breaching confidentiality may rupture the therapeutic relationship, but it does not always have that effect. Although your client may discontinue counseling with you, the need for immediate safety sometimes outweighs longer term treatment and relational considerations.

Competency 8: Document Risk Assessment, the Treatment Plan, and the Rationale for Clinical Decisions

Documentation serves several purposes. Writing down your observations, organizing your inferences, and reflecting on decision-making helps you remember your clients' dynamics and goals. Your notes will provide you with an accurate and efficient method of monitoring client progress or deterioration. Adequate documentation can also mitigate professional liability (Rudd, 2006).

Professional documentation begins with a signed informed consent form that outlines how you work with clients who are suicidal, what clients should do in cases of emergency, and the reasons you would choose or be required to breach confidentiality. You should document everything from case notes to consultations to decision-making rationale. Whatever format you use for intake and progress notes, to help organize your documentation, we offer the following list of items and content to include in your client files (for a comprehensive outline of an intake report, see J. Sommers-Flanagan & Sommers-Flanagan, 2017):

1. Documentation of initial client paperwork, including your client's signature on an informed consent
2. Previous treatment records
3. Information about your suicide assessment, treatment plan, and decision-making, including the following content:
   a. Suicide-related historical information (e.g., suicidal behaviors by family members, client previous attempts, lethality of previous attempts)
   b. Assessment of risk and protective factors
   c. Suicide assessment instruments or questionnaires
   d. Assessment of suicidal thoughts, plan, client self-control (agitation), and intent
   e. A record of consultations with previous counselors and other professionals
   f. Your rationale for the treatment you are providing and your rationale for your treatment disposition and referrals (e.g., day treatment, hospitalization)
   g. Any contacts you have made with authority figures (police officers, administrators, teachers, and/or family members)
4. Your collaborative safety plan, including firearms safety; keep a copy in your files and give your client a copy (If your client reports suicidal ideation and you do not create a safety plan, you should document your rationale for not creating one.)
5. Notes on any review or update of the informed consent and the crisis or safety plan
6. Progress notes that include your client's response (e.g., progress, resistance, deterioration) to your initial suicide assessment as well as ongoing assessment and treatment that you are providing

The preceding list is skeletal. Depending on your setting and needs, to fill in the content, you might elaborate on your rationale for treatment, including describing how and why the treatment you are providing is a good match for your client's unique problems and symptoms. Specifically, you could (a) highlight immediate or prominent risk factors (including suicide triggers) and how you are addressing them, (b) describe how you plan to draw out or activate protective factors to reduce suicidality, and (c) include immediate and longer term interventions you are taking to reduce suicide risk. Using direct quotes or paraphrases from your client that support your evaluation and decision-making is recommended. You can also include mental status observations of physical and nonverbal behaviors, such as lack of eye contact, sighs, or poor hygiene.

Competency 9: Know the Law Concerning Suicide

The laws concerning suicide are simple and complex. The simple part follows court rulings on the duty to protect clients from knowable dangers from self and others (*Tarasoff v. Regents of the University of California*, 1976). The duty to protect is a legal mandate.

In addition to knowing federal guidelines regarding suicide and the law, you also need to know laws and statutes in your specific locality. Jobes and O'Connor (2009) wrote, "All states . . . have explicit expectations of a duty to protect . . . when [clients] pose an imminent danger to self" (p. 165). The state in which you practice has legal statutes covering the involuntary civil commitment process and standards of care for working with clients or minors who are suicidal. Consulting with experienced professionals in your region (and/or seeking training) can help you understand the practical steps you need to cover in your locality.

If you are employed by an agency or school, you will need to know its suicide policy. When you join a new agency or school, read the institution's suicide-related policies and procedures and discuss them with a senior clinician or administrative staff before you even begin seeing clients or students. If your agency or school does not have suicide-related policies and procedures, work with your administration to adopt a temporary working model from a similar agency, and establish a task force to create a more permanent model. You never know when the next client or student will be suicidal. On the first week of his first job, one of our graduates had to manage a student who was actively suicidal. He called and said, "Wow! You guys weren't kidding when you said to know how to handle things before you even open the door!" (see Wheeler & Bertram, 2019, for more information on legal issues in counseling).

Competency 10: Engage in Debriefing and Self-Care

Feeling responsible for life-and-death situations is overwhelming (Cramer et al., 2013). As in the opening case of Kevin, when clients make suicide attempts or die by suicide, practitioners often experience an avalanche of guilt, preoccupation with possible mistakes, and feelings of incompetence. Even though such feelings are natural, they are still extremely difficult. As noted in Chapter 1, self-care is always important for mental health and school professionals, but when suicide is the issue, self-care is especially critical (Binkley & Leibert, 2015).

Debriefings of some sort are important whenever you conduct a suicide assessment. Debriefings may involve you taking the lead and reporting exactly how you handled a particular assessment or intervention. They can also include your supervisor (or classmates or colleagues) asking specific questions. Common debriefing questions include the following:

1. What clinical observations increased your concerns about suicide?
2. What clinical observations decreased your concerns about suicide?
3. What risk and protective factors did you notice through observation? What risk and protective factors did you ask about?
4. How did you directly ask your client about suicide? What was your client's response?
5. What was the quality of your therapeutic relationship or connection?
6. Did you trust that what your client told you was truthful? If so, what made you trust your client? If not, what made you reluctant to trust your client?
7. Did you gather information about the frequency, intensity, duration, and termination of your client's suicidal ideation? What was your client's response to these questions?
8. Did you ask about previous attempts? What was your client's response?
9. Did you ask about suicide plans? What was your client's response?
10. What were your client's reasons for living and reasons for dying?
11. Did you initiate a safety planning intervention? If so, what was your client's response?
12. What was your impression regarding your client's willingness to engage in ongoing counseling?

Suicide-Related Ethical Issues

Imagine you are working as a school professional. Three high school students suddenly pop into your office. They take turns speaking, saying things like the following:

- "Serena is talking about suicide."
- "She posted a creepy thing about death on Instagram that's freaking us out."
- "We think you should talk with her."
- "She's been drinking way too much. We're totally scared."

This case scenario highlights the complexities associated with decision-making around suicidality. Many questions arise. Should you summon Serena from class and meet with her? Serena is 16 years old; does that mean you have a responsibility to contact her parents? What is the school district's policy on suicide risk assessment? If Serena admits to suicidal ideation but assures you she will not act on her thoughts, what discretion do you have as to whether or not you contact her parents? If Serena denies suicidal ideation and says her friends are being silly and stupid, do you have any duty to protect? At a minimum, cases like Serena's reveal the importance of knowing your school's (or agency's) suicide assessment and disposition protocol (including whom to contact first). Here we cover ethical considerations specific to suicidality and related emergent or dangerous clinical concerns.

Is Serena Suicidal?

School counselors and school mental health professionals gain information about students in many different ways. In an ideal world, Serena would approach you, acknowledge suicidal ideation, and ask for help; you would responsibly follow your district's policy for informing your school administrator, contacting the parents, providing referral information, and staying in touch with Serena via your school's suicide-related case management protocol. Unfortunately, the opposite process may unfold. You may hear about Serena's suicidality through her friends or via a teacher. Serena may never approach you and may not be honest with you about her suicidal ideation. To complicate matters further, your district policy may be enigmatic or excessively detailed, Serena's parents may be unreachable or overreactive, referral resources may be nonexistent, and you may not have a case management protocol for students who are suicidal.

In an article in the American School Counselor Association's magazine (*ASCA School Counselor*), Carolyn Stone (2018) described school counselors' responsibilities for reporting suicidal ideation. Her article included the following points:

1. *If you learn that a student is thinking about suicide, contact the parents or other appropriate adults:* "Regardless of whether or not we have a state statute to guide our behavior, we must make certain everyone in our profession understands calling parents whenever we are placed on notice that a suicide is even a remote possibility is not an option or judgment call but an absolute duty" (para. 9).
2. *Do not trust suicide assessment as a reliable method for determining student risk:* "Assessments requiring school counselors to quantify the risk (high risk, medium risk or low risk) based largely on student response is frightening. This is a dangerous practice, and school counselors should consider the information gleaned from a student's self–report as unreliable. To tell a parent the risk is low is to create for a parent a false sense of security when the student may have hidden the real truth" (para. 13).
3. *Lean toward trusting peer reports over student self-report:* "It is a well-known fact that students will say and do whatever they need to if they want to get out from under the school counselor's gaze. Student self-report is not reliable. Peer report is often much more reliable as students will be honest with peers if they are determined to hide their pain from adults" (para. 16).
4. *If you are required to conduct an assessment,* "use assessments as a segue to provide parents everything learned from the assessment, to urge further evaluation, to stress monitoring of their child's safety and to provide resources for mental health" follow up (para. 15).
5. *Call parents, emphasize risk, provide resources, and arrange for the student to be safely transported home:* "School counselors are clear with parents/guardians about a child's expressed, implied or veiled suicidal ideation. This is not the time to soften the message. School counselors stress to parents that expressions of suicide or other warning signs require vigilance. School counselors confer with the appropriate school officials to make certain the student stays in protective custody and is not dismissed to take whatever means the student normally uses to get home" (para. 24).
6. *If necessary, contact child protective services to possibly open a neglect case:* "If the parents/guardians intentionally do not seek help for their child with the first notice, the standard of care for the profession is that the school counselor makes an outreach to the family reiterating the suicide risk, the urgency

to seek help for their child and the acknowledgement that a neglect case has to be lodged with" child protective services (para. 24).

Stone (2018) and the American School Counselor Association (2020) make it clear that whenever suicide is linked to a specific student, professional school counselors are mandated reporters. Although school counselors may participate in formal suicide assessment protocols, if suicidal ideation is reported, parents or caregivers are contacted. The clarity of this position relieves the school counselor of uncertainty. However, this black-and-white guidance on suicide reporting leaves some school counselors wishing they could exercise their judgment. Given that reporting suicidal ideation to parents or caregivers can rupture the therapeutic relationship and initiate a cascade of negative responses, some professionals question the need for school counselors to always report even minor suicidal ideation.

The reason why school counselors need to report is probably best summed up by the Latin phrase *in loco parentis*, which means "in place of a parent." Essentially, when parents are not present, school professionals assume and discharge parental duties. When it comes to suicidal ideation, most professionals, including attorneys, are likely to interpret this principle as meaning that parents or caregivers deserve to be informed when their children talk about suicide. The way we think of this is that school counselors and other professionals working with children should view suicidal ideation as a sign of intense distress, and unless there is evidence of child abuse, parents should be informed when evidence indicates their child is in intense distress. Furthermore, a useful frame to take with parents is to identify support and/or interventions designed to decrease student distress.

Informed Consent

Ethical counseling flows from informed consent. As a counseling professional, it is your job to make sure clients, students, and parents understand and consent to the rules and parameters of counseling—including the limits of confidentiality.

Informed consent is a clinical process that involves written documentation, an oral description, and an opportunity for questions and discussion. The process and documentation capture the professional background, the theoretical orientation(s), agency or school policies, emergency policies and procedures, and other matters specific to your setting, but in this text we only provide guidance for the portions related to potential suicidality.

If you are currently working with clients, students, or patients without a standard informed consent process, we highly recommend you develop one and use it. Both you and your clients are at risk without a clear informed consent document and process. There are three distinct but related components to informed consent. We cover these components here, with examples that may need fine-tuning depending on your setting.

Confidentiality and Its Limits

When clients, students, or others in distress talk with mental health or school counseling providers, they usually assume that what they say will be held in confidence. This is mostly true, but confidentiality exists only when a formal professional relationship has been established. For example, if teachers contact you about student behavior or parents contact you and offer information about their child, you may or may not be required to hold that information confidential. These are situations when you should spell out limits of confidentiality in advance, before inaccurate assumptions take hold.

It is up to you to explain what you can and will keep confidential and what you cannot keep confidential. Intent to harm oneself or others is an almost universal reason for mental health, health, and school professionals to break confidentiality. Some professional ethics codes directly or indirectly allow for maintaining confidentiality when clients are terminally ill and may be considering ending their lives (Werth et al., 2002). Technically, such plans and considerations would be labeled "suicidal," but this is a vastly different situation than the ones we are writing about in this book. State laws, ethics codes, agency policies, and school rules dictate or influence what can and cannot be held in confidence. You should practice presenting information about confidentiality and its limits accurately, in understandable language, to clients, parents, teachers, administrators, and other community or school professionals (e.g., police officers). Here is an example aimed at an adolescent population:

> As your counselor, I will keep nearly everything you tell me private. We call this confidentiality. This is important for a trusting relationship. For example, if we see each other in public, I'll be careful not to greet you unless you greet me first, because the fact that you're seeing me for counseling is nobody else's business. That's how private this relationship is. But there are a few exceptions we should talk about.

1. *Your parents.* Your parents have a right to ask for my counseling records. That doesn't mean I'm going to tell them everything you say, but they can ask to see my notes. Most parents don't ask to see my notes because they agree that what you and I talk about should be just between us. We will work together on reaching an understanding with your parents so we both know what to expect. If your parents, friends, or others tell me things about you that will help in our counseling, I will let you know. They're important people in your life, but they're not my clients. I won't keep secrets for them, and I'll make that clear to them if they speak with me.
2. *Danger.* If what we talk about leads me to believe you're in danger of hurting yourself or someone else, by law I have to act to keep you or others safe. But the first thing I would do is talk directly with you about how to do that. If I believe it's necessary to call someone, I will make every effort to tell you first. My most important priority is to help you. If you're in danger, I may need to contact others to help keep you safe.
3. *Abuse.* If I suspect that you, or anyone, is being abused, the state requires that I make a report to child protective services. This could involve sexual abuse, physical abuse, or neglect. If I suspect this, I'll ask you about it directly and then I'll tell you if I need to make a report.
4. *Questions.* Do you have any questions about your privacy or confidentiality with me?

There are other reasons why counselors breach confidentiality, such as for insurance paperwork or court orders, but these details are typically addressed in written informed consent documents.

Social Media and After-Hours Contact

Social media is now so ubiquitous that school and mental health professionals must address it within the informed consent process (Wheeler & Bertram, 2019). In some cases the messaging can be simple, as in an informed consent form that reads "Please note that because of ethical issues, I don't socialize with clients outside of scheduled professional appointments, including through social media." A specific statement such as the following might be useful:

> In my counseling work, I do not use Facebook, Instagram, Twitter, or other such platforms to interact with clients. I have a Facebook page that I use for personal and social reasons, but I don't friend my clients and I don't accept friend requests from them. My goal is to keep our relationship professional.

Again, there are individual, agency, and professional variations in how clients or students can interact with professionals within the frame of social media. In some cases, it may be an important clinical tool to be used to extend care, but if so, it should be used for specific purposes and professional/personal boundaries should be clear. In other cases, it can be both invasive and worrying to have clients reach out to you via social media.

Emergency Procedures

Emergency procedures should be described in your informed consent document. Your description may be as simple as "In cases of emergency, you should call 911 immediately." When discussing emergency procedures with youth, you might say something like the following:

> If you're feeling suicidal, it's important to have a positive plan for what to do. Of course, you can call 911 or go to the nearest emergency room. You can also call the National Suicide Prevention Lifeline (1-800-273-TALK—a new 988 number for mental health emergencies will be available in 2022) or text the Crisis Text Line (text HOME to 741741 to connect with a crisis counselor). I'm also interested in your ideas about what you would like to do if you're in a crisis. We can talk more about that today.

Creating a collaborative safety plan is an essential clinical skill. We provide guidance on this in Chapter 9.

Ethical Issues Pertaining to Suicide in Online and Other Distance Counseling Formats

Coronavirus-related economic shutdowns, social distancing, and other contemporary factors have quickly increased the use of counseling online and in other distance formats. Going by the names *telehealth*, *telemental health*, and *telebehavioral health*, these counseling platforms follow the same ethics codes and state and federal regulations as face-to-face counseling. However, attention to specific details with regard to informed consent, confidentiality and privacy issues, and emergency procedures is particularly salient when working with clients who are suicidal (Stoll et al., 2020).

Most online, telephonic, or text-based ethical issues in counseling are best addressed by counselor preparation and a clear and thorough informed consent process. Before engaging clients in distance counseling, address the following issues in writing and, when possible, via oral or text-based discussion:

- Before meeting, do a preparation and competence check, including the following:
    a. Learn to use a counseling platform that is compliant with the Health Insurance Portability and Accountability Act of 1996 and has adequate data security and storage.
    b. Establish a clear and secure online payment system.
    c. Develop an electronic informed consent form that clients can review and sign before or at the beginning of counseling.
- Collect information in advance about your client, including identifying information, best contact methods, a home address or location, a personal contact in case of emergency, and contact information of local emergency personnel (e.g., law enforcement, child protective services).
- Describe your strong preference to openly discuss suicide and to work collaboratively, even when clients are in suicidal crisis.
- Make sure your clients know what specific behaviors will prompt an emergency response (e.g., if clients call or text and leave a message that they are suicidal, or if clients hang up or go offline after making a suicide threat).
- Make sure you and your clients agree to an emergency plan (e.g., "I will contact the police and give them your address or your last known location").

Confidentiality is limited when you are using video, online, or telephonic counseling modalities. In particular, you may not be able to ascertain whether your client is in a setting that affords privacy; other people may be present and able to hear or see counseling interactions. In addition, when using text-based platforms, you face the possibility of identity theft—you may not know whether you are really interacting with your client. One method of addressing these limitations to confidentiality is to establish a prearranged challenge question (Rummell & Joyce, 2010).

Directly discussing confidentiality strategies with your clients is recommended. Keep in mind that online and telephonic counseling can be equivalent to face-to-face counseling, but typically the factors that make online approaches effective include (a) establishing and maintaining a therapeutic relationship and (b) implementing evidence-based counseling strategies (Castro et al., 2020; Hanley & Reynolds, 2009). The Zur Institute has a complete comparative list of ethics guidelines pertaining to telehealth counseling across

14 disciplines/organizations, including ACA, the American Psychological Association, the National Association of Social Workers, and the National Board for Certified Counselors (see https://www.zurinstitute.com/ethics-of-telehealth/).

Boundary Setting and Tending

Professional boundaries are a part of all counseling. Appropriate boundaries help clarify the nature of your relationship and aid in establishing and maintaining therapeutic relationships. This is especially true when you are working with clients who may be suicidal. When regularly working with suicidality you might become more easily burned out, your judgment may become impaired, your buttons may get pushed, and in general you may feel increased vulnerability.

Clear boundary setting protects counselors and clients. Boundaries define the parameters of the professional relationship and model clarity, safety, and compassion. The hard truth for all mental health professionals is this: We cannot save people from pain or prevent them from making destructive choices. We can work with people to make changes in their lives—changes that reduce pain and increase joy, changes that may begin a positive momentum—but there are limits, and these limits should be carefully described and observed (see Case Vignettes 2.1 and 2.2).

The Lily and Brian scenario in Case Vignette 2.1 may seem extreme, but in our years of teaching, supervising, and working with difficult populations, we have seen similar (and worse) boundary extensions or breaks (R. Sommers-Flanagan et al., 1998). In telebehavioral health scenarios involving suicidality, you may get many requests to provide immediate assistance via text or telephone. If you respond to such requests with anything that can be construed as providing counseling, you have broken a boundary and begun counseling without establishing informed consent. Whenever clients are suicidal, the temptation to break professional boundaries can be powerful.

Specific circumstances or job demands may require you to give clients your cell phone number or email address, but beware of the implicit messages that accompany this boundary extension. You become responsible for whatever information is communicated through these channels. What are your boundaries for the number of calls a day, or the number of minutes for each call, or the number and length of emails or texts you are willing to read and respond to? Setting and maintaining nuanced boundaries

Case Vignette 2.1
Beyond the Boundaries

Years ago, a kind young volunteer named Lily was working at a homeless shelter. She became close to Brian, a man about her age who struggled with bipolar disorder. Lily was married and had a toddler at home. She spent many hours talking with Brian, trying to convince him to take his medications and get into a rehabilitation program that would train him for entry-level jobs. She was making headway. Brian became med compliant and went on his first job interview, but it did not go well.

After his disastrous interview, Brian called Lily. This was before cell phones. Even though her number was listed in a telephone book, Lily had written her number down for Brian, explicitly giving him permission to call. When she answered, Brian began sobbing, telling her that he was a hopeless case. He thanked her for all she had done, saying, "I just want you to know it's not your fault."

Lily was frightened. She insisted that Brian come to dinner at her house and spend the night on the family's couch. She planned to call her volunteer director in the morning during his office hours. Ironically, calling the director after hours was a boundary Lily did not want to cross.

Brian came to Lily's small apartment, ate dinner, and slept that night on the couch. He did not kill himself, but he did become a demanding force in Lily's life that required several weeks of reboundary setting and extrication assistance from her volunteer director. Lily later went to graduate school in counseling and reflected on her choices with Brian. She was embarrassed by her well-intended but dangerous naiveté. She was grateful that nothing terrible had happened to her or her loved ones.

---

can become slippery. We cannot tell you exactly which boundaries to set, because professional and community norms vary. Our best guidance is for you to consult, read your professional ethics codes, contemplate, and consult again. One more guideline: If you are reluctant to openly consult with colleagues about how you are handling boundaries with clients, then you should probably consult with your colleagues.

Pastoral counselors often have different professional boundaries than rehabilitation, career, school, or mental health counselors.

Case Vignette 2.2
Indirect Giving to Preserve Boundaries

Sharon was a school counselor who regularly visited with Hallie, a 14-year-old girl who lived in a group home because her mother was suffering from meth addiction. Hallie reported occasional suicidal thoughts. She was the brunt of jokes in the hallways because of her weight and wardrobe. Sharon was sympathetic and worried. She asked Hallie whether she could call the group home parents for a consultation. Hallie agreed.

The group home parents, Paul and Michelle, met with Sharon and Hallie. Together they made a plan for Hallie to see a mental health counselor and for Hallie to get an earlier ride home to avoid contact with bullies. Sharon also talked with the school principal about ways to address the bullying directly.

Because access to mental health counseling was limited, Sharon agreed to have Hallie meet with her for brief check-ins until Hallie got her own counselor. Sharon also connected Hallie and her group home parents to a school fund available for students to buy clothes, eyeglasses, and other items. Sharon did not mention that she was a regular donor to this fund.

Sharon was aware that it would feel gratifying to give clothing directly to Hallie, but she also recognized that doing so would be a boundary break. She wanted to preserve the emotionally supportive relationship she had with Hallie. If Hallie knew Sharon was providing clothing, Hallie's expectations might have shifted. Here are two possibilities:

- Hallie might have felt indebted, guilty, or ashamed. She might have pulled back and minimized contact with Sharon, despite her needs for emotional support.
- Hallie could have begun regularly orienting to Sharon for her material needs.

Either way, small boundary breaks can have big implications for counseling and the counseling relationship.

Social workers may have different professional boundaries than psychiatrists or nurses. Licensure laws and ethics codes vary. Make sure the boundaries you set are consistent with the standards of practice in your community and within your professional discipline.

Here are a few basic boundaries we generally recommend:

- Unless your school or agency requires it and provides appropriate liability coverage, do not transport agitated clients who may be suicidal or agree to ride with them in their cars.
- Do not invite clients to join you at social events or places of worship.
- Do not invite clients to your home.
- Do not give your clients your private contact information.
- Do not discuss your family members with clients.

In Case Vignette 2.2, Sharon's school counseling load included 300 students. She could not provide the contact and care for each of them that she was temporarily extending to Hallie. Sharon knew her limits. She brought in the group home parents, had a safety plan in place, and was actively working with Hallie to transition her mental health care to an appropriate community resource.

When Suicide Happens

Having a client die by suicide is an outcome that all mental health professionals dread. Not only will client suicides trigger sadness, anger, guilt, shame, fear, and self-doubt, but sometimes suicides lead to lawsuits or legal inquiries. Other times, suicide survivors or family members will reach out to counselors for support. Whatever the details, the aftermath of a client death by suicide is painful and complex. Several postsuicide measures can help professionals cope with losing a client or student.

Consultation Groups

If your practice includes routinely working with clients who are suicidal, we recommend that you participate in an ongoing peer consultation or peer supervision group. Peer consultation serves two important purposes. Professionally speaking, you need someone to review your assessment and treatment protocols as well as your documentation. If there are gaps in your documentation or questionable professional choices, your colleagues can help you prepare to account for these and orient you toward better practices in the future. Modifying clinical records is illegal, but understanding potential problems can help you focus on how to deal with legal inquiries.

Peer consultation groups also provide professional connection for solace and understanding from friends and colleagues. Emotional support from colleagues who face similar challenges can be especially meaningful. Wellness Practice 2.1 includes a mood management strategy that you can use yourself or with your colleagues.

Wellness Practice 2.1
Happy Songs in Your Life

Music in general, and songs in particular, can trigger happiness, sadness, other emotions, and life memories. Sometimes emotional responses to music are all about the music. Other times emotional responses are about the personal associations or memories that the songs trigger. For example, when John listens to "Joy to the World" by Three Dog Night, he is transported back to positive memories of ninth-grade basketball. It is not unusual for people to turn to music to help regulate emotions or to heighten particular feelings.

For this wellness practice, experiment with the following, and then later consider engaging clients with this activity:

1. Select a song that triggers positive emotions for you.
2. Listen to the song twice in a row and just let the song do its work. You can do this with a friend or by yourself.
3. After you have listened twice and let the positive feelings come, respond to the following prompts:
    a. What emotion does the song bring up?
    b. What is your best guess (hypothesis) for why the song brings up that particular emotion?
    c. Do you usually intentionally listen to this song or just randomly wait for the song to pop into your life?
    d. Optional: Share the song with someone and tell that person why the song triggers positive emotions for you.

At the time of this writing, we have located several articles that illuminate issues that might emerge following a client death by suicide:

- "Facing the Specter of Client Suicide" by Laurie Meyers (2015) in *Counseling Today* (https://ct.counseling.org/2015/10/facing-the-specter-of-client-suicide/)
- "As a Therapist, How Should I Grieve After a Patient's Suicide?" by Lucy Maddox (2018) on *Mosaic* (https://mosaicscience.com/story/therapist-how-should-i-grieve-after-patients-suicide/)
- "Paradise Lost: When Clients Commit Suicide" by Marian Joyce (2013) on Psychotherapy.net (https://www.psychotherapy.net/article/client-suicide-article)

Many other articles are available that focus on how counselors can deal with client suicides. We recommend that you explore this important area and find resources that fit your needs.

Postvention

Postvention is an essential component of dealing with completed suicides. The term *postvention* was first coined by Edwin Shneidman in 1968 at the inaugural gathering of AAS. In 2017, the Psychopathology Committee of the Group for the Advancement for Psychiatry defined and articulated the rationale for suicide postvention: "Postvention, or how clinicians manage the postsuicide aftermath, strengthens suicide prevention, destigmatizes the tragedy, operationalizes the confusing aftermath, and promotes caregiver recovery" (Erlich et al., 2017, p. 507).

Although research on postvention is limited, many different postvention protocols and strategies have been developed. For instance, a 234-page document titled *Coming Together to Care* is available for download at www.texassuicideprevention.org/wp-content/uploads/2013/06/TexasSuicidePrevention-2012Toolkit_8-31.pdf. This document is a postvention toolkit developed in Texas by a consortium of organizations dedicated to suicide prevention.

Postvention is an underdeveloped pillar of suicide prevention (Maple et al., 2019). This is partly because postvention effects are notoriously difficult to assess. Given that every suicide and community or school context is unique, identifying a control group for postvention efficacy research is impossible. In one review of 16 published studies of high research quality, the researchers concluded, "No protective effect of any postvention program could be determined for number of suicide deaths or suicide attempts" (Szumilas & Kutcher, 2011, p. 18). However, "contact with a counseling postvention for familial survivors of suicide generally helped reduce psychological distress in the short term" (p. 18).

Nationally and internationally, beliefs vary regarding how much attention to give a death by suicide. Famous or infamous deaths by suicide get substantial press coverage, and sometimes this raises awareness of the problem. However, the tone of the coverage is influential. A group of 21 academic, community, and not-for-profit organizations published a checklist of dos and don'ts for media reporting on suicide. They recommend that media organizations avoid the following:

- Running sensationalistic headlines
- Including photos of the location, the method, grieving families, or memorials

- Using terms like *epidemic* to describe suicide
- Describing suicides as not explainable or as happening "without warning"
- Quoting from suicide notes
- Using crime investigation reporting styles
- Quoting police or first responders on suicide causes
- Referring to suicides as "committed," "successful," "unsuccessful," or "failed" (this list is adapted from "Recommendations for Reporting on Suicide," n.d.)

Although tragic, suicides are not the fault of loved ones, caregivers, schools, or law enforcement. The best postvention efforts do not level blame or sensationalize but rather encourage grieving, healing, and prevention. (The Suicide Prevention Resource Center has information on an array of suicide-related topics, including postvention, at https://www.sprc.org/news/postvention-prevention.)

Concluding Comments

Competency not only helps ensure that you are meeting professional standards and standards of ethical practice, it also helps reduce anxiety and relieve self-doubt. In this chapter, we summarized competencies for working with clients or students who are suicidal. Although the breadth and complexity of suicide-related competencies may feel overwhelming, as you progress through this book your confidence and comfort with suicide competencies will increase.

Practitioner Guidance and Key Points to Remember

Core suicide competencies, as described by Cramer and his colleagues (2013), include the following:

1. Be aware of and manage your attitude and reactions to suicide.
2. Develop and maintain a collaborative, empathic stance with clients.
3. Know and elicit evidence-based risk and protective factors.
4. Focus on current plan and intent of suicidal ideation.
5. Determine the level of risk.
6. Develop and enact a collaborative evidence-based treatment plan.
7. Notify and involve other persons.
8. Document risk assessment, the treatment plan, and the rationale for clinical decisions.
9. Know the law concerning suicide.
10. Engage in debriefing and self-care.

Along with suicide-related competencies, counselors also need to be well versed in ethical principles and practices associated with suicide assessment and treatment. In addition to knowing your agency's or school's policy and procedures on suicide, you must attend to key ethical issues, including (a) informed consent, (b) confidentiality and its limits, (c) social media policies, and (d) emergency procedures. Several topics specific to online or distance counseling platforms were also discussed in this chapter. Documenting, maintaining professional boundaries, dealing with client or student death by suicide, and engaging in postvention practices are part of functioning as an ethical professional.

Chapter 3

Suicide Assessment

Suicide assessment integrates science and art. Assessment science helps practitioners determine what information is most important during a clinical interview and how to best obtain reliable and valid assessment data (J. Sommers-Flanagan et al., 2020; Wygant et al., 2020). The art of assessment includes how and when to (a) ask questions, (b) be more or less collaborative and relational, (c) offer empathy, and (d) explore client symptoms and strengths in ways that facilitate trust and stimulate honesty (Ganzini et al., 2013). Because suicide is a painful and provocative topic, advanced assessment skills are essential.

When clients or students experience suicidality, exposure to an assessment process can feel threatening. As a consequence, we believe counselors should embrace principles of therapeutic assessment (Fischer, 1970, 1985). Therapeutic assessment originated in the late 1960s, when Constance Fischer began practicing and publishing about a radical new assessment approach. Unlike in traditional objective and unilateral approaches to assessment, Fischer (1969, 1970) began viewing clients as coevaluators. Stephen Finn has extended Fischer's ideas; the approach is now called *therapeutic assessment* (Finn et al., 2012).

The principles of therapeutic assessment are consistent with the professional counseling paradigm (Capuzzi & Stauffer, 2016); they include collaboration, compassion, openness, honesty, and a commitment to valuing clients as the ultimate experts on their lived

• 49

experiences. Although information gathering remains important, relationship connection during assessment interviews takes priority. Every assessment finding needs to be validated and understood within each client's unique personal context. Collaboration is the cornerstone; assessments are done with clients, not on clients (Martin, 2020; J. Sommers-Flanagan & Sommers-Flanagan, 2017). As Flemons and Gralnik (2013) wrote, when conducting suicide assessments, "Our goal is not to remain objectively removed but, rather, to become empathically connected" (p. 6).

Suicide Assessment as Therapeutic Assessment

Suicide researchers, practitioners, and prevention specialists have long held the view that asking about suicide does not increase suicidality. Although we agree that asking directly is essential, we also believe that direct questions about suicidality are sometimes asked in ways that fall short of being therapeutic. Also, standardized assessments can impede empathy and relationship building. While consulting with agencies and schools on their suicide assessment and referral processes, we have often heard from exasperated professionals who dislike trying to connect with students or clients who are possibly suicidal using mandatory, formulaic assessment checklists or protocols.

Suicide assessment does not always have neutral or positive effects (de Beurs et al., 2016). Harris and Goh (2017) conducted a randomized controlled trial evaluating the emotional effects of a suicide assessment protocol on Singapore residents. Although they reported no overall iatrogenic effects, 24% of participants experienced increased negative affect after taking the Suicide Affect-Behavior-Cognition scale, whereas 20% reported increased positive affect. Using a similar protocol, a Dutch research team also found that a subset of participants had increased negative affect after responding to 21 items from the Beck Scale for Suicide Ideation (A. T. Beck, Kovacs, & Weissman, 1979; de Beurs et al., 2016).

For many reasons—including anxiety, inadequate training, client hostility, fears of liability, or countertransference—professionals sometimes engage poorly with clients who are suicidal (Cureton & Clemens, 2015). We firmly believe that school and mental health professionals can do better than following a lock-step suicide assessment protocol. Instead of adopting an authoritative assessment role, we encourage you to apply therapeutic assessment principles to deepen the validity of your suicide assessment interviews.

Suicide Assessment: Process and Protocols

A one-size-fits-all suicide assessment protocol is unrealistic. You should be ready to shift into suicide assessment as needed depending on the clinical situation. Although you will want to prepare an organized interviewing outline, you will need to be equally ready to deviate from your outline depending on how clients respond to your questions, empathic reflections, and efforts to engage in constructive problem-solving. Core components of a comprehensive suicide assessment interview include the following:

1. Know about suicide risk factors, protective factors, and warning signs—and monitor for the individualized manifestation or absence of these factors with each client.
2. Consider using suicide assessment instruments or questionnaires.
3. Ask about and collaboratively explore suicidal ideation, including ideation triggers, frequency, duration, intensity, and termination, using nuanced interviewing assessment skills.
4. Be prepared to deal with irritability and hopelessness.
5. Avoid psychiatric symptom-oriented questioning patterns that overly focus on client distress by also asking about wellness, strengths, and positive experiences.
6. Ask about and explore suicide plans.
7. Ask about and explore previous attempts and client self-control, including client use of substances for the purposes of desensitization.
8. Ask about and explore reasons for living, reasons for dying, the "one thing" question, and suicidal intent.
9. Engage clients in collaborative problem-solving and safety planning for assessment, treatment, and decision-making purposes.
10. Consider contacting collateral informants for assessment and treatment purposes.
11. Consult when possible, and document your decision-making process and recommendations.

Know About Suicide Risk Factors, Protective Factors, and Warning Signs

A *suicide risk factor* is a measurable trait, behavior, demographic, or situation that is statistically associated with higher rates of suicidal ideation, attempts, and/or death by suicide (Erbacher et al., 2015). A *suicide protective factor* is the opposite—a trait, behavior, demographic, or situation linked to prevention or protection. A *suicide warning sign* is a near-term state, behavior, or situation that has been observed in people shortly before they make an attempt or die by suicide (Rudd, 2006).

Researchers and clinicians have developed many acronyms to aid in remembering suicide risk factors. As we reflect on the research, we suspect there are no SIMPLE STEPS (risk factors; McGlothlin, 2008) for determining whether the PATH IS WARM (warning signs; Lester et al., 2011) among SAD PERSONS (risk factors; Patterson et al., 1983).

If you are familiar with research on suicide risk assessment, you probably get the joke embedded in the preceding paragraph. Each of these acronyms orient clinicians to important risk factors and warning signs, but they have little empirical support as suicide predictors and limited practical utility for clinicians who need to make decisions about suicide risk, hospitalization, and treatment planning (Franklin et al., 2017). Suicide researchers and practitioners are mostly in agreement about this: Too much focus on suicide risk factor checklists draws clinicians away from developing therapeutic relationships and offers little assistance in suicide prediction (Franklin et al., 2017; Large & Kapur, 2018; Warden et al., 2014).

Several prominent researchers and practitioners have called for clinicians to stop using suicide risk and protective factors to categorize client risk (Jobes, 2016; Maris, 2019; Nielssen et al., 2017). Their reasoning is that risk categorization results in an unacceptable number of false positives (predicting suicide when it does not occur) and false negatives (not predicting suicide when it does occur). Why then are we now turning to a review (albeit a brief one) of suicide risk factors, protective factors, and warning signs?

Clinicians should be knowledgeable about traditional risk factors (although no one can remember them all) for two reasons. First, your employment situation may require you to make a statement about risk and recommendations for treatment. When this situation arises, we recommend working collaboratively with clients. However, occasionally your setting or the situation will mandate that you make a professional estimate; in such cases, you will want to follow an established risk categorization procedure.

Second, knowledge of suicide risk and protective factors informs your understanding of general suicide-related dynamics as well as your empathic connection and collaboration with individual clients. For example, if you know that cutting functions as both a risk factor and a protective factor, you can talk with clients about their personal use of cutting, emphasizing your respect for your client's unique cutting experiences.

Displaying knowledge while simultaneously deferring to clients for verification is a therapeutic assessment practice that facilitates a deeper conversation about how suicidal impulses manifest within individuals. Collaboratively exploring how risk and protective factors are experienced within an individual client's life aids suicide assessment and treatment planning.

A Brief Overview of Suicide Risk Factors
Hundreds of risk factors are sprinkled throughout the suicide literature (Franklin et al., 2017). Suicide risk factor checklists represent the best science we have for predicting suicide in large groups of people. Although existing risk factors do not account for much variance, as research continues, new risk factors are constantly being identified (Bolton et al., 2012). In the following sections, we organize research-based risk factors into three categories:

1. Demographics
2. Mental disorders and psychiatric treatment
3. Social, personal, behavioral, and contextual risk factors

As you read about risk factors, protective factors, and warning signs, remember that knowledge of risk is foundational, but developing positive therapeutic relationships with clients will make your predictions more accurate and your clients safer. Also, an absence of risk factors and warning signs in individual clients is no guarantee of client safety.

Risk factors related to demographics. Demographics in suicidology generally refer to subpopulations of people—usually based on sex (not gender), age, and race. Consistent with academic/scientific definitions of sex and gender, we use *sex* to refer to biological sex at birth (i.e., male, female, or intersex) and *gender* to refer to sociocultural identities along a broad continuum (Schudson et al., 2019). In this section, we discuss the more stable demographics of sex, age, and race; the more fluid concept of gender is discussed in a later section. In all cases, suicide rates are reported based on the number of deaths per 100,000 people. As a comparator, in 2018 the overall suicide rate in the United States was 14.2 deaths per 100,000.

Across all ages, males are more likely to die by suicide than females. The heightened risk of being male varies from 1.8 times the risk for females (at ages 10–14 years; 3.66 vs. 2.02) to 13.2 times the risk (at ages 85+ years; 47.17 vs. 3.58). In general, in the U.S. population, the risk of death by suicide for males increases with age (from 3.66 at ages 10–14 to 47.17 at ages 85+). Males also die by suicide at higher rates across all categories of race (see Figure 3.1). Although males have higher suicide rates, females are 3 to 4 times more likely than males to make a suicide attempt.

Suicide rates tend to increase with age. Beginning with 2.85 per 100,000 at ages 10–14, the numbers steadily increase until ages 55–59 (21.66) and then level off to range from 16 to 19 per 100,000 through and beyond age 85. Within this general trend there is notable variation. In particular, Native American youth and young adults (especially males) have particularly high suicide rates, followed by White male young adults (see Figure 3.2 for comparisons of Native American and White American males). However, among Native American males the rates eventually level off and decrease (to 7.69 for ages 70–74), whereas the numbers generally trend upward for White males (36–47 per 100,000 for ages from 75 to 85+).

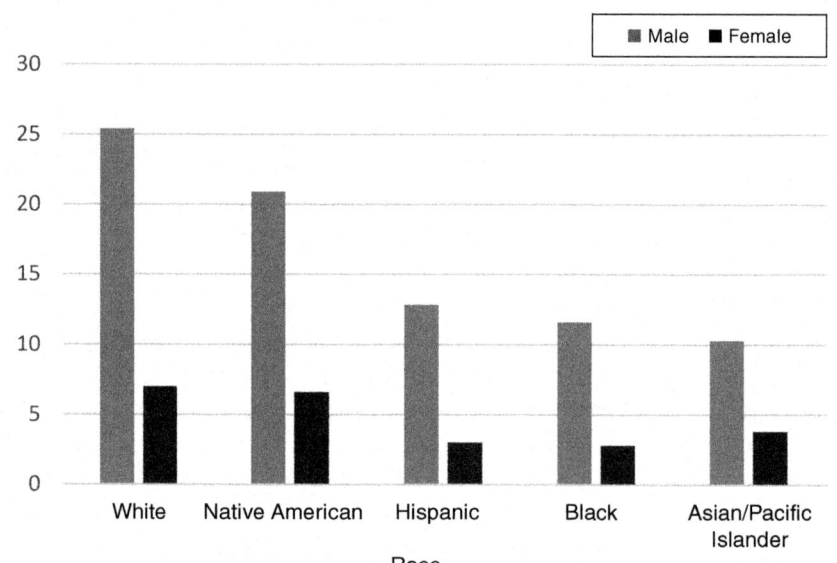

FIGURE 3.1
Suicide Rates by Race and Sex per 100,000

Note. The 2018 suicide death totals in this figure were populated using data from the Centers for Disease Control and Prevention Web-based Injury Statistics Query and Reporting System website at https://www.cdc.gov/injury/wisqars/LeadingCauses.html.

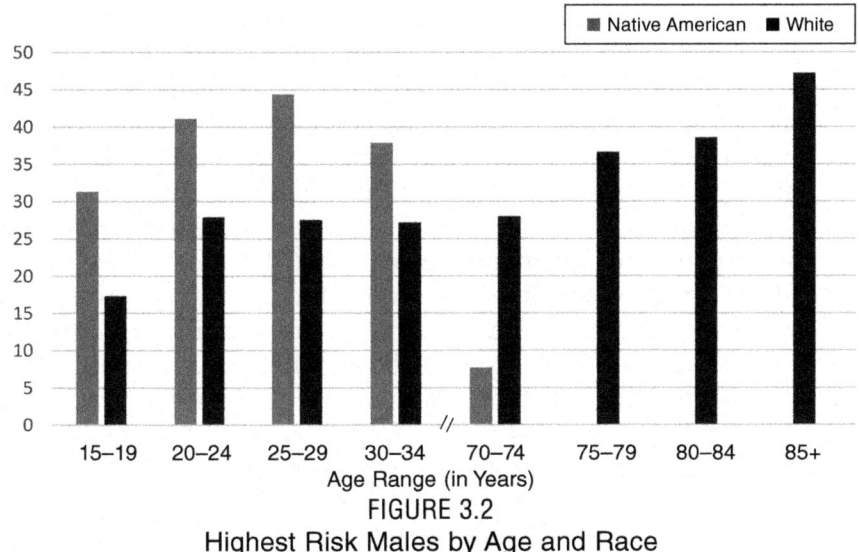

FIGURE 3.2
Highest Risk Males by Age and Race

Note. Data were unavailable for Native American males older than 74 years. Data are from the Centers for Disease Control and Prevention (2020).

Additionally, over the past 15 years, suicide deaths among Black youth have risen at an alarming rate (see *Ring the alarm: The crisis of Black youth suicide in America*, https://watsoncoleman.house.gov/uploadedfiles/full_taskforce_report.pdf).

Definitive explanations for variations in suicide rates among subgroups are sparse and speculative. Although we support the search for explanations of higher and lower rates, when individuals engage in data-free speculation, the outcome frequently leans toward pathologizing individuals based on race, sex, or age. Instead of searching for weaknesses and psychopathology, we prefer focusing on what positive traits or strengths are linked to low suicide rates in specific populations.

Risk factors related to mental disorders and psychiatric treatment. The presence of a specific mental disorder confers greater individual suicide risk. In general, having more than one mental disorder confers greater risk, and risk is further increased as individuals experience greater symptom severity and subjective distress. A list and brief descriptions of mental disorders and situations linked to suicide follow:

1. *Clinical depression.* Although major depressive disorder is linked to suicide, clinical depression plus additional specific distressing symptoms (e.g., severe anxiety or insomnia) increase risk (Bolton et al., 2010; Fawcett et al., 1993).

2. *Posttraumatic stress disorder.* Trauma experiences are associated with later suicide, but more so when trauma begins in childhood and is assaultive, chronic, and severe (Wilcox & Fawcett, 2012). In particular, adult reports of adverse childhood experiences indicate that higher numbers of such experiences are correlated with suicide attempts (Chapman et al., 2007; Shannonhouse et al., 2020).
3. *Bipolar disorder.* Bipolar disorder is linked to the highest suicide attempt rate of all mental disorders (Mazaheri et al., 2019). Specifically, when there is a comorbid mental disorder, and when symptoms are more severe, are unremitting, trigger intense distress, and are associated with low life quality, risk is substantially higher (Cassidy, 2011; Mazaheri et al., 2019).
4. *Substance abuse or dependence.* Alcohol and drug use is linked to suicide, but risk especially increases with comorbid symptoms. Substances reduce inhibition, desensitize clients to pain, and increase immediate risk (Klonsky & May, 2015). In particular, higher opioid doses and discontinuation of opioid treatment—possibly due to associated chronic pain—are associated with greater risk of death by suicide (Ilgen et al., 2016; Oliva et al., 2020).
5. *Schizophrenia.* A diagnosis of schizophrenia increases risk, especially when positive symptoms (e.g., command hallucinations) are present (Hor & Taylor, 2010).
6. *Anorexia nervosa.* Anorexia is linked to higher suicide rates, especially when it is comorbid with anxiety and/or depression (Forcano et al., 2011).
7. *Borderline personality disorder.* Clients with a borderline personality diagnosis have heightened suicide attempt rates and are at higher risk for death by suicide (Linehan et al., 2012).
8. *Conduct disorder.* When depression and substance abuse/dependence are also present, conduct disorder confers particular risk, possibly because of impulsiveness and poor family support (Vander Stoep et al., 2011).
9. *Insomnia.* Insomnia is an independent suicide risk factor but also exacerbates risk when comorbid with other mental disorders (Ribeiro et al., 2012).
10. *Post-hospital discharge.* Individuals are at increased risk following psychiatric hospitalization, possibly because of adverse events that occur during hospitalization or other unspecified factors (Chung et al., 2016; Large & Kapur, 2018).
11. *Use of SSRIs.* SSRI medication labels include a black box warning that suicidal thinking and behavior may increase (U.S. Food and Drug Administration, 2007). Risk is particularly high right after SSRIs are first administered (after 30 minutes and

up to 30 days; Healy, 2009; D. Healy, personal communication, February 17, 2004).

Risk factors related to social, personal, behavioral, and contextual conditions. Various social behaviors and conditions, personal situations, specific behaviors, and sociological contexts are linked to greater suicide risk. Some of these factors are more internalized traits, whereas others involve situations that confer greater risk.

1. *Previous attempts.* Suicide risk is higher when there has been a previous suicide attempt (Brown et al., 2020; Fowler, 2012). Previous attempts are "one of the most reliable and potent predictors of future suicidal ideation, attempts, and death by suicide across the lifespan" (Van Orden et al., 2010, p. 577). Although previous attempts are generally associated with increased risk, in some cases they function as a protective factor.
2. *Nonsuicidal self-injury.* Self-mutilation or nonsuicidal self-injury is not necessarily indicative of increased suicide risk. However, repeated self-harm predicts eventual suicide, especially in young women (Zahl & Hawton, 2004). When self-harm progressively escalates, it may constitute a rehearsal behavior that leads to death by suicide. However, like previous attempts, for some people, nonsuicidal self-injury can protect against suicide.
3. *Social isolation/loneliness.* Divorced, widowed, and separated people are at higher risk for suicide. Single, never-married individuals die by suicide at nearly double the rate of married individuals (Van Orden et al., 2010).
4. *Physical illness.* Physical illness and suicide are linked. Specific illnesses that confer increased suicide risk include brain cancer, chronic pain, stroke, rheumatoid arthritis, hemodialysis, dementia, and others (Jia et al., 2014).
5. *Unemployment or personal loss.* Losses that are associated with increased suicide risk include loss of (a) employment, (b) status, (c) a loved one, (d) physical health or mobility, (e) a pet, and (f) face through shameful events (Mandal & Zalewska, 2012; Maris, 2019).
6. *Military or veteran status.* Being a veteran in general, and being a young veteran in particular, appears to elevate suicide risk. The reasons for this may have to do with (a) posttraumatic stress (including traumatic brain injury), (b) access to firearms, (c) difficulties adjusting to civilian life, or (d) reluctance to acknowledge emotional problems or seek help (Bongar et al., 2017).

7. *Availability of firearms.* Access to firearms is a suicide risk factor in the United States and in other countries (Runyan et al., 2015). Firearms safety and restriction are associated with reduced suicide rates, especially among males (Houtsma et al., 2018). More than 50% of deaths by suicide in the United States involve firearms.
8. *Sexual orientation, sexuality, and gender identity.* Individual characteristics related to sexuality and gender are linked to increased suicide risk. Individuals who identify as lesbian, gay, bisexual, transgender, queer, or questioning (or other sexual and gender minorities; LGBTQ+) have significantly higher suicide attempt rates; they also may have higher completion rates (although empirical data on completion rates are less clear). In particular, sexuality-related verbal abuse, parental rejection, depression, hopelessness, and societal oppression substantially increase suicidality among people who identify as LGBTQ+ (Kaniuka et al., 2019).
9. *Suicide contagion.* Suicide contagion is defined as an indirect or direct passing on of suicidal behavior from one person to another. Whether it is a local suicide or a highly publicized one (e.g., that of Robin Williams), individuals who have a previous history of depression and suicide attempts have the highest risk of being affected by contagion (Lake & Gould, 2014).
10. *Abuse and bullying.* Social trauma and bullying (both online and in person) are contextual factors linked to suicidal ideation, attempts, and death by suicide. Some researchers describe a phenomenon referred to as "spontaneous, unplanned adolescent suicides" that appear unrelated to depression and other traditional risk factors (Reed et al., 2015, p. 128).
11. *Sociopolitical, astronomical, and geographic conditions.* Suicide rates vary by region, country, and season and appear to increase during significant astronomical events, such as the passing of Halley's Comet. Although precipitation and cloudy days are unrelated to suicide, the month of April (in the Northern Hemisphere) and sparsely populated rural settings are correlated with increased rates. Some U.S. states have suicide rates 3 times higher than rates in other states.
12. *Occupation.* Similar to military status, specific occupations are linked to higher suicide rates. Data from 2016 indicated that individuals employed in mining and other extraction industries had the highest suicide rates (54.2 per 100,000). Individuals

employed in the construction industry had the second highest suicide rates (45.3 per 100,000; Peterson et al., 2020).
13. *Poverty.* Although poverty may or may not be a suicide risk factor among adult populations, researchers have reported that suicide rates are significantly higher among children living in poverty (Hoffmann et al., 2020).

A Brief Overview of Suicide Protective Factors

There are two types of protective factors: (a) factors linked to reduced suicide risk in the overall U.S. population and (b) factors identified as protective for individuals within specific populations (e.g., Native American youth, military personnel, transgender individuals).

General protective factors (see Rudd, 2014)

- Reasons for living (e.g., being a role model for others, having children or loved ones)
- Higher global functioning (i.e., individuals who score higher on overall life functioning tend to have lower suicide rates)
- Presence of social support (e.g., reporting many friendships)
- Life satisfaction (e.g., viewing life as meaningful)
- Frequent attendance at religious services
- Suicide-related beliefs (e.g., believing that suicide is an unacceptable life choice)
- Children present in the home
- Hopefulness
- Active participation in treatment

Specific protective factors

- Parent connectedness (for adolescents)
- Neighborhood safety (for adolescents)
- Academic achievement (for adolescents)
- Supportive school climate (for sexual minority youth)
- Supportive/accepting family climate (for youth with diverse sexual identities)
- Coming out/disclosing (for transgender adults)

Like risk factors, protective factors only account for a small portion of the variance associated with death by suicide (Franklin et al., 2017). However, being informed of protective factors in general can help you identify what might help protect individual clients from suicide. In addition, exploring protective factors with clients provides a foundation for identifying, nurturing, and growing individualized protective factors.

A Brief Overview of Warning Signs

Warning signs are limited in many of the same ways as risk and protective factors. Although they intuitively seem important to suicide prevention, in practice they have not been shown to have much clinical significance (Franklin et al., 2017).

In 2003, the American Association of Suicidology brought together expert suicidologists and asked them to develop an evidence-based list of suicide warning signs. The goal was to provide a suicide warning signs checklist that could be used to flag individuals at immediate suicide risk. The work group reduced hundreds of potential warning signs from the literature to their 10 top suicide-specific warning signs. These warning signs were organized into the acronym IS PATH WARM:

I = Ideation
S = Substance use
P = Purposelessness
A = Anxiety
T = Trapped
H = Hopelessness
W = Withdrawal
A = Anger
R = Recklessness
M = Mood change

IS PATH WARM is broadly evidence based because it is derived from empirical research. However, despite its research foundation, IS PATH WARM has little empirical support. In one study, only anger/aggression distinguished suicide attempters from suicidal ideators (Gunn et al., 2011). In another study, IS PATH WARM did not adequately discriminate genuine and simulated suicide notes (Lester et al., 2011). These studies capture how difficult it is to anticipate suicidal behavior, even when using state-of-the-science warning signs.

Suicide Assessment Instruments or Questionnaires

Many standardized suicide screening and assessment instruments exist. These instruments can be used to efficiently gather information regarding suicidality (Erford et al., 2018). Although we prefer using face-to-face assessment interviews, we also recognize that some clients may find it easier to disclose suicidal ideation on a questionnaire.

Using standardized instruments allows clinicians to quickly gather lots of information. On the down side, questionnaires are mechanized; they do not flex or provide clients with empathy or support. The information obtained is only useful if clients respond honestly. Also, clinicians must review the client's responses before the session starts. Although checklist procedures and questionnaires are useful for uncovering suicidality, if clients indicate suicidality, the baton must be passed to a competent clinician for a clinical interview and a crisis or safety planning intervention.

Columbia-Suicide Severity Rating Scale (C-SSRS; Posner et al., 2011)

In the world of suicide assessment instruments, the C-SSRS is considered the gold standard. The C-SSRS has been recommended or adopted by several large-scale organizations, including the Centers for Disease Control and Prevention and the National Institute of Mental Health. Many school districts throughout the United States also use the C-SSRS.

The C-SSRS has two opening questions: One assesses for passive suicidal ideation, and the other assesses for active suicidal ideation. If respondents answer "yes" to the active suicidal ideation question, four follow-up questions are administered. The final question is a preparation question: "Have you ever done anything, started to do anything, or prepared to do anything to end your life?" Responses to the C-SSRS are color-coded to indicate low risk, moderate risk, or high risk. Despite its gold-star status, it is worth noting that in a recent study of 1,376 adult patients in an emergency room setting, the C-SSRS exhibited weak psychometrics and performed poorly as a predictor of future suicide attempts. The researchers concluded, "The utility of the C-SSRS in an [emergency department] setting is inadequate in terms of predictive power, though may be useful for classification of suicidal thoughts and behavior" (Brown et al., 2020, p. 7).

Reasons for Living Inventory (Linehan et al., 1983)

The Reasons for Living Inventory is a 48-item inventory that focuses exclusively on protective factors (i.e., reasons for living). It includes six factors: (a) Survival and Coping, (b) Responsibility to Family, (c) Child-Related Concerns, (d) Fear of Suicide, (e) Fear of Social Disapproval, and (f) Moral Objections (Linehan et al., 1983, p. 283). Administering the Reasons for Living Inventory can stimulate discussions of what your client finds meaningful in life.

Beck Hopelessness Scale (A. T. Beck & Steer, 1988)
The Beck Hopelessness Scale is a 20-item true/false self-report questionnaire focusing on hopelessness. The item content includes negative and positive beliefs about the future. It has high reliability (.87–.93) and predicts suicide attempts and death by suicide (Brown et al., 2000). A. T. Beck (2009) has long considered hopelessness the central cognitive factor linked to suicide.

Suicide Status Form (SSF; Jobes et al., 1997)
Jobes developed the SSF as the centerpiece of his collaborative assessment and management of suicidality model. The SSF has six self-report and six clinician-administered items rated on a 5-point Likert-type scale; items measure psychological pain, external pressures, agitation, hopelessness, low self-regard, and overall risk of suicide. The SSF is a monitoring device used in the collaborative assessment and management of suicidality model to focus in on and intervene with suicidality. It has weak reliability but is sensitive to change and has high utility for working directly on an ongoing basis with clients who are suicidal.

Patient Health Questionnaire–9
The Patient Health Questionnaire–9 is widely used to screen for depression and suicide, especially in health care settings. It includes nine items rated on a 4-point Likert scale. Patients estimate how often over the past 2 weeks they have experienced depressive symptoms (i.e., "not at all," "several days," "more than half the days," or "nearly every day"). All items come directly from *Diagnostic and Statistical Manual of Mental Disorders* (5th ed.; American Psychiatric Association, 2013) diagnostic criteria for major depression. Item 9 is a multidimensional question about suicide: "How often have you had . . . thoughts that you would be better off dead or of hurting yourself in some way?" Although popular in medical settings, Item 9 is generally considered "an insufficient assessment tool for suicide risk and suicide ideation" (Na et al., 2018, p. 34).

Ask About and Collaboratively Explore Suicidal Ideation

Asking directly about suicide while maintaining a compassionate and calm demeanor requires practice. As reassurance, it is good to know that Hahn and Marks (1996) reported that 97% of clients who were previously suicidal were either receptive to or neutral about discussing suicide during intake sessions. What follows are three approaches for bringing up the topic and asking clients about suicide (adapted from J. Sommers-Flanagan, 2018a).

Use a Normalizing Frame

Prevention and intervention programs often recommend asking clients, "Have you been thinking about suicide recently?" If you are with someone from whom you can expect an honest response, this is an adequate approach. However, in a meta-analysis of 70 studies, about 60% of people who died by suicide denied suicidal ideation when asked by a general practitioner or psychiatrist (McHugh et al., 2019). Asking directly is fine, but psychological and interpersonal barriers can stop people from openly sharing suicidal thoughts. When asking directly about suicide, we recommend using a normalizing frame. For example:

> I asked this question since almost all people at one time or another during their lives have thought about suicide. There is nothing abnormal about the thought. In fact it is very normal when one feels so down in the dumps. The thought itself is not harmful. (Wollersheim, 1974, p. 223)

Here are three more examples of using a normalizing frame:

- "I recently learned that up to 50% of teenagers have had thoughts about suicide. Is that true for you?"
- "It's not unusual for people who are feeling down to also have thoughts about suicide. Have you had any thoughts about suicide?"
- "I ask everyone I meet with about suicide, and so I'm going to ask you: Have you had any thoughts about death or suicide?"

Normalizing suicidal thoughts will reassure clients that you are comfortable with the subject, in control of the situation, and capable of dealing with the problem.

Use Gentle Assumption

Based on two decades of clinical experience, Shea (2011) recommended using a framing strategy called *gentle assumption*. To use gentle assumption, you presume that potentially embarrassing thoughts or behaviors are already occurring. Instead of asking "Have you been thinking about suicide?" you would ask, "When was the last time when you had thoughts about suicide?" Gentle assumption makes it easier for clients to disclose suicidal ideation.

Use Mood Ratings With a Suicide Floor

In our work with adolescents and young adults we developed a mood rating procedure to initiate conversations about suicide. It includes eight steps.

1. "Do you mind if I ask a few questions about your mood?" (This is an invitation for collaboration; clients can say "no," but they rarely do.)
2. "I'd like to take a rating of your mood using a scale from 0 to 10. Zero is the worst mood possible. A rating of 0 would mean you're totally depressed and you're just going to kill yourself. At the top, a 10 is your best possible mood. If you're a 10, you're in the best mood possible. You might be dancing or singing or doing whatever you do when you're in your best mood. So on that 0-to-10 scale, where 0 is depression and suicide and 10 is the best mood ever, what rating would you give your mood right now?" (Each end of the scale is anchored for mutual understanding. We have done this assessment procedure hundreds of times; clients usually understand the question and answer immediately.)
3. "What's happening now that makes you give your mood that rating?" (This question links the mood rating to an external situation or experience. After you ask, "What's happening now?" you should use reflective listening skills and open questions to facilitate understanding of your clients' emotional state.)
4. "What's the worst or lowest mood rating you've had over the past 3 months?" (This informs you of the lowest lows. Although this example uses "the past 3 months," you can use whatever time period is relevant; for example, "in the past year" or "in your whole life.")
5. "What was happening that made you a _____?" (This question links clients' lowest rating to a situation or experience and can lead to a discussion of previous attempts. If it does, you can shift from the rating process to discussing a previous attempt or return to talk about the previous attempt later, depending on your clients' preference.)
6. "For you, what would be a normal mood rating on a normal day?" (This question lets clients define their normal. You can ask this "normal" mood question at any point in the scaling process. For example, if a client begins with, "I'm a 5 today, so I'm feeling good," you might immediately say, "It sounds like 5 is above average for you. What's your usual or average rating?" During the whole process you should go with the clients' flow as they rate their mood.)
7. "What's the best mood rating you've had in the past 3 months?" (Again, asking about "the past 3 months" is not set in stone. What is important is to end your rating process on a positive

mood rating and an exploration of what is linked to positive mood ratings.)
8. "What was happening then that helped give you such a high mood rating?" (This last question links the positive rating to an external situation or experience. After hearing about whatever improves your clients' mood, use your active listening skills to prompt your clients to elaborate on details associated with their positive mood rating.)

The mood rating with a suicide floor tool facilitates a deeper understanding of life events linked to negative and positive moods and suicidal ideation. Although eight steps are described, do not be rigid about sticking with the steps or the ratings. For example, if, when providing the low rating, your client begins talking about a trauma, you may take a side road to explore the traumatic experience and related symptoms. You can always come back to the rating process later. The rating process can lead you toward further assessment, formal counseling, or safety planning.

Responding to Suicidal Ideation

If you use a standardized questionnaire or clinical interviewing strategy to broach suicide and your client responds, in essence, with, "Yes, I think about suicide," what's next?

First, remember that hearing about your client's suicidal ideation is good news. If your client discloses suicidal ideation, some trust has been established, and that is a positive sign. Also, remember that depressive symptoms and suicidal thoughts are normal responses to distress. Then, provide emotional validation as you normalize your client's response: "Given the stress you're experiencing, it's not unusual that you're sometimes thinking about suicide. It sounds like things have been really difficult lately."

Recently, Bella, one of our first-year counseling graduate students, encountered a client who was suicidal during practicum. Although she was instantly anxious, Bella remembered the normalizing frame. She started with, "It's not at all unusual for college students to have suicidal thoughts," moved to, "You know, it's really pretty normal for people to think about suicide," and added, "If you're feeling distressed, it's perfectly natural to think about suicide," along with several more variations of the same message.

Bella's client (a 20-year-old White, cisgender lesbian female) showed visible relief. In response, she shared that she had never spoken of her suicidal thoughts to anyone. She thanked Bella for listening. She returned for future sessions and continued to work on her suicidality. At the end of eight sessions, the client was less depressed and reported that she no longer felt suicidal.

Many individuals who experience suicidality also feel socially disconnected, emotionally invalidated, and as if they are a burden (Joiner, 2005; Linehan, 1993). Efforts to normalize, validate, and provide empathic reflections are essential to helping clients feel more normal. When clients feel normal, they are less likely to feel shame and more likely to work productively on the internal or situational stressors driving their suicidal ideation.

Gathering Useful Details About Suicidal Ideation

For most clients, suicidal ideation comes and goes. Suicide assessment protocols traditionally include questions about the frequency, duration, and intensity of ideation. We think it is wise to add questions about what triggers suicidal ideation and what helps to diminish (or eliminate) it.

- *Frequency.* Ask, "How often do you think about suicide?" If an open-ended question seems too difficult, you can ask this as a closed question: "Do you think about suicide every day . . . or less often?" If clients report thinking of suicide every day, follow up with, "How often during an average day?"
- *Triggers.* Ask, "What usually triggers your suicidal thoughts?" or "What's happening when you start thinking about suicide?"
- *Intensity.* Ask, "How intense are your thoughts about suicide? Do they gently pop into your head and drift around at a distance, or do they have lots of power and intensity and become the only thing you can think about?"
- *Duration.* Ask, "Once they start, how long do thoughts about suicide stay with you?"
- *Termination.* Ask, "What's happening when your suicidal thoughts stop? Are there some strategies or situations that help them go away or stay away?"

As you explore suicidal ideation, it helps to display calmness and curiosity rather than judgment. Instead of thinking, "We need to get rid of these thoughts," focus on how you can collaboratively and empathically explore the suicidal thoughts. The last question (about what helps suicidal thoughts go away) is central to the strengths-based approach.

Some clients will deny suicidal ideation. If this happens, and their denial feels genuine, acknowledge and accept the denial while noting that you were just using your standard practice (e.g., "OK. Thanks. Asking about suicide is just something I do with everyone."). If the denial rings false or is combined with severe distress or other risk factors, acknowledge and accept the response, but then find a way to return to the topic of suicide later in the session.

Be Prepared for Irritability, Hostility, and Hopelessness

Thoughts about suicide are often natural manifestations of depressed moods or depressing or invalidating situations and may be linked to a depressive disorder. Irritability is a common depressive symptom. Among children and adolescents, irritability is a central feature of depression (see Case Vignette 3.1).

A Strategy for Responding to Irritability or Hostility
Client irritability or hostility may interfere with rapport and provoke negative emotional reactions. If a client is insulting you (e.g., "Everything you say is bullshit. I'll kill myself if I want to."), you can try a three-part strategy: (a) use reflective listening, (b) validate and gently interpret, and (c) express your commitment to working with your client regardless of their irritability:

Case Vignette 3.1
Intense Irritability

A school counseling colleague of ours shared a story about her work with a 16-year-old adolescent.

> I got a referral from the industrial arts teacher. He had seen fresh cuts on her arms and sent her to me. The student arrived at my office, refused to enter, and literally screamed from the doorway: "I hate counseling! I hate you! You're an ugly old lady! I'm not telling you anything!"
>
> I thought there was no way I was getting this girl into my office. But after 5 minutes of me nodding, smiling, and paraphrasing from my chair with her in the doorway, she began inching into the room. Eventually she slumped into a chair. I asked if I could shut the door. She consented. As soon as the door was shut, she burst into tears.
>
> What helped me in this situation was being patient and not taking her anger and hostility personally. Typically there is pain and vulnerability just beneath student anger. All I had to do was be kind, use reflective listening skills, and let her know I was not afraid of her hostility.

1. "As you talk, I hear annoyance and irritability in your voice." (Reflective listening)
2. "When I hear your annoyance, I feel like it's partly an expression of how tired you are of feeling bad and sad. So I don't blame you for feeling annoyed with me. Being annoyed is part of being depressed." (Validation and gentle interpretation)
3. "I want to work with you. I'm sure you'll be annoyed with me sometimes. That's OK. If you're unhappy with something I say, please tell me, because I want to be helpful, and I'd rather be less annoying than more annoying." (Statement of commitment)

Being prepared to deal with irritability will help you feel more competent as you work with clients who are suicidal.

Hopelessness

One especially important cognitive symptom linked to suicidality is hopelessness (Van Orden et al., 2010; Wenzel et al., 2009). To assess for hopelessness, you can use the Beck Hopelessness Scale (A. T. Beck & Steer, 1988), look at Item 2 on the Beck Depression Scale, ask directly, or observe your client's language. A. T. Beck (2009) and others (Klonsky et al., 2012) regard hopelessness as the most important predictor of suicide.

Clients express hopelessness in different ways. They might say, "Things will never be different" or "I've felt like this for as long as I can remember." Students may say things like "My life sucks." When you inquire further, they will say they think their life will suck forever.

Your client's ability to make constructive or pleasurable future plans—even plans for the short-term future—is an important gauge of hopefulness. Future-oriented questions include the following:

- "What are your plans for tomorrow?"
- "What do you think you'll be doing 5 years from now?"
- "What might help you feel hopeful again?" (adapted from J. Sommers-Flanagan & Sommers-Flanagan, 2017)

Questions that require clients to reflect on past successes or third-person situations can be useful for evaluating whether hopefulness can be stimulated:

- "You've been down before. How did you get yourself to feel better last time around?"

- "If you had a really good friend going through what you're going through, what would you tell your friend?" (adapted from J. Sommers-Flanagan & Sommers-Flanagan, 2017)

Consistent with the therapeutic assessment framework and a strengths-based approach, queries about hopelessness provide intimate information about depression and suicidality but also can be used to focus on how to regain hopefulness.

Ask About Wellness, Strengths, and Positive Experiences

To maintain balance and avoid inducing negative affect, you should intermittently and systematically include questions with a positive focus during your assessment. As a general guide, we recommend one positive-oriented question for every symptom-oriented question. If you ask whether the client has been feeling down, depressed, or hopeless (Item 2 from the Patient Health Questionnaire–9), then, after using your active listening skills to explore your client's response, follow that question with, "What lifts you up?" or "What's happening on your good days?" or "What gives you hope?"

Positive mood questions pull clients toward positive moods and are an essential part of a comprehensive strengths-based depression and suicide assessment. If clients cannot answer positive questions, or if they answer but their affect does not brighten, they may be experiencing a more severe depressive state. Consider integrating some or all of the following positive questions into your usual suicide assessment protocol:

1. "What's happening in your life when you feel happy or joyful?"
2. "Over the past 2 weeks, when have you felt good?"
3. "Some people feel especially good when they do something nice for someone else . . . does that help put you in a good mood too?"
4. "What recreational activities do you enjoy?"
5. "What do you do for fun?"
6. "Who do you look forward to spending time with?"
7. "When do you sleep best?"
8. "What thoughts are you thinking on the nights when you're able to drop off to sleep?"
9. "When was the last time you had your normal appetite? What was happening then?"
10. "If you could wish for something to change, and that change would make your life better, what would you wish for?"

In addition to asking the preceding questions, as you become more comfortable interviewing clients about suicide you can spontaneously use a positive psychology or solution-focused mindset to create new questions that fit with your client's struggles and strengths.

Ask About and Explore Suicide Plans

After exploring suicidal ideation, the next step is to ask about suicide plans. Responses to questions about suicide plans vary widely. Some clients will say, "I don't have a plan and don't want to die." This is often true of youth, partly because students often express their distress by using the words *suicide* or *suicidal*. Older clients are more likely to say they would never act on their thoughts because of their children, religion, fear, or other reasons for living. When clients deny having a plan, you should reflect that and pause. The pause gives clients a few moments to possibly revise their denial. Then you can move on, but circle back later to ask the question again, if needed. You can use a normalizing frame, as described earlier. Wollersheim (1974) recommended the following:

> You know, most people who have thought about suicide have at least had passing thoughts about how they might do it. What kinds of thoughts have you had about how you would [kill yourself] if you decided to do so? (p. 223)

You can also accept their denial: "Sounds like you don't have a specific plan." In some situations, you might ask a hypothetical, "If you did decide to kill yourself, what method would you use?" Then listen for the SLAP factors.

M. Miller (1985) recommended four areas of inquiry regarding suicide plans: the (a) specificity of the plan, (b) lethality of the method, (c) availability of the method, and (d) proximity of social or helping resources. These four areas form the acronym SLAP.

Specificity

Clients can have vague and passive thoughts about dying (e.g., "I'd like to fall asleep and never wake up") or more clear, specific, and actionable plans (e.g., "I'll take my gun, go to the woods, and shoot myself"). If clients are not explicit and clear about their plan, traditional assessment protocols encourage clinicians to press for details. We prefer a collaborative approach. Aggressive questioning about the specificity of a plan can feel adversarial;

clients might think you are trying to take away their right to die by suicide, which leads to greater secrecy. When clients are vague about their plans, collaborative assessment principles call for stepping back and commenting on the process instead of taking on an investigative role. You might say, "You seem reluctant to share details. That's OK. My goal is to work with you to keep you safe. I'm not into interrogation. We can move on. I'm less interested in details and more interested in you and me partnering to keep you safe."

If your client appears uncomfortable, and you explicitly move on, you are not avoiding the hard issues. Instead, if you wait until you have more rapport or you skip over unneeded details that raise anxiety, you are likely to be perceived as being sensitive and respectful of your client's discomfort. You can remain calm and work on relational connection because you know that later you will be initiating a collaborative safety planning intervention anyway (see Chapter 9).

From a risk assessment perspective, specificity is judged on a continuum from vague thoughts to detailed planning and preparation. When clients begin rehearsing plans, risk is high.

Lethality

Suicide methods are more lethal or less lethal. In a review of 309,377 deaths by suicide and 3,348,509 nonfatal attempts in the United States, firearms had an 89.6% lethality rate (Conner et al., 2019). If you are doing a traditional risk assessment and your client says that she has a gun and is keeping it close in case she feels like killing herself, you will immediately think about lethal means restriction. However, depending on your rapport, how much time you have left in the session, and other factors, you may or may not immediately talk about gun safety. Strategies for discussing lethal means restriction are in Chapter 9.

Availability

Knowing the availability of the method is useful for assessment and therapeutic purposes. Like specificity and lethality, you can address availability during safety planning (Stanley & Brown, 2012). The last step in Stanley and Brown's (2012) safety planning intervention focuses on making the environment safe.

Proximity

Proximity refers to the accessibility of social support. Proximity is relevant because greater social connection and contact confers greater safety. In addition, having others nearby can work into your safety planning and overall suicide prevention strategy. When clients are further from people who might intervene, suicide risk increases.

The purpose of evaluating your client's plan in general and the specificity of the plan in particular has to do with much more than risk assessment. Your purpose is also therapeutic. You can focus narrowly on estimating risk, but risk estimation is relatively useless if you have sacrificed your therapeutic relationship in favor of information gathering.

If you are working with clients on an ongoing basis, you should regularly check in regarding suicidal ideation and plans. One recommendation is for collaborative reassessment at every session until suicidal thoughts, plans, and behaviors are absent from three consecutive sessions (Jobes et al., 2007).

Ask About and Explore Previous Attempts, Client Self-Control, and Agitation

Previous suicide attempts and client self-control are associated with disinhibition. Most clients are reluctant to act on their plans. However, a subset of clients with suicidal thoughts and plans are disinhibited and desensitized (Klonsky & May, 2015; O'Connor, 2011). Disinhibition occurs when clients lose inhibition and act impulsively or do not feel normal fears of pain and fears of death. Desensitization makes it easier for clients to cross the threshold of normal inhibition and make suicide attempts. Among other factors, alcohol and repeated cutting can contribute to disinhibition and desensitization.

Exploring Previous Attempts

Previous attempts are often considered the most significant suicide predictor (Brown et al., 2020; Fowler, 2012). You can gather information about previous attempts through your client's medical or mental health records, from an intake form, or during the clinical interview. During clinical interviews, clients may spontaneously tell you about previous attempts; other times you will need to ask directly. Again, using a normalizing frame can be facilitative: "It's not unusual for people who are feeling very down to have made a suicide attempt. I'm wondering if there have been times when you were so down that you tried to kill yourself?"

Once you have knowledge of a client's previous suicide attempt, you can explore several dimensions of the attempt:

- "What was happening that made you want to end your life?"
- "When you discovered that your suicide attempt failed, what thoughts and feelings did you experience?"
- "Some people report learning something important from attempting suicide. Did you learn anything important? If so, what did you learn?" (see Case Vignette 3.2).

Although the preceding questions are important for assessment, once you are ready to move beyond an exploration of a previous attempt, you should ask a therapeutic solution-focused question similar to the following: "You've tried suicide before, but you're here with me now . . . what has helped?" (J. Sommers-Flanagan & Sommers-Flanagan, 2017, p. 373). Asking "What helped?" is central to a strengths-based or solution-focused model and sometimes illuminates a path forward toward living. However, if your client is depressed, in response you may hear, "Nothing helped. Nothing ever helps" (p. 373).

In the context of an assessment protocol, the "What helped?" question and its sidekick "What have you tried?" are important because they assess for two core cognitive problems associated with suicidality: hopelessness and problem-solving impairments. Clients who respond with, "Nothing ever helps" are communicating hopelessness. Clients who claim, "I've tried everything" or "There's nothing left to do" are communicating hopelessness plus the narrowing of cognitive problem-solving that Shneidman (1996) called *mental constriction*. Addressing hopelessness and problem-solving impairments should be integrated into your suicide treatment plan.

Evaluating Self-Control and Impulsivity

Self-control is difficult to assess. Among clients who have a documented history of impulsive behavior, deficits in self-control are predictable. However, sometimes clients who appear well controlled or overcontrolled suddenly display lapses in control. These uncharacteristic lapses may arise in response to big environmental or external stressors (e.g., the breakup of a romantic relationship, a sudden job loss, the death of a family member, or family/community/cultural pressures).

One means of assessing self-control is through client self-report. You can ask directly, in a positive, strengths-focused way: "You've mentioned that you have thoughts about suicide and a plan for killing yourself. What stops you from killing yourself?" You can also ask about self-control in a less positive way: "Do you ever worry that you might lose control and try to kill yourself?" (J. Sommers-Flanagan & Sommers-Flanagan, 2017, p. 370).

Case Vignette 3.2
A Previous Attempt and Posttraumatic Growth

Exploring previous suicide attempts can illuminate past stressors, but it is equally useful for helping clients articulate past, present, and future coping responses as well as the potential for posttraumatic growth.

Counselor: You wrote on your intake form that you attempted suicide about a year and a half ago. Can you please tell me about that?

Client: Right. I shot myself in the head. It's obvious. You can see the scar right here. [*Client points to a scar on his forehead*]

Counselor: What was happening in your life that brought you to that point?

Client: I was getting bullied in school. I hated my stepfather. Life was shit. One day after school I took the pistol out of my mom's room, aimed at my head, and shot.

Counselor: What happened then?

Client: I woke up in the hospital with a very bad headache. Then there was rehab. It was a long road, but here I am.

Counselor: Right. Here you are. What do you make of that?

Client: I'm lucky. I'm bad at suicide. I don't know. Maybe I'm supposed to be alive.

Counselor: Tell me more about that. You're supposed to be alive?

Client: Yeah. I figure because I shot myself in the head and lived to tell about it, that must mean I've got a reason to live. Maybe it's God or the universe, but I just feel like it's a message that my life is worthwhile and I'm supposed to do something with it.

Counselor: That's cool. What do you think you're supposed to do?

Client: At the very least, I should love the people who have shown love to me.

Counselor: I think that's a great message that you've taken from your suicide attempt. Even so, I need to ask you this question that I ask everyone. Have you had any thoughts about suicide recently?

Client: Nope. Nada. Not one.

Counselor: Nice. Another question I have is about you having been bullied and having family problems. How do you cope with those problems now?

Client: I've got friends. I've got my sister. I talk to them. You know, after you do what I did, you find out who really cares about you. Now I know. That's another thing I learned. I've got people who love me.

This vignette was adapted from from *Clinical Interviewing*, sixth edition (pp. 375–376), by J. Sommers-Flanagan and R. Sommers-Flanagan, 2017, New York, NY: Wiley.

Exploring both sides of self-control (what helps with maintaining self-control and what triggers a loss of self-control) can be therapeutic. Rudd (2014) recommended having clients rate their self-control using a scale from 1 to 10. However, like all risk factors, in isolation "impulsivity provides little, if any, information about differences between suicide attempters and suicide ideators" (Klonsky & May, 2014, pp. 2–3). Despite the statistically nonsignificant relationship between impulsivity and suicide attempts, if your clients doubt their self-control and you cannot address their doubts therapeutically, discussing hospitalization or an alternative structured setting is reasonable.

Observing for Arousal/Agitation
Arousal and agitation are physical states that contribute to suicide potential. One example of arousal or agitation is akathisia—a common side effect among patients who are prescribed SSRI antidepressant medications.

Agitation adversely affects self-control. Evidence of client agitation or arousal includes the following:

1. Observations of increased client psychomotor activity during the clinical interview
2. Client talk about feeling unsettled, hyper, or unusually overactive
3. Client endorsement of questionnaire items indicating agitation
4. Client statements indicating a push to act (e.g., "I need to do something about this!")
5. Historical evidence of suicide gestures or attempts related to agitation

Ask About and Explore Reasons for Living, Reasons for Dying, the "One Thing" Question, Suicidal Intent, and (Maybe) Trauma

Asking "What helped?" orients clients to the past and fits well when talking about previous attempts; it is also a therapeutic question, because what helped in the past is likely to be helpful going forward. "What's helping now?" is a different question that functions in a more explicitly therapeutic way. Asking "What's helping now?" along with several variations orients clinicians and clients to reasons for living, reasons for dying, that "one thing," and suicidal intent.

What's Helping Now?
Some clients respond affirmatively to questions about what is helping them cope and stay alive. They may identify specific activities

(e.g., going to church) or treatments (e.g., counseling or medications) that help them get through the daily grind. However, clients who are in the midst of a suicidal crisis and feeling hopeless may be unable to generate ideas of what helps. Along with using the hopelessness protocols described in Chapter 5, you can use the "one thing" question.

The "One Thing" Question
Jobes (2016) described the "one thing" question in his SSF. The "one thing" question is a "magic wand assessment" (p. 63). Jobes uses the following wording: "If we could somehow magically change just one thing in your life that would eliminate your suicidal risk all together, what would that be?" (p. 63).

Jobes has a substantial cache of data pertaining to client responses to the "one thing" question. He codes client responses along three dimensions: whether the response focuses on (a) self versus other(s), (b) something reasonably attainable versus unrealistic, and (c) something clinically useful versus not useful. Consider the following examples:

1. "Have someone who really loves me." (This response focuses on someone else, and is not directly attainable, but could be clinically useful.)
2. "Change the past so that I didn't get involved with an abuser." (This response focuses on self and other, and is not attainable, but could be clinically useful.)
3. "Bring back my father so I can make peace with him." (This response focuses on someone else, and is not attainable, but could be clinically useful.)
4. "To be less depressed." (This response focuses on the self, is potentially attainable, and is clinically useful.)

Consistent with SMART (specific, measurable, achievable, relevant, time bound) goals and reality therapy (Glasser, 1998), the best client goals are those within the client's behavioral control. When clients respond to the "one thing" question, they may describe scenarios that focus on others, are not attainable, and appear—on the surface—clinically irrelevant. In general, other-focused, unattainable, and low-clinical-utility responses are linked to higher suicidality. However, it is important not to let the magical quality of client responses lull you into ignoring their potential deeper meaning. In fact, even if your client says something apparently superficial, like "Win a million dollars" (Jobes, 2016, p. 203), the million-dollar response tells you something about your client's fantasies, which could contribute to treatment planning. If the client sees winning a million dollars as the one thing that would make life worth living, there may be ways to integrate concrete goals pertaining to financial stability or comforts related to wealth into the treatment plan.

Let's take another example that might be categorized as unrealistic and not attainable. In Example 2, the client wants to "Change the past so that I didn't get involved with an abuser." This response might indicate a need for trauma treatment (e.g., trauma-focused cognitive behavior therapy, cognitive processing therapy, or eye-movement desensitization and reprocessing are all options). In addition, active behavioral work on how to increase safety and avoid abusive people in the future could become a treatment goal that increases hope and resonates with the client's wishes.

Like most projective questions, the "one thing" question provides rich and potentially clinically useful material. Client responses, even when seemingly unrealistic, can point toward specific treatment goals and meaningful counseling interventions.

Reasons for Living and Reasons for Dying

In 1983, Linehan and her colleagues developed the Reasons for Living Inventory. This inventory was based on the observation that clients who are suicidal have fewer positive life goals and experiences, and consequently, helping clients elaborate or expand on their reasons for living might decrease suicidality.

Most clients who are suicidal are ambivalent about living and dying. They are experiencing intense psychological pain, dissatisfaction, and hopelessness, which fuels their impulses to die. However, they also have reasons to live, because, without any reasons to live, they would have likely already died by suicide (Jobes, 2016).

On the SSF, Jobes (2016) has clients list and rank their reasons for living and reasons for dying. If clients list more reasons for dying than reasons for living, greater suicide risk is inferred.

Therapeutic assessment principles and practices can be integrated into your process for evaluating clients' reasons for living and dying. We recommend questions that orient clients toward coping responses. If a client's top reason for dying is to stop the pain, then counseling goals and tasks should be oriented toward distress tolerance; if the top reason for dying is "I'm always alone," then counseling goals and tasks on developing social connections may be useful. We also recommend individualized client goals and strategies for mindfully focusing on and expanding reasons for living. See Wellness Practice 3.1 for more information on tips for mood enhancement.

Suicidal Intent

Suicidal intent is an active planning state in which clients are cognitively (and possibly behaviorally) moving toward death by suicide. Intent is often evaluated following a suicide attempt. Higher suicidal intent is inferred when clients use or plan highly lethal means; higher intent is also associated with rehearsal

Wellness Practice 3.1
Your Happy Places

More often than not, your environment, setting, or context directly influences your mood and sense of well-being. This is most obvious when you are in settings or environments that you find aversive. After having subjected you to a long chapter on suicide assessment, we are tempted to ask whether your immediate surroundings, right now, are triggering happy feelings or something else.

For this activity, reflect briefly on environments, settings, or contexts that you find aversive. For example, some people find cloudy days, rain, smoky skies (or rooms), or particular temperatures aversive or uncomfortable. Other people might find churches, gyms, or libraries aversive.

Now consider the opposite: What environments, settings, or contexts do you find pleasurable, comforting, or energizing?

After reading and reflecting on the above, write a few words (short answers) in response to the following prompts:

1. List three settings that usually trigger negativity or discomfort in you.
2. List three settings that usually trigger happiness and well-being in you (and be specific). These are your happy places.
3. What can you do to prepare for or cope with challenging settings that usually cause you discomfort (other than avoiding them)?
4. What can you do to increase the frequency of time you spend in environments that contribute to your feelings of wellness?
5. What can you do to create places or spaces in your mind that you can use (anywhere and anytime) to increase your sense of comfort and wellness in the moment?

behaviors, extensive and detailed planning, and a negative reaction to surviving a suicidal act. In a small longitudinal research study, suicidal intent, as measured by the Beck Suicide Intent Scale, was a moderate predictor of death by suicide (Stefansson et al., 2012).

Assessing suicidal intent prior to a potential attempt is challenging and less well researched. The question can be placed on a scale and asked directly: "On a scale from 0 to 10, with 0 being you're absolutely certain you want to die and 10 being you're absolutely certain you want to live, how would you rate yourself?"

You can also infer intent based on the SLAP assessment. This has broad evidentiary support because the suicide-planning items on the Beck Suicide Intent Scale are the strongest predictors of death by suicide (Stefansson et al., 2012).

Asking About Trauma

Asking about or screening for trauma makes intuitive sense because trauma in childhood or adulthood is statistically linked to greater suicide risk. However, asking directly about trauma also has several downsides. Specifically, many clients find that talking about trauma experiences is destabilizing. That being the case, it is probably better practice for clinicians to wait and ask about trauma after a therapeutic alliance has been established. Also, if counselors routinely ask about trauma, they should do so only if they have time to process the emotional distress that asking about trauma might trigger. In the context of an initial interview, the timing of asking about trauma is challenging: You want to wait to ask until after you have established rapport, but you do not want to wait too long and emotionally activate your client too close to the end of a session.

In other situations, clients will make it clear that they are willing and able to talk about their trauma experiences. When clients say something like "I've had a difficult past" or otherwise imply a trauma history, they may be indirectly asking to be asked about their trauma history. If so, gently asking about trauma may be the right thing to do.

Overall, we advise against asking about trauma in a routine manner. Instead, we advise watching for signs or signals of trauma (see Chapter 7) and waiting until the therapeutic relationship has strengthened. Talking about trauma is, by default, emotionally activating. In many cases, clients are not ready to talk about trauma with a relative stranger during an intake interview. Thus, waiting until a second or third session to ask about trauma in the context of broader treatment planning is probably preferable.

Engage in Collaborative Problem-Solving and Safety Planning for Assessment, Treatment, and Decision-Making Purposes

Traditional suicide assessment protocols usually end with risk categorization. In contrast, the strengths-based protocol we are describing ends with collaborative problem-solving, safety planning, and treatment planning. Rather than determining risk, the assessment provides foundational knowledge about clients and helps counselors respond therapeutically and initiate treatment. If decision-making around hospitalization is needed, we recommend proceeding with collaborative decision-making for as long as possible. We recognize that in lethal situations you may need to call 911 or pursue involuntary hospitalization.

For about two decades, no-suicide contracts were standard practice in suicide prevention and intervention (Drye et al., 1973). These contracts consisted of signed statements like "I promise not to commit suicide between my medical appointments." In a fascinating turn of events, during the 1990s, no-suicide contracts came under fire as (a) coercive and (b) focusing more on practitioner liability than client well-being (Rudd et al., 2006). Suicide experts no longer advocate using no-suicide contracts. Instead, collaborative problem-solving and safety planning are recommended.

Risk Categorization

An array of risk factors were reviewed earlier in this chapter, and a plethora of suicide risk factor checklists are available online. The general guideline is that more risk factors equates to more risk, despite lack of much empirical evidence supporting that guideline (Franklin et al., 2017). Although all risk factors may be important, clinicians have identified some risk factors as especially salient. These include the following:

- *Previous attempts.* Having one previous attempt increases risk, but having two previous attempts is especially predictive of suicide because it represents chronic or repeated intent. Also, when previous attempts were severe, and the client was upset about not dying, risk is high.

- *Command hallucinations.* When clients are experiencing a psychotic state accompanied by command hallucinations (e.g., a voice that says, "You must die"), risk is high.
- *Severe depression with extreme agitation.* The combination of depression and agitation is especially lethal. Agitation can take the form of extreme anxiety or extreme anger.

Any single protective factor may outweigh many risk factors, but it is impossible to know the depth or meaning of any individual protective factors without discussing them with your client. Warning signs are also relevant to decision-making, despite the fact that they have only minimal empirical support (Franklin et al., 2017). IS PATH WARM (discussed previously in this chapter) represents the most common warning signs.

Whether or not observable warning signs are present, intense distress (Shneidman's, 1993, psychache) plus suicidal intent often moves clients toward lethal attempts. Intense distress is always subjective and variable; it ranges from the memory problems, emotional dysregulation, and social alienation that combat veterans experience to the relationship breakups and family/spiritual rejection that LGBTQ+ youth experience, and much more. Assessment of suicidal intent can be based on objective or subjective signs and symptoms. Objective signs of intent include one (or more) previous lethal attempt(s). Subjective signs of intent include client ratings of intent or reports of preparation behaviors linked to highly lethal plans.

Final Clinical Decision-Making

Using a traditional assessment approach, you can estimate your client's suicide risk as fitting into one of three categories:

- *Mild.* Minimal risk. The situation may be managed with weekly monitoring and an emergency plan. Make sure firearms and lethal means are safely stored.
- *Moderate.* The situation should be managed with an active safety plan. Depending on your client's preference, engaging family or friends as support may be advisable. Make sure firearms and lethal means are safely stored.
- *High.* Treatment is likely to include hospitalization, residential treatment, and/or an intensive safety plan implemented with family/friends. Firearms and lethal means should be safely stored.

Many clients will not report suicidal ideation. If so, you should document "No suicidal ideation" but avoid using the language "No risk." Instead, as with most counseling scenarios, suicidality will simply not become a part of the treatment plan.

Contact Collateral Informants

Sometimes clients are socially isolated and have few, if any, supportive family members or friends. Other times, there are worried loved ones, work associates, teachers, or others available to help, both for assessment and for safety planning. With your client's permission, you can contact potential informants to gather details about client risk and the presence (or absence) of protective factors.

If you do not have client permission but believe you need collateral information, it is advisable to consult with a colleague or supervisor before breaking confidentiality. State laws, school policies, and licensing rules will guide your decision-making around maintaining or breaching confidentiality. Your own informed consent process (see Chapter 2) plays a role in decisions around confidentiality. Violating your client's trust often results in relational ruptures and may irreparably damage the therapeutic relationship, but sometimes you will need to put client safety ahead of therapeutic issues. Reminding clients that you are legally obligated to call family, friends, or the police can be helpful. Making telephone calls in your client's presence may build a foundation for working through therapeutic ruptures (see Case Vignette 3.3).

Engage in Consultation and Documentation

Consultation and documentation are integral to suicide assessment. Before you begin seeing clients who may be suicidal, you should have a formal or informal list of colleagues, supervisors, and former professors to call for consultation. You should have an outline or assessment form that you can complete during or after assessment sessions.

Determining which assessment outline or form to use is a function of several variables. Schools often mandate that school counselors and school psychologists use their district forms and protocols. However, because every student or client you assess will be unique, if you use overly formulized procedures that limit your

Case Vignette 3.3
Calling in Mom

A 15-year-old heterosexual cisgender female rape victim began talking with her counselor about passive suicidal impulses. She said, "Maybe I'll get run over by a car" or "Maybe if I was driving and I forgot to wear my contacts I might accidentally drive off a cliff."

The client's mother was aware of the rape, but, according to client reports, her mom had little empathy and minimized the trauma. When the passive suicidal talk began, the counselor decided to bring the client's mother into a session. Although the client adamantly opposed having her mother attend, the counselor's decision to reach out to a parent was supported by law and the counselor's informed consent form. The counselor said, "I know you disagree with me, and I know you may forever hate me for this, but what you've said makes me worry about your safety. We need to have a session with your mom to make sure we're all on the same page."

During the joint session, the mother expressed awareness and concern about her daughter's suicidality but said that her daughter had "prohibited" her from contacting the counselor. When this information came out, the client was furious and vowed never to speak to the counselor again—and she made good on her vow. In the end, a new counselor was selected who specialized in family counseling, and the mother and daughter attended counseling together.

---

empathic engagement, therapeutic opportunities will be sacrificed. Our advice for resolving this conundrum is to find the middle way, simultaneously honoring the protocol and the person.

Concluding Comments

We strongly recommend that when providing assessment services to clients who struggle with suicide you use a therapeutic assessment model, normalize suicidal ideation, and work explicitly from a collaborative frame. Assessment is essential, but interpersonal connection, rapport, and empathy will facilitate your ability to gather valid and reliable assessment data. Remember that assessment is threatening and that some clients will have negative affective responses to being asked about suicide.

Practitioner Guidance and Key Points to Remember

Engaging in an assessment process with clients who are suicidal is daunting, partly because of the need to balance relational connection with intensive information gathering. Combining an array of nuanced interviewing strategies with a positive attitude toward your clients is crucial. In this chapter, we reviewed the following 11 components of a comprehensive suicide assessment process:

1. Prepare yourself with knowledge of suicide risk factors, protective factors, and warning signs—and use that knowledge to monitor for individualized manifestations or absence of these factors and signs.
2. As needed, use suicide assessment instruments or questionnaires, but complement their use by adopting a therapeutic assessment model.
3. Ask about and collaboratively explore suicidal ideation. To do this well you will need to use a variety of sophisticated interviewing assessment skills. Include an assessment of the frequency, triggers, duration, intensity, and termination of ideation.
4. Prepare yourself to deal with client or student irritability, hostility, and hopelessness.
5. Weave questions about wellness, strengths, and positive experiences into your suicide assessment process—even if you are operating from a psychiatric symptom-oriented questioning paradigm.
6. Ask about and explore suicide plans. Collaboratively exploring the plan's specificity, lethality, and availability and the proximity of social support (SLAP) is advisable.
7. Ask about and explore previous attempts and client self-control, including clients' use of substances for the purposes of desensitization.
8. Ask about and explore reasons for living, reasons for dying, the "one thing" question, and suicidal intent.
9. Engage clients in collaborative problem-solving and safety planning for assessment, treatment, and decision-making purposes.
10. Consider contacting collateral informants for assessment and treatment purposes. When suicide risk exists, you should obtain previous and current mental health and medical treatment records and engage supportive family members as appropriate.

11. Consult colleagues whenever possible, and then document your consultations as well as your decision-making process and recommendations.

Then, after conducting a state-of-the-art comprehensive suicide assessment, go find your happy place (see Wellness Practice 3.1).

Chapter 4

The Emotional Dimension

In many cases, emotions drive behavior. For clients struggling with suicide, suicidal acts are often viewed as a means of escaping intense emotional pain (Baumeister, 1990). Edwin Shneidman, author of *The Suicidal Mind* (1996), believed that when clients report suicidality, the first and most important priority is to shrink or shift their experiences of emotional or psychological pain: "What I think is crucial here is the conscious focus . . . on the psychic pain (psychache), on the reduction . . . of that pain, combined with the necessary redefinition and reconceptualization of that pain as somehow bearable" (Shneidman, 2004, p. 160). To address suicidal pain, Shneidman (2004) pointed to three treatment targets:

- *Focus on the pain.* Do not minimize or dismiss the pain. Address emotional pain as a central issue in treatment.
- *Reduce the pain.* Find ways to help clients experience reductions in the triggering, frequency, intensity, and duration of their emotional pain.
- *Redefine or reframe the pain.* Change ways in which clients think about and cope with their emotional pain.

In this chapter we follow Shneidman's guidance. How can we focus on, reduce, and redefine the suicidal pain that clients or students are experiencing? From a strengths-based perspective, another important question follows: How can we prioritize suicidal pain while still embracing positive wellness and client strengths?

Working in the Emotional Dimension

When clients are depressed and suicidal, everyone—including family, friends, coworkers, counselors, and clients—wishes for an improved emotional state. But often the process is slow, and as a result the very people on whom the client relies for support may lose patience. Supportive people, even counselors, may feel urges to say things that are emotionally dismissive, like "Cheer up" or "Come on, you need to exercise!" or "Why can't you do something to make your life better?"

Moving clients out of despair and into the light is difficult; if it were otherwise, clients would resolve suicidality on their own. Directly or indirectly suggesting to clients in suicidal pain to "cheer up" often backfires, creating anger, hostility, and resistance to treatment; this resistance is a powerful phenomenon called *psychological reactance* (Brehm & Brehm, 1981).

Psychological reactance occurs when clients perceive their ultimate freedoms as threatened. If clients sense that clinicians want to coerce them to stay alive, they may dig in their heels in response and engage in behaviors designed to restore feelings of autonomy. Psychological reactance is one explanation for why clients who are suicidal sometimes vehemently resist help, insisting on their right to think about and act on suicidal impulses. Repeatedly displaying empathic acceptance of your client's emotional pain is one way to avoid activating reactance; empathic acceptance also allows clients to begin exploring and addressing key emotional issues in counseling.

Key Emotional Issues to Address

Many emotional issues are relevant to suicide treatment planning. These include (a) excruciating distress; (b) specific disturbing emotions, such as acute or chronic shame and guilt, anger, or sadness; and (c) emotional dysregulation. In this section, we briefly review core emotional issues that may guide your treatment planning. Later in the chapter we provide case examples and vignettes illustrating methods for working in the emotional dimension.

Excruciating Distress

Shneidman (2001) referred to the emotional state surrounding suicide as "psychache," or unbearable distress. He wrote, "The suicidal drama is almost always driven by psychological pain, the pain of negative emotions—what I call psychache. Psychache is at the dark heart of suicide; *no psychache, no suicide* [emphasis added]" (p. 200).

Even when using a strengths-based or wellness model, exploring the "pain of negative emotions" or excruciating distress is usually your first focus. Sometimes, to avoid activating reactance or resistance, you will need to stay with your client's emotional pain longer than you would prefer. Staying with your client's pain not only helps bypass resistance, it also models that facing negative affective states without fear, avoidance, or dissociation requires personal strength. Even so, as you focus on suicidal pain, you might wish that the client would immediately adopt a more positive mindset, or you might find the process difficult to bear. You also might need to turn to colleagues or your self-care plan for support. Nevertheless, your first priority in the emotional dimension is to recognize and resonate with your client's emotional pain.

Acute or Chronic Shame and Guilt

Shame and guilt are nonprimary emotions because they involve significant self-reflection. Shame connotes beliefs of being unworthy, defective, or bad. Shame is often directly linked to core beliefs about the self and activated by particular life situations. In contrast, guilt is more specific, often associated with certain actions or lack of actions (e.g., "I should be doing more to fight racism" or "I shouldn't have been so critical of my professor"). Guilt can lead to shame, and shame is more likely to ignite suicidality. Reducing or resolving shame or guilt may be a crucial therapeutic goal.

Suicidal thoughts are often accompanied by shame. Cultures around the world have historically judged death by suicide as a shameful or sinful event, and many still do. Your client's experience may be something like "Not only do I have suicidal thoughts, which are terrible in their own right, but the fact that these thoughts exist in my mind also makes me a bad person." This double dose of negative judgment—emotional pain plus self-condemnation—often needs to be addressed in counseling. One strategy that may fit into your treatment plan is to help clients develop greater self-compassion as a method for countering their self-condemnation.

Anger

In graduate school, we had a professor who suggested we consider this question: "Who is this client planning to commit suicide at?" Often people who are suicidal carry great anger toward one or more friends, lovers, or family members and thus think of suicide as an act of revenge. Counselors should listen for underlying themes that involve using suicide as a behavioral goal for getting even or intentionally hurting others (Marvasti & Wank, 2013).

Thoughts of dying by suicide sometimes emerge as a revenge fantasy. Thoughts like "I'll show them" or "They'll suffer forever" represent anger along with the desire to punish others. It can be tempting to point out to clients that death is an irrationally high price for fulfilling revenge fantasies. However, helping clients express, accept, and understand the depth of their anger will usually reduce suicidality more efficiently than pointing out that death is a maladaptive revenge strategy. If revenge is central and forgiveness is not a viable option, then an apt philosophy to gently infuse into your clients is that the best revenge is a well-lived life.

Sadness

Major depression is the psychiatric diagnosis most commonly linked with suicide attempts, especially among older adults (Melhem et al., 2019). Clients who present with sadness as a dominant emotion may or may not meet diagnostic criteria for major depression. However, when sadness and the associated emotions and cognitions of irritability, regret, discouragement, and disappointment are central sources of distress, we recommend targeting those symptoms with evidence-based counseling interventions. Weaving positive psychology or happiness interventions into treatment planning is especially appropriate for clients struggling with sadness and depression (Rashid & Seligman, 2018; Seligman, 2018). More information about evidence-based approaches and positive psychology interventions is provided later in this chapter and in upcoming chapters.

Emotional Dysregulation

Clients who are suicidal may exhibit emotional dysregulation during counseling sessions and in their everyday lives. Clients may be emotionally labile, shifting from expressing anger to expressing feelings of affection, appreciation, and deep connection. Clients may share stories of repeated maladaptive emotional overreactions to life's challenges. When these stories include examples of unstable relationships, emotional swings, and explosive anger, it may be tempting to label clients as having borderline personality disorder. However, because excruciating distress can trigger borderline-like behaviors, we recommend that clinicians exercise caution before assigning personality disorder labels. Given enough situationally based stress—including, as Linehan (1993) noted, emotionally invalidating environments—nearly everyone becomes dysregulated and appears unstable. Normalizing dysregulation as a natural response to intense distress helps to maintain a strengths-based perspective.

Treatment plans for clients who are suicidal often include teaching emotional regulation skills; this translates to helping clients become more capable of regulating themselves in the face of emotionally activating circumstances. Linehan's (1993, 2015) protocols for working with clients with characteristics of borderline personality are recommended for emotional regulation skill development. However, alternative approaches exist, some of which come from positive psychology, happiness, and well-being literature (Hays, 2014; Lyubomirsky, 2007, 2013; see Wellness Practice 4.1 for savoring interventions used for reducing emotional distress).

Interventions in the Emotional Dimension

Consistent with Shneidman's views on suicidality, counselors should initially focus on emotional distress. Reducing emotional (or suicidal) distress is your first priority.

Empathic Responding to Client Distress

Sometimes clients—especially teenagers—avoid talking about anything, including their distress. However, clients who are

Wellness Practice 4.1
Savoring the (Positive) Moment

Too often we gulp down tasty portions of life and let bitter experiences linger and spoil. Remember to savor. Slow down. Be mindful of the beautiful and good. Let the upsetting or ugly stuff drift away, like leaves floating down the river.

Savoring

Everyone knows how to savor chocolate or wine or the cheesecake that tastes like heaven. When it comes to gustatory experiences, savoring feels natural.

But savoring positive experiences, successes, beautiful scenery, or a poem on the radio often feels less natural. That is too bad, because researchers repeatedly report that taking time to savor the moment in the midst of a busy day increases happiness, decreases depression, and enhances resilience and optimism (Sytine et al., 2019).

(continued)

Wellness Practice 4.1
Savoring the (Positive) Moment (*continued*)

Taking time to practice positive savoring is good for counselors and clients. If you are willing, pick one savoring assignment from the following menu of research-based savoring activities. Each activity has research support. We encourage you to experiment with savoring yourself but also to do so with students and clients. Here are your options:

- *Engage in mutual reminiscence.* Mutual reminiscence happens when you get together with someone (in person or online) and talk about fun, positive, or meaningful memories. Pick someone with whom you have done this before, or pick someone new. At the least, you will build positive memories of remembering shared positive memories. In our University of Montana happiness class, many students not only felt good reminiscing but also increased their motivation to plan future positive shared experiences.
- *Make a list of positive memories.* After making the list, transport yourself back to one of the memories. Do this one by yourself. Retrieve the memory. Play it back in your mind. Explore it. Feel it. Let your brain elaborate on the details. Notice what made that experience positive. Can you replicate parts of that experience in the future?
- *Celebrate good news longer than you normally would.* First watch for positive news in your life that feels good. Then let your mind linger on it. Notice how you feel. What parts of the news are especially meaningful or pleasant? Extend and celebrate the good news. Happiness researcher Sonja Lyubomirsky (2007) wrote, "You shouldn't shy away from pride: Pat yourself on the back; tell yourself how hard you've worked for this moment; imagine how impressed people might be" (p. 197).
- *Notice and observe beauty.* This activity is mostly visual, but you can listen for beautiful sounds too. Let yourself see color, patterns, and nuanced beauty in nature or in art. Linger with that visual and let its pleasant effects be in your eyes, brain, and body. Notice and feel your sensations and thoughts related to color and beauty (Lyubomirsky, 2007).

suicidal usually want to talk about their emotional distress and unhappiness. Although it may not seem strengths based, if you do not empathize with your clients' distress from the beginning, you may never learn the depth and details of their pain. Even worse, if you try shifting to positivity, strengths, and solutions too soon, you may activate resistance, or, even worse, your client will drop out of counseling.

Emotional pain is mostly subjective. Life experiences that cause emotional pain for a 65-year-old male, heterosexual, cisgender wheat farmer may not be the same as what causes emotional pain for a transgender college student or a military veteran suffering from a traumatic brain injury. In addition, what causes emotional pain for you may be extremely dissimilar to what causes pain for your client. These subjective differences may cause you to minimize your client's pain, or you may find their pain overwhelming. No matter what, it is your job to bracket your judgments and instead do what Carl Rogers (1957, 1961) did: Let yourself partially inhabit the psyche of your clients so you can approximate their unique emotional "nooks and crannies." Rogers (1961) said this so well that it bears repetition and contemplation:

> Acceptance does not mean much until it involves understanding. It is only as I understand the feelings and thoughts which seem so horrible to you, or so weak, or so sentimental, or so bizarre—it is only as I see them as you see them, and accept them and you, that you feel really free to explore all the hidden nooks and frightening crannies of your inner and often buried experience. (p. 34)

Accepting your clients' emotions and cognitions is essential and is especially important when your clients are having emotions and cognitions that they evaluate as horrid, weak, and bizarre. By accepting your clients' shameful inner experiences you promote their self-acceptance, and self-acceptance can help them reduce their emotional pain, principally because harsh, negative judgments of the self (e.g., shame) nearly always magnify emotional pain.

Rogers's language around empathic understanding requires a warning: In an effort to convey empathy, avoid the words "I understand." Saying "I understand" can trigger dramatically hostile interpersonal interactions with clients; they may respond by saying things like "How the hell do you think you can understand what I'm going through?" The general rule is to convey empathic understanding without ever using the words "I understand" (J. Sommers-Flanagan & Sommers-Flanagan, 2017). However, you do not want your clients to think that no one will ever understand them and their experiences. Using phrases like "Help me understand more about what you're going through" signals your willingness to try as well as your belief that you are capable of at least partially understanding the world through your clients' eyes.

Focus First on Exploring Emotional Distress
Your first focus with clients who are suicidal includes three main parts:

1. Recognize or identify your clients' emotional or suicidal pain.
2. Resonate with the pain.
3. Explore the pain, and identify factors unique to your clients that increase and decrease it (i.e., this is how you individualize the risk and protective factors currently operating in your clients' lives).

To illustrate how to work with emotional distress, in the following pages, we feature a 15-year-old girl, whom we call Sophia, referred by her parents for suicidal ideation (see J. Sommers-Flanagan, 2018b). (To preserve anonymity, this and all case examples and vignettes in this book are composites of video simulations, clinical work, supervision experiences, and previously shared clinical anecdotes.)

When parents refer children for counseling, you and the parents may choose individual or family counseling. Whichever modality you choose—and there are benefits to both options—you need to establish regular methods for communicating with the parents. Having the parents and child together provides an optimal snapshot of family systems dynamics and a foundation for family systems interventions (e.g., functional family therapy, multisystemic family therapy). However, some parents and families oppose family sessions, and pushing parents to fit into our optimal intake scenario may heighten the risk of them choosing a different provider. In every case involving children and teenagers, you should emphasize to parents or caregivers the need for ongoing monitoring and maintenance of a safe home environment.

In the case of Sophia, the clinician sensed parental resistance to family therapy. Rather than insisting that the whole family come for counseling, the clinician chose to see Sophia alone. Depending on the outcome of the first session, the treatment plan will incorporate the parents directly in future sessions or through regular communications about safety planning.

The opening exchange with Sophia is important because it shows how clinicians—even when operating from a strengths-based foundation—address emotional distress. In the beginning the counselor drills down into the negative (e.g., "What's making you feel bad?"), even though the plan is to develop Sophia's strengths and resilience. By drilling down into distress and emotional pain, and then later identifying what helps the client cope, the counselor is individualizing risk and protective factor assessment.

> *Counselor:* Sophia, thanks for meeting. I know you're not super excited to be here. I also know your parents said you've been talking about suicide off and on for a while, so they wanted me to talk with you. But I don't know exactly what's happening in your life. I don't know how you're feeling. And I'd like to be of help. If you're willing to talk to me, the first thing I'd love to hear is what's going on in your life, and what's making you feel bad or sad or miserable or whatever it is you're feeling.

The counselor begins with an acknowledgment and quick summary of what he knows. This is a basic strategy for working with teens (J. Sommers-Flanagan & Sommers-Flanagan, 2007) but also can be helpful when working with adults. If counselors withhold what they know about clients, rapport and relationship development suffers.

The opening phrase "I don't know . . ." acknowledges the limits of the counselor's knowledge and offers an invitation for collaboration. Effective clinicians initially and intermittently offer invitations for collaboration to build the working alliance (Parrow et al., 2019). The underlying message is "I want to help, but I can't be helpful all on my own. I need your input so we can work together to address the distress you're feeling."

The opening question for Sophia is negative (i.e., "What's making you feel bad or sad or miserable or whatever it is you're feeling?"). This opening shows empathy for the emotional distress that triggers her suicidality and clarifies the link between her emotional distress and the triggering situations. By tuning into negative emotions, the counselor hones in on the presumptive primary treatment goal for all clients who are suicidal—to reduce the perceived intolerable or excruciating emotional distress (Shneidman, 1993).

Sophia: I think I'm just like really busy every day. I'm in volleyball, and I got a lot of homework, and I don't get a lot of sleep. So it's really stressful getting up early, and my parents are always fighting, and sometimes I miss the bus, and they don't want to drive me. So sometimes I'm late. It's stressful, and the teachers get mad.

Counselor: So you've got stress piling up, volleyball, school, sometimes being late, and your parents arguing. Of those, which one adds the most misery into your life?

Asking "Which one adds the most misery?" continues the focus on distress and is a method for seeking greater specificity regarding what triggers Sophia's distress.

Sophia: Being at home is hardest. In volleyball at least, I find some joy. I enjoy being on the court and playing with my team. They lift me up. I don't like being at home.

Counselor: OK. What do you hate about being at home?

When Sophia says, "I don't like being at home," she is being vague about the trigger for her distress. The counselor stays with the negative and uses a word ("hate") that is a good match for how teenage girls sometimes feel about being with their family.

Sophia: They're always fighting. My dad's just mean, and my mom is too. They're both mean to each other. I just lock myself in my room.

Counselor: So as I listen, it feels like being around fighting feels bad. I don't know what other feelings are there. Any other feelings come up when that happens?

If you are unclear about a client's emotion or do not want to rush in with an emotional reflection, saying something like "I don't know for sure what you're feeling" is a way to invite collaboration on deeper emotional exploration. Early in this session the counselor is tentatively exploring emotions and behaviors associated with Sophia's suicidal distress.

Sophia: I don't know. Just sometimes I don't feel like I have a home, or my family is not there for me, and sometimes I just don't feel like living anymore.

Counselor: When the family stuff feels so bad, you start thinking about suicide.
Sophia: Yeah.

Based on initial interactions with Sophia, the counselor is already building a working alliance, identifying Sophia's primary problems, conceptualizing these problems as potential goals, and considering therapeutic interventions. Here is an early, tentative reflection on what is happening with Sophia:

- *Working alliance.* Sophia is responding to the questions. The counselor should continue to be open with her, seeking input to help further understand her suicidal distress.
- *Primary problem.* Sophia's suicide risk is linked to her parents' fighting, because their fighting increases her distress. This is an initial formulation; more information is needed.
- *Primary goal.* Work with Sophia on specific coping skills for how she can deal with her parents' fighting when it occurs.
- *Possible therapeutic interventions.* If parental fighting is the main trigger for Sophia's suicidal distress, the counselor may need to propose couples or family counseling. At a minimum, using Sophia's personal strengths, the counselor can help her develop distress tolerance skills and establish a workable safety plan.

Therapeutic obstacles and concerns will inevitably emerge. Because autonomy is so important for teens, it may be difficult to get Sophia on board for doing the work needed to enact a distress reduction plan. It also may be difficult to get Sophia's permission to speak with her parents and recruit them to counseling. Knowing how fragile the therapeutic relationship between teenagers and counselors can be, the counselor needs to be creative, empathic, and affiliative with both Sophia and her parents.

A summary of how Sophia's emotional distress might be incorporated into an initial treatment plan is in Table 4.1.

Shifting From Distress to Positive Problem-Solving

If you are working with Sophia, your next step after initially exploring her emotional distress is to pivot toward the positive. Pivoting to the positive might involve a direct and open question like, "What helps?" or "What has helped in the past?" Although this is the

TABLE 4.1
Treatment Plan for Sophia—Emotional Dimension

Problem	Goals and Strengths[a]	Interventions/Plan
1. Sophia reports emotional distress linked to hearing her parents argue and fight.	1. Develop distress tolerance strategies.	1. Brainstorm with Sophia to identify and practice distress tolerance/coping strategies.
	2. Parents will stop or reduce their fighting in Sophia's presence.	2. Get Sophia's permission to meet with her parents about their fighting.
		3. Refer Sophia's parents for couples counseling.

[a]Sophia's strength is that she is able to immediately engage in thoughtful discourse and problem-solving.

next logical step, each client is unique; therefore, you may or may not quickly transition to asking about what helps. For example, if you are working with a client who has a trauma history, and the client wants to talk about past trauma experiences, you may need to linger and listen for longer than you would if you are working with a client without a trauma history.

Exploring what helps now or what has helped in the past is a cognitive problem-solving process. You will read more about problem-solving with Sophia and other clients in Chapter 5. In the meantime, we review other interventions to help clients work through emotional pain.

Using Motivational Interviewing (MI)

MI is an evidence-based approach to working with clients on substance issues and health behaviors (W. R. Miller & Rollnick, 2013). Two foundational principles that underlie MI are crucial to working effectively with clients who are suicidal:

- *Ambivalence is ubiquitous.* When it comes to healthy behaviors, people tend to be of two minds. MI practitioners refer to this as *ambivalence*. Even if humans want to engage in healthy behaviors, there is often another part of them that resists. W. R. Miller and Rollnick (2013) put it this way: "Ambivalence is simultaneously wanting and not wanting something, or wanting both of two incompatible things. It has been human nature since the dawn of time" (p. 6).
- *Clients should make the case for change.* Given the ubiquity of ambivalence, MI is oriented toward creating the following condition for change: "Ideally, the client should be voicing

the reasons for change" (W. R. Miller & Rollnick, 2013, p. 9). MI practitioners tap into client motivation instead of applying external pressure on clients to change.

W. R. Miller and Rollnick (2013) described MI as "a person-centered counseling style for addressing the common problem of ambivalence about change" (p. 29). The relationship elements that MI practitioners value most include the following:

- *Collaboration.* MI is described as dancing, not wrestling. Instead of behaving like they have the answers to clients' problems, MI counselors honor clients' perspectives and use open questions, affirmation, reflections, and summarizing to gain access to what clients are thinking and feeling.
- *Acceptance.* MI counselors hold an "attitude of profound acceptance of what the client brings" (W. R. Miller & Rollnick, 2013, p. 16). This profound acceptance includes an emphasis on (a) absolute worth, (b) accurate empathy, (c) autonomy support, and (d) affirmation.
- *Evocation.* Because clients are experts on their own experiences, MI practitioners assume they have explored both sides of their ambivalence. A major task of counselors is to draw out clients' wisdom instead of imposing their own wisdom on clients.
- *Compassion.* In 2013, W. R. Miller and Rollnick added compassion to their original list of collaboration, acceptance, and evocation. Compassion orients counselors toward carrying the pain alongside their clients and helps make certain that practitioners focus on clients' interests first.

Our reasons for reviewing MI and providing an example (see Case Vignette 4.1) are to illustrate (a) why MI skills are essential for working with suicidality, (b) how MI skills help clinicians focus on client suicidal distress, (c) how the MI attitude of profound acceptance guides clinicians in fulfilling the suicide competency of accepting client suicidal distress (Cramer et al., 2013), and (d) how MI clinicians engage clients to establish goals and voice reasons for change.

Although MI allows for the use of technical strategies, overall, the MI philosophy is person centered: "It is the client who knows what hurts, what directions to go in, what problems are crucial" (Rogers, 1961, pp. 11–12). If the client knows what "directions to go in," MI skills can be used to identify client goals and values.

Case Vignette 4.1
Motivational Interviewing (MI) With an Emergency Room Referral

A 17-year-old lesbian female named Melanie arrived at a local hospital emergency room (ER) accompanied by her mother. Melanie had reported suicidal ideation to her high school counselor. Melanie refused to engage in safety planning. Instead, she kept insisting "I'm going to kill myself, so all this bullshit is pointless." Further assessment was needed. The counselor consulted with Melanie's mom, who had picked her up and taken her to the ER.

Melanie admitted to a recent suicide attempt (i.e., she took 10 tablets of her fluoxetine prescription). She reported current suicidal ideation and intent. She also reported binge drinking; she scored as having major depression on the Patient Health Questionnaire–9.

Melanie was placed in the Teen Options for Change (TOC) intervention arm of a clinical trial. In the TOC intervention, all patients received the following:

- An information card with crisis phone numbers and a brochure with information about depression, suicide risk, local mental health services, and firearms risk;
- Personalized feedback on ER screening results;
- A 40-minute motivational interview with a mental health professional who had received 40-plus hours of MI training that resulted in the development of personalized goals accompanied by an action plan to achieve patient goals;
- A follow-up handwritten note from the mental health professional; and
- A follow-up telephone call from the mental health professional 2 to 5 days after the emergency contact to "support and facilitate implementation" of the patient's "action plan" (King et al., 2015, p. 98).

During the motivational interview, the mental health professional used a therapeutic assessment approach to give Melanie feedback on her ER screening (Finn et al., 2012; Fischer, 1985). The clinician said things like, "You reported on the alcohol screening that you've been binge drinking. My impression, as well as research on binge drinking, suggests that sometimes people binge drink to numb painful feelings. Does that fit for you, or is the binge drinking about something else?" Or, "On this questionnaire called the Patient Health Questionnaire, you answered in ways that indicate you have symptoms of depression. From your perspective, how do sadness and depression affect you in your life?"

(continued)

Case Vignette 4.1
Motivational Interviewing (MI) With an
Emergency Room Referral *(continued)*

> The MI protocol also emphasized identifying client values and goals and exploring whether clients saw themselves as moving toward or away from their values and goals. For Melanie, the following goals and discrepancies were observed and reflected back to her:
>
>> You said that one thing you wish for in your life is to be more open about your sexuality. You don't think your family will accept you. That feels bad. I'm wondering what you've tried to achieve that goal for yourself.
>
> After Melanie responded by describing her thoughts, hopes, and fears about being open with her family about her sexuality, the clinician continued:
>
>> One question that comes to mind about that is "How can you begin to be more open about your sexuality?" But I don't think we can just focus on that. We should also be asking, "What can you do to feel safe as you try to be more open? How can you take care of yourself in case of rejections or negative reactions?"

Case Vignette 4.1 was extrapolated from a research study on the efficacy of the TOC program versus ER contact and follow-up (King et al., 2015). In the study, clients who received MI were likely to experience a significant reduction in depressive symptoms compared to typical ER outcomes. In addition, TOC patients had more improvements in (a) hopelessness, (b) suicidal ideation, and (c) alcohol misuse. In conclusion, a brief ER-based MI intervention may be an effective treatment for suicidal ideation in adolescents.

Separating the Pain From the Self and Other Emotional Reframing Strategies

Shneidman (1993) recommended that clinicians partner with clients and with members of the client's support system (e.g., their family) to do whatever possible to reduce emotional pain. He also recommended that clinicians assist clients in reframing or redefining their suicidal pain.

Rosenberg (1999) and others have described a helpful cognitive intervention for reframing emotional pain. She wrote that counselors can help clients understand that what they really want "is to eradicate the feelings of intolerable pain *rather than to eradicate the self* [emphasis added]" (p. 86). Similarly, Rosenberg recommended that counselors help clients reframe what is usually meant by the phrase *feeling suicidal*. She noted that clients benefit from seeing their suicidal thoughts and impulses as a communication of their depth of feeling rather than an "actual intent to take action" (p. 86). Rosenberg's reframe—illustrated in the following case example—can decrease clients' need to act, partly because of the cognitive reframe and partly because of the therapist's empathic message of siding with the client to battle the pain.

How to Separate the Pain From the Self

Katie was a 44-year-old heterosexual, cisgender married female with two children. She arrived for counseling in extreme emotional distress. She stated, "It hurts so bad to be alive."

Much of Katie's emotional pain came from the recent death of her mother. Katie had provided in-home care for her mother for 7 years. Katie had an ambivalent relationship with her mother, who had been diagnosed with schizophrenia. Katie's acute emotional distress was accompanied by the thought of reuniting with her mother: "I need to be with her."

To help Katie separate her intense emotional pain from the self, the counselor began by noticing two different parts of Katie with distinct ideas about how to move forward. The counselor said, "Sounds like a part of you feels this big and overwhelming pain and then thinks the solution is to die, to stop the pain. Does that sound about right?"

Katie affirmed this perspective, and the counselor continued, "But there's another part that says, maybe the solution isn't to die. Maybe I can come here and talk. Maybe talking can shrink the pain. I should shrink my pain because my kids and husband would suffer if I die."

Katie accepted that she was "of two minds" about how to go forward. Next, the counselor asked for an agreement to work together with the part of Katie that wanted to shrink the pain. "How about, for now, we listen to that second voice. We can be a team and work to decrease the pain you're feeling. It might not go away immediately, but if you stay alive, we can chip away at the pain. Together, we can try all sorts of things that might make it shrink."

Framing Pain and Suicidality as Evidence of a Normal Self-Care Impulse

Another reframe involves viewing suicidality as coming from a place of self-care or self-compassion. Using your own words, you might try a reframe like this: "As you talk about wanting to die, I'm struck that your wish for death also comes from your wish to *feel better* . . . and your wish to feel better is normal, natural, and healthy. What I'd like to do for now is to partner with you on the healthy goal of feeling better. I need your help on this. For now, we can put your wish to die on the sidelines and focus on feeling better. We can't expect immediate positive results. Will you work with me to battle your pain and, little by little, to help you feel better?"

This reframing message is intentionally repetitive and almost hypnotic. The purpose is to engage with and activate the healthy part of the self that wants to feel better. When clients respond to this message, hope for positive outcomes may increase. If clients reject this reframing message, suicide risk may be high.

Framing Pain as Meaningful

Viktor Frankl (1967) used reframing to address depressive symptoms in the following case:

> An old doctor consulted me in Vienna because he could not get rid of a severe depression caused by the death of his wife. I asked him, "What would have happened, Doctor, if you had died first, and your wife would have had to survive you?" Whereupon he said: "For her this would have been terrible; how she would have suffered!" I then added, "You see, Doctor, such a suffering has been spared her, and it is you who have spared her this suffering; but now you have to pay for it by surviving and mourning her." The old man suddenly saw his plight in a new light, and reevaluated his suffering in the meaningful terms of a sacrifice for the sake of his wife. (pp. 15–16)

Consistent with Frankl's existential perspective, his reframe involves viewing suffering as meaningful. If clients view suffering as meaningful, life can feel more bearable.

When Reframes Fail

Reframing and redefining client emotional distress takes many forms, but sometimes reframes do not fit and do not work. Reframes may be ineffective because of (a) cultural insensitivity, (b) symptom severity, (c) inadequate rapport or alliance, or (d) countertransference (Lenes et al., 2020; Parrow et al., 2019). When your efforts to reframe fail, clients may withdraw or become agitated, and you may be at risk for a relationship rupture (Safran & Kraus, 2014). If the reframe does not fit, process the issue (e.g., "Based on your reaction, it doesn't seem like the idea I shared fits well for you"). After listening to your client's response, you might need to proceed with strategies for rupture repair (see J. Sommers-Flanagan & Sommers-Flanagan, 2017). Relationship repair might include a direct apology and further processing. For example, "I'm sorry my idea for how to think about your pain wasn't a good fit. But I'm glad you let me know it doesn't fit. Lots of counseling is like an experiment. Sometimes we discover something doesn't work. If you think something doesn't fit or work for you, I will always want to know. Thank you for telling me."

When it comes to using reframing and redefinitions, your theoretical foundation is less important than the pragmatics of finding something that works for your client. The process involves (a) identifying a potential reframe, (b) asking clients for permission to try it out, (c) sharing the reframe, (d) observing client reactions, (e) verbally checking in on client reactions and goodness of fit, (f) continuing to collaboratively experiment with the reframe or collaboratively discarding it as a bad idea, and (g) addressing the relationship rupture—if one has occurred.

Mindfulness, Distress Tolerance, and Emotional Regulation

Linehan (1993), the developer of dialectical behavior therapy (DBT), wrote, "DBT emphasizes learning to bear pain skillfully" (p. 147). As you can see from that quotation, DBT includes emotional pain management as its central focus. If you are planning to work with suicidality in clients or students, training and practice in DBT can be very helpful.

DBT practitioners work hard to get client buy-in. Linehan sometimes says things like, "Getting through this is like going through hell. Therapy can help, but only if you stay alive. Therapy never works on dead people. So I want you to stay alive and work with me on attacking your pain. Will you give me 6 months for us to go through hell together so we can get control of your pain?"

Clients are also involved in group work aimed at developing cognitive behavioral skills to manage excruciating distress. These skills include mindfulness, emotional regulation, distress tolerance, and interpersonal effectiveness (content focusing on interpersonal effectiveness is in Chapter 6).

Mindfulness

Counselors who use DBT break mindfulness skills into three "what" skills and three "how" skills (Linehan, 1993). "What" skills focus on teaching clients to observe, describe, and participate. *Observing* involves getting distance from one's own experiences and noticing what is happening, even when the situation is distressing. *Describing* involves using verbal labels to describe cognitive, affective, and physiological experiences. The emphasis is on accurate and objective description of experiences. *Participating* involves engaging spontaneously in activities without self-consciousness.

"How" skills include taking a nonjudgmental stance, focusing on one thing in the moment, and being effective. *Taking a nonjudgmental stance* involves accepting life, events, and the self as is. When practicing being nonjudgmental, clients are encouraged to recognize and let go of their tendency to automatically evaluate and ruminate on their experiences. *Focusing on one thing in the moment* involves focus and absorption. The goal is to keep attention on one thing rather than experiencing divided attention. *Being effective* involves focusing on what works in specific situations rather than obsessing on what is fair or right. Given that much of life is unfair and emotionally destabilizing, being effective counters the idea of "I must be right" with the practical doing of "whatever gets you through an experience."

As a skill, mindfulness is impossible to completely attain and sustain. Helping clients accept imperfection is an ongoing part of mindfulness training. DBT practitioners use a concept called *onemindfully* to illustrate that mindfulness is a process and that this process includes imperfection. Clients are asked to do one thing at a time and, while doing that one thing, to not think of anything else. For example, if a client is knitting, the client practices thoughts of "knitting, knitting, knitting." When other thoughts emerge, even emotionally neutral thoughts like "I need to go to the store at 4 p.m.," clients are instructed to notice the distracted thought, accept it, and then go back to "knitting, knitting, knitting." Developing and practicing mindfulness skills in and out of therapy fits well into treatment plans for handling and decreasing excruciating emotional distress and improving emotional regulation.

Distress Tolerance

Distress tolerance is an extension of mindfulness into especially difficult and emotionally provocative situations. Clients learn to accept their current environment, their emotional state, and their thoughts and actions; they are also taught that acceptance does not mean approval. For example, clients who face a chronically critical work environment but cannot quit because they need the income can practice affirmations that include acceptance, not approval. For instance: "Working in a difficult situation is part of my life right now. I accept that. I will use my coping skills to deal with work. But I don't think my work situation is good for me in the long run. While I'm coping with work difficulties, I'll be keeping my eyes open for more validating work opportunities in the future."

Emotional Regulation

Emotional regulation can be improved through mindfulness training, but DBT also involves directly teaching clients seven specific emotional regulation skills:

1. *Identifying and labeling affect:* "What am I feeling?"
2. *Identifying obstacles to changing emotions:* "What's stopping me from feeling differently?"
3. *Reducing vulnerability to "emotion mind":* "What physical and wellness self-care activities (e.g., sleeping, eating) can I build into my life?"
4. *Increasing positive emotional events:* "What short-term and longer term pleasant activities can I weave into my life?"
5. *Increasing mindfulness to current emotion:* "How can I observe and experience my emotions and love my emotions while recognizing that I'm more than my emotions?"
6. *Taking opposite action:* "What if I did the opposite of how I usually respond to problematic emotions? Perhaps approaching fear (instead of retreating), taking a step back from anger (instead of raging), or facing up to shame (instead of avoiding) will help with difficult emotions?"
7. *Applying distress tolerance techniques:* "What unpleasant experiences do I need to radically accept, and how will I apply self-soothing strategies when needed?"

DBT was developed to treat borderline personality disorder, although there is growing evidence that it is effective in addressing other problems, especially problems linked to emotional dysregulation (Berk et al., 2019; Hollenbaugh & Lenz, 2018; Maffei et al., 2018). Many clients who are suicidal experience problems with emotional regulation. Regardless of your client's diagnosis, if emotional dysregulation is the problem, consider integrating DBT skills training into your treatment plan.

The Three-Step Emotional Change Trick

Affect regulation implies affect elevation (see Wellness Practice 4.1). The three-step emotional change trick is an Adlerian-based intervention that teaches youth how to use cognitive behavioral skills to improve their mood (Mosak, 1985; J. Sommers-Flanagan & Sommers-Flanagan, 2007). Youth and many adults find emotions such as fear, sadness, guilt, and anger difficult to tolerate. For some clients, feeling emotionally out of control contributes to suicidality. Learning skills to improve mood contributes to larger emotional regulation goals.

The three-step emotional change trick is about emotional education and regulation. This intervention breaks emotion management into three easily understood steps.

Step 1: Feel the Feeling

Step 1 involves labeling the emotion, honoring its existence, and being with the emotion (instead of immediately trying to change it). Counselors begin by asking, "Have you ever had someone tell you to cheer up?" Young clients usually share that they "hate" being told to cheer up, and discussion ensues. Then, instead of asking them to cheer up, counselors ask, "Can I teach you a trick that will help you get in a better mood, but only when you're ready?" Actively honoring and being with the emotion and noticing what its presence might mean could involve talking, crying, making faces, or using any method that is safe and consistent with the emotion.

Step 2: Think a New Thought or Do Something Different

Clients are coached to start Step 2 when they (not others) have decided to move away from the unpleasant emotion. During Step 2, clients can distract themselves with fun, funny, or meaningful thoughts and/or do something that grabs their attention and draws them away from the disturbing emotion (and accompanying thoughts). Young clients might focus on jokes, riddles, or funny stories from school. Creative brainstorming is important during this step.

Step 3: Spread the Good Mood

Once the unpleasant or disturbing mood has passed (more or less), young clients can focus on other people and on spreading their good mood. As long as they avoid using the "just cheer up" strategy, encourage youth to identify ways they can have a positive emotional influence on others. Usually this involves smiling, doing a favor, offering a surprise compliment, saying "I love you" to a parent or caregiver, and other creative ideas.

Step 4: Teach Someone the Three Steps

When teaching this emotion management skill, we like to surprise clients by including a fourth step (even though it is a three-step technique). Typically young clients immediately protest, saying, "You said it was three steps!" We compliment them for noticing and then explain that emotions are so complex that we needed four steps, even for a three-step technique. Step 4 is a homework assignment to teach the three-step technique to someone.

A video example of the three-step emotional change technique is available at https://johnsommersflanagan.com/2017/03/12/revisiting-the-3-step-emotional-change-trick-including-a-video-example/.

Additional Interventions in the Emotional Dimension

Many other interventions and therapeutic models for working with clients on emotional issues are available (Capuzzi & Stauffer, 2016). However, because the therapeutic alliance predicts positive outcomes across counseling approaches, we have three rules to apply when choosing your interventions. First, be a friendly, compassionate person who displays excellent listening skills. Make it clear that you want to work with the client and that you believe you have strategies and tools to help clients address and reduce their emotional pain. These behaviors will help you develop a positive emotional bond with your clients (Parrow et al., 2019).

Second, explicitly and collaboratively identify counseling goals. Goal consensus facilitates positive outcomes (Tryon et al., 2018). Within the emotional dimension, together with your client, identify emotions that are most disturbing; identify their triggers; and set goals to reduce the frequency, duration, and intensity of emotional distress. As noted previously, tracking and addressing negative affect will help you individualize large-group, nomothetic risk factors in ways that become meaningful to your treatment plan.

Third, identify and practice tasks that are rationally and logically linked to your mutually identified goals. For example, if anger and rage are problematic, you should help your client see how developing relaxation and mindfulness skills along with better communication skills can help with anger management. Engaging in collaborative and meaningful tasks is central to positive counseling outcomes (J. Sommers-Flanagan, 2015b; Tryon et al., 2018).

A positive emotional bond, goal consensus, and collaborative therapeutic tasks are derived from Bordin's (1979) formulation of the working alliance. When engaging with clients who are experiencing intense emotions, it is especially critical to integrate principles from research on the working alliance into your clinical practice. The three relational components from Bordin's working alliance are robust predictors of positive treatment outcomes (Flückiger et al., 2018).

Concluding Comments

In this chapter, we began our analysis of the seven life dimensions with a focus on all things emotional. In subsequent chapters, we review the remaining six life dimensions, but none of these other dimensions independently drive suicidal behavior. Clients can cope with experiences of extreme cognitive or social dysfunction, physical illness, spiritual malaise, cultural disconnection, behavioral impulsivity, or disturbing contextual factors—as long as those experiences are not accompanied by unbearable emotional distress. By default, emotional pain is the central focus to which your counseling always returns.

Practitioner Guidance and Key Points to Remember

When working in the emotional dimension, reducing and redefining your client's emotional pain is your primary focus. In this chapter, we described three key emotional issues to address in counseling: (a) excruciating distress; (b) specific disturbing emotions, such as shame, guilt, anger, and sadness; and (c) affect dysregulation. Interventions in the emotional dimension include the following:

- Collaboratively identify factors that contribute to your client's emotional pain so you can understand and individualize your client's unique risk and protective factors.
- Avoid activating psychological reactance or resistance by focusing first on your client's emotional distress.
- Use empathic responses and emotional acceptance to resonate with your client's emotional pain.
- When the timing is right, shift your focus from emotional distress to positive problem-solving (more on this in Chapter 5).
- Apply MI skills to identify goals and enhance your client's interest in positive change.
- Separate your client's pain from the self so you can work along with your client on reducing emotional distress.
- Frame your client's emotional pain as a normal self-care impulse or as conferring particular meaning.

- When your efforts to reframe your client's pain fail, shift to relationship repair and refocus counseling on goals and tasks of value to the client.
- Teach DBT skills for mindfulness, emotional regulation, and distress tolerance.
- Use the three-step emotional change trick to respectfully engage young clients or students in an emotional education process.
- When using alternative emotionally oriented interventions (and there are many), follow Bordin's (1979) guidance on the treatment alliance by establishing a positive emotional bond, engaging in mutual goal setting, and developing collaborative therapeutic tasks.
- Teach yourself and your clients how to practice positive savoring.

Chapter 5

The Cognitive Dimension

In the introduction to *Cognitive Therapy for Suicidal Patients* (Wenzel et al., 2009), Aaron Beck (2009) wrote of his discovery of hopelessness:

> Early in my work, I became aware of the central role of hopelessness, or negative expectations for the future, in my depressed suicidal patients. I observed that the greater the hopelessness, the greater these patients' wish to kill themselves. I also found that if I successfully targeted patients' hopelessness in therapy, their suicidal wishes appeared to subside. (p. iv)

The flip side of Beck's discovery of hopelessness is his identification of hope as an effective treatment for suicidality. In this chapter, we follow Beck's lead and focus on client cognitions—including hopelessness and hope—as the royal road to assessment and treatment planning with clients who are suicidal. Although we are discussing hopelessness in the cognitive dimension, clients and practitioners often talk about "feelings of hopelessness." Hope is a cognitive experience laden with emotion. If you (or your clients) feel hopeful, you are probably experiencing a combination of optimism and happiness. Experiencing hopelessness combines pessimistic expectations and sadness. Adler (1938), whose work predated the cognitive revolution in psychotherapy, believed, similarly to Beck, that discouragement was at the heart of all psychopathology and encouragement was the foundation for all therapeutic change. In

• 111

the spirit of Adler, Beck, and positive psychology, we recommend that your work in the cognitive dimension be saturated with encouragement (with *encouragement* defined as the instilling of "courage, perseverance, confidence, inspiration, or hope in a person [for] addressing a challenging situation or realizing a potential"; Wong, 2015, p. 182).

Working in the Cognitive Dimension

The cognitive dimension includes thoughts, images, and perceptions. Clients who are suicidal usually report negative, aversive, or self-loathing thoughts that shape their emotions and behaviors. As clients recognize and change their maladaptive thoughts, they will likely experience greater control over the emotional and behavioral dimensions of their lives.

When he was a practicing psychoanalyst, A. T. Beck (1976) discovered the ubiquity of evaluative cognition. As his clients free associated, Beck noticed they were simultaneously evaluating themselves (e.g., "I said the wrong thing . . . I shouldn't have said that . . . I'm wrong to criticize him . . . I'm bad . . . I have no excuse for being so mean"; A. T. Beck, 1976, pp. 30–31). Beck decided that psychotherapy was more effective when clinicians focused on clients' ongoing judgments of themselves, others, and their expectations for the future.

Key Cognitive Issues to Address

Cognition is nearly always part of the complex dynamic that ends in suicide. Researchers and clinicians have identified four cognitive factors drive suicidal behavior: (a) hopelessness, (b) problem-solving impairments, (c) maladaptive thinking, and (d) negative core beliefs and self-hatred. In general, these factors are considered disturbances in information processing and should be integrated into suicide-focused treatment plans. Next, we briefly review these four core cognitive issues. Later, we provide in-depth case examples.

Hopelessness

Hopelessness is a broad cognitive variable linked to elevated suicide risk (Bedrosian & Beck, 1979). In many cases, clients hold a hopeless view of the future, even when rational justifications for hope exist. Countering hopelessness with hope is crucial; hope functions as a protective factor against suicide (Hagan et al., 2015).

Hopelessness cognitions can be related to any of the seven life dimensions:

- Emotional: "I'll never feel any better. I'll always be sad."
- Cognitive: "I'll always make bad decisions in my life."
- Interpersonal: "I'll never be in a healthy, loving relationship or have any real friends."
- Physical: "This pain will only get worse."
- Cultural-spiritual: "Life and death have no meaning whatsoever."
- Behavioral: "I can't control these urges to kill myself."
- Contextual: "The world is a wreck and will never get better."

The ways in which clients articulate hopelessness can illuminate their underlying core beliefs and provide you with ideas about where to focus your interventions.

Problem-Solving Impairments

Shneidman (1996) hypothesized that intense emotional distress adversely affects information processing, resulting in mental constriction. Research supports Shneidman's hypothesis: Negative moods adversely affect cognitive content, especially for individuals with a history of depression and suicidal ideation (Lau et al., 2012). As emotional distress increases, problem-solving skills diminish. Over time, thinking narrows and people begin believing they have only two choices: They can continue living in miserable pain, or they can end their lives.

Collaborative problem-solving—illustrated later in case examples—is a method for assessing and treating problem-solving impairments. Clients who cannot problem solve are at higher risk; you may need to involve others to keep them safe. If clients are able to engage in problem-solving, then problem-solving becomes an intervention for decreasing suicidality. Collaborative problem-solving is nearly always central to treatment for suicidality.

Maladaptive Thinking

Traditional cognitive therapy targets maladaptive or irrational thinking (A. T. Beck, 1976; Ellis, 1962). Modern cognitive therapy is combined with behavior therapy and referred to as *cognitive behavior therapy* (CBT; J. S. Beck, 2011). CBT is used to help clients monitor and evaluate automatic thoughts, maladaptive thinking patterns, core beliefs, and specific behaviors; counselors then guide clients to determine whether their thoughts and behaviors are (a) accurate and (b) useful. If thoughts and behaviors are inaccurate or not useful, clients are coached to develop and practice more adaptive ways of thinking and behaving.

Several new (third-wave) cognitive approaches that emphasize mindfulness are available (Hayes, 2004/2016). These new approaches include mindfulness-based cognitive therapy (Segal et al., 2013), dialectical behavior therapy (Linehan, 1993), and acceptance and commitment therapy (Hayes et al., 1999). Instead of coaching clients to counter their cognitions, third-wave CBT practitioners teach clients to adopt an attitude of mindful acceptance. In particular, clinicians who practice acceptance and commitment therapy believe that clients often fail at their efforts to eliminate negative thoughts and end up feeling even worse about themselves. We view both approaches—countering negative thoughts and mindfully accepting negative thoughts—as alternative strategies that may be more or less effective, depending on the preference and disposition of your client. When deciding which approach to take, we encourage you to use Aaron Beck's concept of collaborative empiricism. Collaborative empiricism involves working alongside clients to test and determine what works best for each individual client.

Negative Core Beliefs and Self-Hatred

Clients who are suicidal frequently suffer from negative core beliefs that are activated by specific environmental triggers. For example, failing an exam can activate deep core beliefs of being unworthy or stupid. When activated, core beliefs permeate daily life and contribute to excruciating distress.

Negative core beliefs can also be viewed through all seven dimensions:

- Emotional: "I'm permanently emotionally flawed."
- Cognitive: "I'm stupid."
- Interpersonal: "I'm unlovable, useless, and unworthy of friendship."
- Physical: "I'm unattractive, weak, and genetically inferior."
- Cultural-spiritual: "I am unworthy. I am a misfit in the human race."
- Behavioral: "I cannot control myself."
- Contextual: "The deck [world] is stacked against me."

Core beliefs are difficult to change. Experts in cognitive therapy have noted that complete alteration of core beliefs may be an unrealistic treatment goal (Dobson & Dobson, 2017). Rather than putting "Change core beliefs" on your problem list, it is more realistic (and encouraging) to focus on "Coping with or mindfully accepting core beliefs."

Interventions in the Cognitive Dimension

Many different interventions address hopelessness, problem-solving deficits, maladaptive thinking patterns, and negative core beliefs. Determining which interventions to use with clients should involve collaboration. Rather than insisting that clients use a particular treatment model or technical strategy, you and your clients can use collaborative empiricism to experiment with various techniques and decide together which approaches have the best chance for success.

Showing Empathy for Cognitive Impairments

Showing empathy for client cognitions and perceptions is as important as displaying emotional empathy. Case Vignette 5.1 includes an example using an empathic metaphor.

In Case Vignette 5.1, the clinician is not minimizing the client's depression and hopelessness. Instead, depression, hopelessness, as well as cognitive and memory impairments are framed as natural by-products of a difficult situation. The metaphor allows the counselor to express acceptance and a willingness to join and collaborate—thus loaning the client hope.

Being with clients in their pit of despair requires a willingness to connect with and accept your clients' emotional and cognitive experiences. In some situations, you may need to sit with clients in their confusion before illuminating potential solutions. For example, military veterans who have been traumatized and who have experienced a traumatic brain injury may experience memory problems and disorientation that erodes their confidence and deepens hopelessness. In contrast, adolescent clients may wallow in their powerlessness, insist that adults will never understand them, and reject every possible option for improving their lives. Although we encourage you to take a strengths-based approach with clients, before focusing on potential positive experiences and hope you will need to spend time alongside clients in their uniquely personal pit of despair, confusion, and hopelessness. Eventually, after resonating with your clients' despair, you may be able to begin using homework assignments that orient your clients toward monitoring positive experiences and events. See Wellness Practice 5.1 for more information on collaborative problem-solving.

Case Vignette 5.1
The Pit of Despair

Carl Rogers often used metaphors to show empathy. The pit of despair is a metaphor that often resonates with clients who struggle with suicidal thoughts (see also Brené Brown's empathy video at https://www.youtube.com/watch?v=1Evwgu369Jw).

Counselor: Many people who are suicidal say their brains feel shut down. It can feel like being in a dark pit. Can you relate to that at all?

Client: My brain is definitely pathetic. There's no way out of my shitty life.

Counselor: And so one goal might be to think of ways to get out of that pit, right?

Client: That'd be nice, but I can't even imagine it.

Counselor: That's totally natural. If you're trapped in a dark pit of depression, it's normal to think there's no way out, because if you're in the pit, you can't see a positive future, you can't look back and see anything positive from the past. You've been trying to get out of the pit on your own but feel stuck and hopeless.

Client: That pretty much describes it. I've tried everything to get out. I can't. Nothing works. I don't think anything can ever help get me out of this place.

Counselor: You feel like you've tried everything and nothing has worked. I'm guessing you might think counseling is pointless too.

Client: No offense. I'm sure you're good at what you do. It just won't work for me.

Counselor: Sure. I don't blame you. Given what you've been through, being discouraged seems perfectly natural.

Client: So what's the point then?

Counselor: The point is that I'm planning to get into the pit with you, and I've got a few tools. One of the tools is a flashlight. I hope we can look around this pit together. We'll look for openings. We'll look for footholds and ladders. At first, we might not see much that looks hopeful. That's because we're in a pit and it's hard to see good things when we're in a pit. But over time, we'll figure out which tools work best for you. We'll get to the surface once in a while and see a better future. We may have to go through hell together, but by working together we can get out of this.

Wellness Practice 5.1
Witness Something Inspiring

A traditional cognitive therapy homework assignment is for clients to self-monitor positive experiences and events that happen in their lives. One variation on this assignment is to have clients focus on inspiring things that are constantly happening in the world.

In our Art and Science of Happiness course at the University of Montana, we gave students the assignment to witness something inspiring over the Martin Luther King Day weekend. Our only requirement: The inspirational moment had to be live and in vivo, not via the internet.

The students' responses were surprising. Instead of going to Martin Luther King Day activities (which we thought was a natural choice), most students simply set their minds to finding something inspiring in the context of a normal (long) weekend. What they discovered were multiple examples of small but inspiring observations each day. Examples included "I saw someone spontaneously pick up some litter" and "I went to a campus event on Black Lives Matter" and "My dad told me he loves me and believes in me." Your goal for this activity is similar: We want you to watch for and observe something inspiring that is happening in the real world. We also want you to try this for 1 week.

The inspiring event that you notice may be small or it may be big. The key part of this assignment is that it involves intentionally watching for that which will inspire. Keep all your sensory modalities open for inspiration. Then, as you are going to bed each night, think or write about what you observed and contemplate what in particular it was that felt inspiring.

Collaborative Problem-Solving

Problem-solving therapy is an evidence-based therapeutic approach (Nezu et al., 2013). As Reinecke (2006) noted, "From a problem-solving perspective, suicide reflects a breakdown in adaptive, rational problem solving. The suicidal individual is not able to generate, evaluate, and implement effective solutions and anticipates that his or her attempts will prove fruitless" (p. 240). Problem-solving with clients has assessment and treatment potential.

In Chapter 4 we emphasized that clinicians should initially focus on and show empathy for clients' excruciating distress and suicidal thoughts. However, there comes a moment when a pivot toward positive problem-solving can occur. Questions to facilitate this pivot include the following:

- "What helps, even a tiny bit?"
- "When you've felt bad in the past, what helped the most?"
- "How have you been able to cope with your suicidal thoughts?"

In response to these questions, clients who are suicidal often show you their hopelessness, mental constriction, problems with information processing, or selective memory retrieval. Statements like "I've tried everything," "Nothing helps," and "I can't remember ever feeling good" represent cognitive impairments. Even though your clients may think they have tried everything, no one can possibly try everything. Similarly, although it is possible that nothing helps much, it is doubtful that all your clients' efforts to feel better have been equally ineffective. These statements are black-and-white or polarized thinking and signal hopelessness and memory impairments (A. T. Beck, Rush, et al., 1979; J. Sommers-Flanagan & Sommers-Flanagan, 2018).

Pivoting to the Positive

Recall the case of Sophia introduced in Chapter 4. After exploring distress linked to Sophia's suicidal ideation, the counselor pivots to asking about the positive ("What helps?") and proceeds with problem-solving for assessment and intervention purposes. One trigger for Sophia's suicidal thinking is her parents' fighting. She may not be able to do anything about their fights, but she can do other things to shield herself from the downward cognitive and emotional spiral that the fighting activates.

> *Counselor:* Let's say your parents are fighting and you're feeling suicidal. You're in your room by yourself. What could you do that's helpful in that moment?
>
> *Sophia:* I have a cat. His name is Douglas. Sometimes he makes me feel better. He's diabetic, so I don't think he'll live much longer, but he's comforting right now.
>
> *Counselor:* Nice. My memory's not perfect, so is it OK with you if I write a list of all the things that help? Douglas helps you be in a better mood. What else helps?
>
> *Sophia:* I like music. Blasting music makes me feel better. And volleyball is a comfort, but I can't play volleyball in my room.

Counselor: Yeah. Great. Let me jot those down: music and being with your cat. And volleyball, but not in your room! I guess you can think about volleyball, right? How about friends? Do you have friends who are positive supports in your life?

Sophia immediately engages in problem-solving. She identifies Douglas and other things that help. At least for now, Sophia does not appear to have a problem-solving impairment.

During problem-solving, regularly repeating positive coping strategies back to the client is important. In this case, the counselor summarizes Sophia's positive ideas and then asks about friends and social support—an important dimension in suicide treatment and safety planning.

Sophia: My friend Liz and I hang out quite a bit. I can walk into her house, and it will feel like my house. But we're both in volleyball, so we're both really busy.
Counselor: OK, the list of things that help, when you're in a hard place with your parents fighting: Douglas the cat, music, volleyball, and friends. Anything else to add?
Sophia: I don't think so.

The next step in collaborative problem-solving is to ask clients for permission to add to the list, thus turning the process into shared brainstorming. At no time during the brainstorming should you criticize client-generated alternatives, even if they are dangerous or destructive. However, clients sometimes criticize your ideas. When clients criticize, just agree with a statement like "Yeah, you're probably right, but we're just brainstorming. We can rank and rate these as good or bad ideas later."

Brainstorming is used to break open mental constriction. During brainstorming, Sophia and her counselor generate the following list:

- Be with the cat, Douglas
- Sing
- Blast music
- Play volleyball
- Go to a friend's house
- Go walk by a creek near our house
- Clean my room when I don't know what else to do
- Mess around with makeup
- Try on clothes, or anything to keep me not thinking about it
- Call a friend
- Do Snapchat or games on phone

Sophia responded well to list-making as a problem-solving method. She agreed to take the list home to remind herself of different coping options.

Using Motivational Interviewing (MI) During the Problem-Solving Process

MI was developed in part to manage or reduce client resistance (W. R. Miller, 1978). Using MI skills during brainstorming and problem-solving can be beneficial. For instance, prelabeling your own ideas as possibly negative works like an amplified reflection, making it easier for clients to accept the ideas. Here is an example:

Counselor: I suggested this one—calling a friend—but it's probably a bad idea. I can think of reasons it might not work. And I have another bad idea that I'd like to share. You alright with that?

Labeling the option as "another bad idea" is beneficial in several ways, especially with adolescents. Offering a bad idea sidesteps authority issues and circumvents resistance by negatively prejudging the idea before the client gets a chance to pass judgment. With Sophia, the counselor wants to address the parents' arguing and uses the bad-idea frame:

Counselor: I'm super glad to see Douglas and singing and music on the list of things you can do to deal with your parents' fighting. But I'd like to get your parents to stop fighting in front of you. If you're willing, I'd like to have a meeting with the four of us. My plan is to see if they would stop fighting so much because I hear you saying that the fighting is what makes you think about suicide. Is that right?
Sophia: Yeah.
Counselor: I'd like your permission to say to your mom and dad, "Hey, we need a family session with Sophia." And then I'll talk about how they can avoid fighting in front of you. I'll probably recommend counseling so they can learn to communicate respectfully. I know this might be a bad idea. What do you think?

The preceding exchange captures the underlying spirit of MI (W. R. Miller & Rollnick, 2013). First, the counselor is transparent and collaborative with Sophia. Second, he accepts her views as valid. Third, he shows compassion. Fourth, he is interested in evoking her strengths and empowering her to provide feedback after the experience.

In the end, Sophia reluctantly agrees to a meeting with her parents. She is not optimistic about a positive outcome, which is understandable. Nevertheless, when working with youth, incorporating parents into your treatment plan is essential. If you decide not to engage parents in your work with teenagers who are suicidal, you will need to support your decision with a very strong (and documented) rationale (e.g., previously reported parental abuse). See Table 5.1 for Sophia's initial treatment plan.

Alternatives to Suicide, Part I

In the previous case, Sophia was able to participate in brainstorming and problem-solving. In the next example, Katie is significantly more suicidal and less able to engage in problem-solving.

Shneidman (1980) wrote of a procedure for assessing and intervening with clients who are experiencing mental constriction. This procedure is called *alternatives to suicide* (J. Sommers-Flanagan & Sommers-Flanagan, 2017). Alternatives to suicide is similar to problem-solving. With Sophia, problem-solving focused on behavioral coping in the moment of distress. With alternatives to suicide, the focus is on making choices other than suicide. As with the problem-solving procedure, the brainstorming principle of no criticism is central.

Counselor: You said the only way to make things better in your life is to kill yourself. Obviously, killing yourself is one option. But I wonder what you might do instead of killing yourself. I'd like to make a list, if that's OK. I'll put "Suicide" here on top, but let's make a list of the alternatives.

Katie: I don't know. Maybe there's nothing else.

TABLE 5.1
Treatment Plan for Sophia—Cognitive Dimension

Problem	Goals and Strengths[a]	Interventions/Plan
1. Sophia lacks coping skills for dealing with distress.	1. Develop skills for coping with distressing situations.	1. Actively practice coping and distraction techniques during each session.
2. Sophia is unable or unwilling to speak with her parents about their arguing in front of her.	2. Provide Sophia with a safe situation in which she can communicate with her parents about how their fighting affects her.	2. Give homework for distraction and distress tolerance strategies at home and have Sophia and/or her parents report on her success.

[a]Sophia's strengths include her problem-solving skills and her engagement in counseling.

Depending on the severity of the depression and associated problem-solving deficits, the client's willingness to engage may be minimal or nonexistent. To start the process, you may need to provide more structure or to begin listing alternatives yourself. If you begin listing alternatives, be prepared for the client to immediately say "no" in response. With Katie, the counselor provides more structure.

Counselor: Maybe suicide is your only option. But we're just making a list of possible alternatives. We don't have to be realistic, and you don't have to do any of the ideas we come up with. It's just a list. We can work on it together.
Katie: I don't know.
Counselor: That's OK.
Katie: Maybe to focus on other things and keep coming here.
Counselor: So you could kill yourself, but instead of that you could come here. And you could also focus on other things. What else?
Katie: Yeah, but it's just so hard. It's hard to focus right now.
Counselor: It's hard to focus. But let me ask this. You've got a husband and kids. If you could have quality time with them, would that be something we put on the list?
Katie: Yes. Being with my family, my husband, and my kids. Maybe my brother.
Counselor: I'll put quality time with your family, OK?
Katie: Uh-huh.
Counselor: I'm also putting down quality time with your brother.
Katie: Uh-huh.

As you build a list of alternatives to suicide, it is acceptable to begin with vague statements. In the preceding interaction, the counselor puts "quality time" on the list without defining what quality time might entail. Later the counselor can go through the list two or three more times to define quality time with each of these four people. Until then, the list-building continues.

Counselor: Anything else we could add?
Katie: Uh . . . maybe . . .
Counselor: Any kind of employment or volunteer activities?

Because Katie continues to struggle to come up with specific alternatives to suicide, the counselor continues to draw her out with structure and suggestions.

Katie: I haven't been volunteering for a long time now. I just can't do it anymore.
Counselor: OK. Can't do that.
Katie: Yeah.
Counselor: I'm going to put it on the list anyway, because this is just a list. You don't have to do it. We're just listing things that might be an alternative to death.

Even when clients say, "I just can't do it anymore," the content should go on the list because clients are simply responding with their first negative impulse. They often need your help to open up their constricted thinking and glimpse possible behavioral alternatives.

Katie: Yeah.
Counselor: I'm putting volunteering down. What's something you've had passion for?
Katie: In the past?
Counselor: In the past, sure.
Katie: Horses.
Counselor: OK. Maybe some kind of activity with horses. That's on the list now.
Katie: Uh-huh.
Counselor: So we've got kill myself, talk through it, focus on other things. We have quality time with your family and your brother. I put down volunteering. And now we're talking about things you've had passion for. You said horses, and that made me think of recreational activities.
Katie: Uh-huh.
Counselor: Anything else we would put on this list?
Katie: Uh-huh. Yeah, I don't know. Horses used to be a passion of mine. But my friends took me out for a day, we rode horses, and it didn't really work. Didn't help.

Here Katie displays a cognitive distortion. She is using what we call a *spoiling cognition*. A spoiling cognition is a thought that spoils or undermines an otherwise positive experience. Spoiling thoughts can be future focused (e.g., "Riding horses won't make me feel better"), or they can undermine positive experiences from the past (e.g., "I rode horses with my friends, and I still felt depressed"). When clients display cognitive distortions, you can immediately focus on and collaboratively examine the accuracy and usefulness of the cognitions. You can also provide psychoeducational information about how depressive states affect memory and can result in cognitions that preemptively spoil events that would otherwise be pleasant.

> *Counselor:* Yeah. Riding with your friends didn't fix things, didn't make things better. So I have horses down here. I put it in the recreation category.
> *Katie:* Yeah.
> *Counselor:* Because we're just making a list, and none of the things on the list have to be things you're going to do. I also put volunteering. I remember earlier when we were talking, you said you had interests in the arts.
> *Katie:* Uh-huh.
> *Counselor:* Could I put volunteering for the arts? There are lots of art galleries in town.

This exchange is an example of interactive problem-solving with a client who is severely depressed. The counselor alternates between leading, following, checking in, connecting throughout the brainstorming process, and adding ideas that match with the client's interests and ideas. Sometimes it helps to write down the idea and then double back to ask permission. Being redundant, hopeful, positive, and encouraging is essential. With Katie, the alternatives include social connection (interpersonal dimension), distress reduction (emotional dimension), and meaningful life activities (spiritual dimension).

Psychoeducation on Behavioral Activation

In the previous exchange, Katie peeked out from behind her depression and shared something that may be useful in counseling. Consistent with MI, even though the counselor might be enthused about a given alternative, it is important to let clients decide what works best. However, it is also important to provide psychoeducation, especially when clients use cognitive distortions. Here is an example:

> *Counselor:* There's a puzzling thing about depression, and research bears this out. People stop doing things that are naturally rewarding. And when naturally rewarding behaviors decrease, like you don't go horseback riding, depression increases. You start thinking nothing will help. If you reinsert those things into your life, at first it will seem like nothing is happening. But if you keep doing the activities that should be pleasant or meaningful, eventually your mood lifts back up.

Katie: Hmm.
Counselor: We call this *activity scheduling*. It doesn't involve thinking. You just plan and do a horse activity every week, right?
Katie: Uh-huh.
Counselor: Let's plan volunteering with doing art with kids, right?
Katie: Uh-huh.
Counselor: Let's plan quality time with the family.
Katie: Uh-huh.
Counselor: And when you put those things back into your life, it's not a magic pill, but over a few weeks almost everyone starts to feel better.
Katie: It feels so hard, though, to get it planned. Someone else has to plan it.
Counselor: Yeah. OK. So get someone else to plan. I'm putting that on the list, too.

When Katie says, "Someone else has to plan it," she provides an important insight. She cannot imagine planning healthy activities in her life, even though these activities might be natural antidepressants. She needs support. Because behavioral activation is an excellent strategy for improving Katie's mood, one key strategy in her treatment, at least in the beginning, is to find a person who can act as her planner.

Alternatives to Suicide, Part II

Following this interaction, the counselor continues with alternatives to suicide and asks Katie to rank order her choices.

Counselor: What I'd like you to do now is rank these items on the list one through whatever number we have there, and then we can look at your rankings.
Katie: You want me to go all the way to 10?
Counselor: Sure. Let's give it a try.
Katie: OK. [*reviewing the list*] One, two, three. Well, don't you think this should be last? [*Katie points to the "Suicide" option*]
Counselor: Do you think it should be last?

Although the counselor has helped generate many of Katie's alternatives, it is important that Katie do the ranking. This process is used to reduce her mental constriction but also to get her to genuinely rank where suicide fits for her. In this way, this activity also provides assessment data.

Katie: No.

Counselor: Where would you put it? Are there some things here you'd put before it? Like before you were to kill yourself, would you like quality time with your family?

Katie: Yeah, of course I want more time with my family.

Katie ends up ranking "Suicide" fourth on her list (see the following list for Katie's final rankings). Nevertheless, Katie's stability and safety are of concern. To address safety concerns, the counselor decides, with Katie's permission, to call Katie's husband and discuss her need for extra support. The husband agrees to be supportive and to come with Katie for her next counseling session. Integrating a spouse or significant friend or relative into the treatment plan is an interpersonal intervention that is often recommended when safety is in question.

Katie's Ranked Alternatives to Suicide

Ranking	Alternative
4	Suicide
10	Focus on other things
5	Keep coming for counseling
1	Quality time with husband and children
7	Quality time with brother
8	Volunteer work in general
9	Recreation with horses
3	Volunteer work with art and children
6	Couples counseling
2	Ask husband for help with activity scheduling

Decision-Making Dilemmas

When discussing Katie's situation and other scenarios that involve outpatient work with clients who are highly suicidal, the following question usually comes up: "What if the counselor's judgment is wrong and Katie makes a suicide attempt or kills herself before the next session?" This question gets to the core of practitioner anxiety.

The truth is that Katie could kill herself, and if she does, it will cast doubt on her counselor's clinical judgment. Completed suicides are terrible, emotionally wrenching outcomes that might involve lawsuits, professional self-doubt and sorrow, or even the choice to leave the mental health profession. Suicide tragedies happen; when they do you will probably feel it was partly your fault and could have been prevented. Self-blame is a natural reaction, but suicides are mostly unpredictable. Many high-risk clients do not die by suicide, and some low-risk clients do.

Even more disturbing is the reality that hospitalization is not very effective at treating suicidality and preventing suicide (Large & Kapur, 2018). Hospitalization sometimes causes clients to regress and destabilize; suicide risk is often higher after hospitalization. Because hospitalization is not a good fit for many clients who are suicidal, and because we cannot predict suicide very well anyway, some respected suicide researchers recommend intensive safety planning as a viable (and often preferred) alternative to hospitalization. In the case of Katie, as long as she is willing to collaborate, and the counselor has obtained Katie's husband's agreement to support a safety plan, the counselor is on solid professional ground (or at least as solid as professional ground gets when working with clients who are highly suicidal).

Working With Hopelessness as It Emerges During Sessions

Client hopelessness manifests in different ways. Sometimes hopelessness statements have depressing content (e.g., "I've never been happy and I'll never be happy"); other times they include irritability (e.g., "Counseling has never worked for me. I hate this charade. It won't help."). Either way, hopelessness statements can be provocative and can trigger unhelpful responses from counselors. Preparing yourself to respond therapeutically is important.

Hopelessness among clients who are depressed and suicidal also manifests as an ongoing, long-term cognitive style linked to cognitive distortions wherein clients have difficulty (a) recalling past successes, (b) noticing signs of hope in the immediate moment, or (c) believing that their emotional state or life situation could ever improve. We address acute hopelessness next and hopelessness as a longer term cognitive distortion in a subsequent section.

Resonating With Hopelessness

Imagine you are working with a new client. You want to be encouraging, so you make a statement about the potential for counseling to be helpful.

Counselor: After getting to know you a bit, and hearing what's been happening in your life, I want to share with you that I think counseling can help.

Client: I know you mean well, but this is a waste of time. My life sucks and I want to end it. Popping in to chat with you once a week won't change that.

When clients make hopelessness statements, you may feel tempted to counter with a rational rebuttal. After all, if hopelessness represents a pervasive depression-related cognitive distortion or impairment, it makes sense to offer a contrasting rational way of thinking. Although rational rebuttals reportedly worked for Albert Ellis, for most counselors, immediately disputing clients' global, internal, and hopeless cognitions will create resistance. Offer empathy instead. For example:

Counselor: I hear you saying you don't think counseling can help. You feel hopeless, like your life sucks and won't ever change and so you just want it to end.

Staying empathic requires accurately reflecting hopelessness in sessions. You may even use MI amplification (i.e., using the phrase "never going to change" could function as an amplification). Mirroring your clients' hopelessness will likely stand in stark contrast to what your clients have been experiencing in their lives. In most situations, if your clients have spoken about their depression and suicidality with friends or family, they will have heard reassuring platitudes and emotional minimization (e.g., "I'm sure things will get better" or "You're a wonderful person, you shouldn't think about suicide" or "Let's talk about all the blessings you have in your life").

Remaining steadily empathic with clients as they express hopelessness is an intentionally courageous way to do counseling. Staying empathic means you are sticking with your clients in their despair. You are not running from it; you are not minimizing it; you are not brushing it aside as insignificant. Instead, you are resonating with your clients' terribly depressive and suicidal cognitive and emotional experiences.

Following this empathic path can take you deep into depressive ways of thinking and emoting. This can affect you personally; you may begin adopting your clients' impaired depressive thinking and feel depressed yourself. Part of being a conscious and intentional counselor means you are choosing to temporarily step alongside and into your clients' depressive mindset. You need to be clear with yourself: "I'm stepping into the pit of depression with my client, but even as I'm doing this, my intention is to initiate Socratic questioning or cognitive restructuring or collaborative problem-solving when the time is right."

Integrating Solutions

You might wonder how long you need to stay alongside your client in the depressive mindset. The answer varies. Sometimes as soon as you step alongside your clients' hopelessness, they rally and say something like "It's not like I'm completely hopeless" or "Sometimes I feel hope here or there." Gently nurture such statements with a reflection (e.g., "I hear you saying that once in a while, a bit of hope comes into your mind"), and then explore (and possibly grow) the positive statement with a solution-focused question designed to facilitate elaboration of the exceptional thought (e.g., "What's different between now and a time when you were feeling hopeful?"). Then, for as long as you can manage, you should follow Murphy's (2015) solution-focused model for working with client exceptions:

1. *Elicit exceptions.* Ask questions like "What was different . . .?" and use the MI techniques of coming alongside or amplified reflection.
2. *Elaborate exceptions.* Ask questions like "What's usually happening when you feel a bit of hope peek through the dark clouds?"
3. *Expand exceptions.* Move exceptions to new contexts and try to increase their frequency: "What might help you feel hope just a tiny bit more?"
4. *Evaluate exceptions.* Collaboratively monitor the usefulness of the exception: "If you create reminders for being hopeful all day, would that be a plus or minus for you?"
5. *Empowering exceptions.* Give clients credit for their exceptions and ask what they did to make the exceptions happen: "How did you manage to get yourself to think a few positive thoughts when you were in that conflict with your supervisor?"

Sometimes you will need to stick with your clients' misery and hopelessness longer. However, because this is a strengths-based model, and because the evidence suggests that clients who are suicidal sometimes need counselors to explicitly lead them toward positive solutions, you should watch for opportunities to turn or nudge your clients away from abject hopelessness.

Matching Client Language and Using Validation
As you watch for the right moment to nudge clients toward the positive, more empathy may be required. Although traditional Rogerian empathy primarily involves mirroring surface feelings or deeper emotions, with clients who are depressed and suicidal your empathic responding may need to be explicitly validating. In the following interactions, counselors use empathic validation while also matching their clients' language:

Interaction 1

Client: I know you mean well. But this is a waste of time. I'm depressed and suicidal. Popping in to chat with you once a week won't change that.

Counselor: It's normal to feel doubts about whether counseling can help. If I were in your shoes, I'd also be wondering if weekly counseling could work.

Interaction 2

Katie: Riding horses used to be a passion of mine. My friends took me out for a day. But it didn't really work. It didn't help.

Counselor: You tried something you felt passion for before, but it didn't help. I'm guessing that experience felt disappointing and you felt even more hopeless.

Interaction 3

Client: I've tried counseling. I've tried different medications. I even tried electroconvulsive therapy. But nothing worked. I still feel depressed.

Counselor: You've tried many things. That's a lot of effort, and you still feel depressed. I see your point. No wonder you feel hopeless.

Each of these examples illustrates how to use empathic reflection, match client language, and make validation statements. Validation statements often use words like "I don't blame you" and "No wonder you feel . . ." and "It seems perfectly normal that you would feel. . . ." Validation statements accomplish two things. They demonstrate empathy, and they involve you in being a companion to your clients in their gloom. As a companion, from that place of gloom, you can begin taking small steps toward hope along with your clients. Also, as a companion, you can see the obstacles that get in the way of your clients' journey toward hope.

Working From the Bottom Up to Build a Continuum of Hope

When clients are depressed and suicidal, they often think and talk about depressing thoughts and feelings. We should not expect otherwise. Even so, when clients ruminate on the negative, it fogs the window through which positive feelings and experiences are viewed. Within counseling, a potential conflict emerges: Although clinicians want clients to problem solve, focus on their strengths, and have hope for the future, clients are unable to generate solutions, cannot focus on their strengths or positive attributes, and seem unable to shake their hopelessness.

As discussed earlier in the case of Sophia, after an initial discussion of suicidality, there may come a natural time to pivot to the positive. One common strengths-based tool for exploring what helps clients overcome their suicidality is a solution-focused question (J. Sommers-Flanagan, 2018a). If you are working with a client who has made a previous attempt, you might ask something like, "You've tried suicide before, but you're here with me now, so there's still a chance for a better life. What helped in the past?"

Although this is a perfectly reasonable question, it may fall flat, and your client might respond with a hopelessness statement: "Nothing really ever helps." This puts you in a predicament. Should you use Socratic questioning to identify a cognitive distortion? Should you interpret the distorted thinking in the here and now? Or should you retreat to empathy?

No matter what theoretical model you are using, the predicament of how to deal with client nonresponsiveness, negativity, or cognitive distortions remains. Say you are operating from a solution-focused or strengths-based model and you ask the miracle question:

> I'm going to ask you a strange question. What if, after we get done talking, you go back to doing your usual things at home, go to bed, and get some sleep. But in the middle of the night, a miracle happens, and your feelings of depression and suicide go away. You were asleep, and so you don't know about the miracle. When you wake up, what will be the first thing you notice that will make you say to yourself, "Wow. Something amazing happened. I'm no longer depressed and suicidal"? (Adapted from Berg & Dolan, 2001, p. 7)

Although the miracle question might do its magic and your client will respond with something positive, it is equally possible that your client will say something like "Not possible" or "The only way that would happen would be if I died in the night." When clients are pervasively negative and hopeless, one error clinicians often make is to get into a yes/no questioning process that looks something like this:

Counselor: I'm sure there must be something that helps you feel more positive.
Client: I can't think of anything.
Counselor: How about time with friends, does that help?

Client: No. I don't have any real friends left.
Counselor: How about exercise?
Client: I can't even get myself to exercise.
Counselor: Being in the outdoors helps with depression. Does that help?
Client: Nope.
Counselor: Have you tried medications?
Client: I hate medications. They made me feel like a zombie.

Entering into this exchange is unhelpful. In the end, both you and your client will be more depressed. Rather than continuing to ask what helps, try changing the focus to what does not help. This shift is useful because when clients are experiencing suicidal depression, they are more likely to resonate with negativity, and connecting with your client at the negative bottom is better than not connecting at all. The goal is to collaboratively build a continuum from the bottom up. By starting at the bottom, you are simultaneously assessing hopelessness and intervening on the black-and-black (as opposed to black-and-white) distorted thinking that you are witnessing in session. Here is an example:

Counselor: You've tried lots of different strategies to deal with your suicidal thoughts, without success. You've tried medications, you've exercised, and you've talked to your rabbi. Let's list these and other things you've tried and see which strategies were the worst. Of all the things you've tried, what was worst?
Client: I really hated exercising. It felt like I was being coerced to do something I've always hated. And it made me sore.
Counselor: OK then. Exercise was the worst. You hated that. Of the other things you've tried, what was a little less bad than exercising?
Client: The medications. I just didn't feel like myself.
Counselor: So that didn't work either. So of those three things, talking with your rabbi was the least bad?
Client: Yeah. It didn't help much. But she was nice and supportive. I felt a little better, but I didn't want to keep talking because she's busy and I was a burden.

Focusing on the worst option resonates with a negative emotional state. For clients who are unhappy with the results of previous therapeutic efforts, beginning with the most worthless strategy of all is easier than talking about positives and possibilities, provides useful information, and is usually answered quickly. Subsequently, clinicians can move upward toward strategies that are "just a little less bad." Building a unique continuum of what is more and less helpful is the goal. Later you can add new ideas that you or your client identify and put them in their place on the continuum. If this approach works well, together with your client you will have generated several ideas (some new and some old) that are worth experimenting with in the future.

Beginning from the bottom puts a different spin on the problem-solving process. Even extremely depressed clients can acknowledge that every attempt to address their symptoms is not equally bad. Using a continuum is a useful tool for working with hopelessness and is consistent with the CBT technique of thinking in shades of gray.

Using CBT for Questioning, Countering, Modifying, and Accepting Maladaptive Thinking

Two CBT approaches for working with suicidality have been broadly identified as evidence based: brief cognitive behavior therapy for suicide (Bryan & Rudd, 2018) and cognitive therapy for suicide (Wenzel et al., 2009). Aaron Beck's original approach to cognitive therapy for depression emphasized collaborative empiricism (A. T. Beck, Rush, et al., 1979). Collaborative empiricism occurs when, operating from clients' frames, clinicians present scenarios and ask questions to help clients evaluate the accuracy and usefulness of their thoughts. Beck's approach is nonconfrontational; it involves clinicians and clients looking together at whether particular thoughts are accurate and/or helpful.

Cognitive Reappraisal and Socratic Questioning

Instead of collaborative empiricism, Bryan and Rudd (2018) use the term *cognitive reappraisal*. They wrote, "The primary purpose of cognitive appraisal is to replace core suicide beliefs with more adaptive beliefs and positive cognitive styles that reduce risk for suicide" (p. 198). Using a collaborative, educational process, Bryan and Rudd move clients away from unhelpful and inaccurate cognitive distortions and core beliefs and toward positive and adaptive beliefs, including optimism, meaning in life, hope, pride, and self-efficacy.

Bryan and Rudd (2018) use worksheets and other methods to help clients evaluate their beliefs and engage in cognitive reappraisal. One of their worksheets, designed to modify clients' suicidal beliefs, is called the *Challenging Questions Worksheet*. Inspired by Bryan and Rudd's Worksheet, we offer an alternative: the *Strengths and Solutions Worksheet* (see Figure 5.1).

Worksheet

Challenging Situation	Strengths and Solutions
For each challenging situation, list at least two strengths or solutions that you could use to improve the challenging situation.	
1. You're stuck home all weekend without friends.	A. I can finally read some books I've been wanting to read. B. I'll call some old high school friends. C. This will be a good weekend to learn to meditate.
2. You've been drinking too much, and you know it.	A. I'm aware of the problem, and that's the first step. B. I'm smart enough to make a plan to cut down or quit. C. I can force myself to attend Alcoholics Anonymous.
3. You just got fired from a job.	A. _____. B. _____.
4. You've been experiencing racial oppression.	A. _____. B. _____.
5. Your parents have rejected your sexuality.	A. _____. B. _____.
6. Your romantic partner cheated on you.	A. _____. B. _____.
7. You just had a family member die.	A. _____. B. _____.
8. You had a panic attack at work.	A. _____. B. _____.

FIGURE 5.1
The Strengths and Solutions Worksheet

In their worksheet, Bryan's and Rudd's challenging questions are called Socratic questions. Socrates (470–399 B.C.) taught by asking questions to stimulate his students' rational thinking. Socratic questioning is a central cognitive therapy tool for dialoguing about the accuracy and usefulness of thoughts (Beck et al., 1979). The Strengths and Solutions Worksheet is an alternative that focuses on helping clients practice positive problem-solving.

For some clients, the straightforward process of using worksheets to explore cognitions may be less threatening than open exploration. Other clients will find cognitive monitoring and reappraisal worksheets tedious and unhelpful. You may need to convince clients to give worksheets a try. It is helpful to work on them together. We have found that clients respond positively to a request like this one: "Let's do this worksheet and critique it in the process."

Even if you do not use worksheets, you can integrate cognitive principles into counseling in other ways. For example, hopelessness is a common cognitive problem that includes using a cognitive distortion called *negative prediction*, which refers to the tendency to anticipate or prophesize bad outcomes—even when no data exist to support the negative prediction. Here are several worksheet-free examples of collaborative empiricism for negative prediction:

- "For many of us, predicting the future is automatic. Do you think your predictions affect events? Do you think making a prediction changes how things come out?"
- "You've said that you think the conversation you want to have with your son will go badly. That's a reasonable worry, especially if we don't develop a good strategy. How about, before you make your prediction, we develop a strategy that gives you the best possible chance of having a good conversation with your son?"
- "You're convinced you'll be unsuccessful in your career. That's an interesting prediction. Let's break it down. First let's define success. Then let's look at the evidence that suggests you'll be unsuccessful, the evidence that suggests you might be successful, and the evidence that suggests that sometimes you'll be successful and sometimes you'll be unsuccessful."

Although Bryan and Rudd's (2018) worksheets have a specific format, their ABC (Activating event, Beliefs, Consequences) worksheets are consistent with Ellis's cognitive model. Many different versions of ABC worksheets are available, including alternative versions downloadable from the internet (we explain a six-column cognitive and behavioral monitoring worksheet at https://johnsommersflanagan.com/2014/02/18/how-to-use-the-six-column-cbt-technique/).

Questioning and Modifying Core Beliefs

Most clinicians hope their work with clients will produce lasting psychological, emotional, and behavioral change. When working in the cognitive dimension, there is a temptation to go deeper than worksheets and to try and address core cognitive beliefs about the self, about others, and about the future.

Some clinicians believe that core beliefs (sometimes referred to as *schemas* or *schemata*) are at the root of dysfunctional thoughts. Young and his colleagues (2003) developed schema therapy to address deeper, long-standing, or underlying client beliefs. Resources for schema therapy are available online (see www.schematherapy.com).

Although you may be tempted to go deep into clients' foundational beliefs, the evidence supporting schema change is not strong (Dobson & Dobson, 2017). Challenging client core beliefs, even when the beliefs are palpably dysfunctional, can be destabilizing for clients. Dobson and Dobson (2017) cautioned, "Changing schemas may require clients to modify their social circles, confront people from the past, and even to face rejection from others . . . and may in the short term actually increase rather than decrease distress" (p. 215).

Deconstructing and reconstructing negative core beliefs is associated with longer term counseling. However, acknowledging negative core beliefs early in counseling, even in short-term counseling models, can be beneficial. Talking about core beliefs helps clients feel known and understood on deeper levels.

Abuse and trauma may be at the root of self-hatred or chronic negative core beliefs. If so, initiating a trauma-oriented treatment (e.g., trauma-focused CBT [Cohen et al., 2012], eye-movement desensitization and reprocessing [Shapiro, 2001]) can relieve distress and reduce negative thoughts. Alternatively, to address negative core beliefs, the cognitive therapies—including suicide-specific treatment protocols (i.e., Bryan & Rudd, 2018; Wenzel et al., 2009)—schema therapy (Young et al., 2003), as well as the narrative therapies (Schauer et al., 2011) are the treatments of choice.

Concluding Comments

Elizabeth M. Gilbert (2009), an American author, wrote,

> There is so much about my fate that I cannot control, but other things do fall under the jurisdiction. I can decide how I spend my time, whom I interact with, whom I share my body and life and money and energy with. I can select what I can read and eat and study. I can choose how I'm going to regard unfortunate circumstances in my life—whether I will see them as curses or opportunities. I can choose my words and the tone of voice in which I speak to others. And most of all, I can choose my thoughts. (p. 186)

We share Gilbert's optimism about changing thoughts but also recognize that individuals who are suicidal may have long-standing thinking patterns that resist modification. When working in the cognitive dimension, the therapeutic focus is squarely on the remarkably difficult and remarkably rewarding task of changing client thinking patterns.

Practitioner Guidance and Key Points to Remember

In this chapter we described four key cognitive issues to address in counseling: (a) hopelessness, (b) problem-solving impairments, (c) maladaptive or irrational thoughts, and (d) negative core beliefs and self-hatred. Interventions in the cognitive dimension include the following:

- Begin with empathy for the cognitive struggles your clients may be experiencing.
- Engage in collaborative problem-solving by finding the right time to pivot to the positive with a question like "What helps?"
- Develop a wellness practice for witnessing something inspiring and, if appropriate, share that practice with clients.
- Use MI skills to facilitate the problem-solving process.
- Help clients identify positive alternatives to suicide.
- Provide psychoeducation on behavioral activation.
- Recognize that you will face decision-making dilemmas around the appropriate level of care and that you will not always make the perfect decision.
- Work with hopelessness as it emerges during sessions by resonating with hopelessness, integrating solutions into problem-solving, matching client language, using validation, and working from the bottom up to build a continuum of hope.
- Use CBT for questioning, countering, modifying, and accepting maladaptive thinking.
- Use worksheets and in vivo interactions to implement Socratic questioning and modify core beliefs.

Chapter 6

The Interpersonal Dimension

In 2005, Thomas Joiner published his interpersonal theory of suicide in the book *Why People Die by Suicide*. Joiner summarized the interpersonal theory with these words: "The desire for death is composed of two psychological states—*perceived burdensomeness* and *failed belongingness* [emphasis added]" (p. 136). Although perceived burdensomeness and failed belongingness are psychological states, they illuminate social or interpersonal relationship dynamics that Joiner, his colleagues, and other suicide researchers have repeatedly linked to death by suicide (Hagan et al., 2015; Van Orden et al., 2010). Joiner's theoretical principles are foundational to the interpersonal dimension as we describe it in this book.

Clients who are suicidal nearly always have interpersonal issues that fuel their emotional distress. For 15-year-old Sophia (featured in Chapters 4 and 5), exposure to parental conflict triggered her suicidal thoughts. At one point she articulated how her emotional distress was related to a shattered sense of belonging, stating, "I don't feel like I have a family anymore." Operating from Joiner's interpersonal theory, when working with clients like Sophia, counselors should monitor their relationships and include therapeutic interventions that enhance social connections in general and a sense of family belonging in particular.

Also in Chapter 4, we introduced Katie, a wife, mother, and grieving daughter. Katie's situation illustrates how life dimensions interact and operate together to increase or reduce depression and suicidality. Katie felt excruciating emotional distress over the loss of her mother (emotional and interpersonal dimensions). She felt disconnected from her deceased mother (interpersonal dimension) and wished to reunite with her mother in the hereafter (interpersonal and spiritual dimensions). Then, as Katie engaged in the alternatives to suicide intervention (cognitive dimension), it became clear that Katie might benefit from behavioral activation (behavioral dimension); it was equally clear that she could not complete a behavioral activation plan without assistance from her husband (interpersonal dimension). However, even if Katie garners the support and connection she needs to complete a behavioral activation plan and her depressive symptoms lift, there is a danger that she will begin seeing herself as a burden to others (a cognitive-interpersonal dynamic with emotional ramifications). Because therapeutic interventions often play out in interpersonal contexts, assessing, intervening, and monitoring interpersonal functioning will be a common theme in your work with clients who are suicidal.

Working in the Interpersonal Dimension

Interpersonal relationships are central to most therapeutic approaches. That said, some approaches (psychoanalytic, attachment-based therapies) emphasize the client's past relationships, others (existential, reality therapy) focus on present relationships, and still others (Adlerian, solution-focused therapies) look toward future relationship goals. Despite these different perspectives, nearly every theoretical orientation holds healthy interpersonal relationships as key to psychological health and well-being in the present. Several interpersonal issues are especially salient for suicide-focused treatment planning and interventions.

Key Interpersonal Issues to Address

Interpersonal or social relationships contribute to human growth and suffering in many ways. As a broad umbrella, Joiner's failed belongingness and perceived burdensomeness encompass nearly every potential disturbance clients might have within the interpersonal dimension. To make Joiner's formulations more treatment specific, we have divided his two broad interpersonal themes into four categories that link to particular therapeutic approaches:

- Social disconnection
- Interpersonal loss and grief

- Social skill deficits
- Repeating dysfunctional relationship patterns

Next we briefly describe these four interpersonal categories. Later in this chapter we go into greater detail regarding how to integrate interpersonal relationship issues into suicide-related treatment planning.

Social Disconnection
Individuals with positive social connections or relationships live longer and report greater wellness (Holt-Lunstad et al., 2010). Some researchers hypothesize that interpersonal relationships function as a social buffer, protecting individuals from the adverse effects of stress (Tran et al., 2018). Social relationships are beneficial for many reasons and are an especially effective cushion against stress when individuals experience relationships as supportive and available (Szkody & McKinney, 2019).

Social connection may also cultivate social interest or *Gemeinschaftsgefühl* (Adler, 1938; Ansbacher, 1968). *Gemeinschaftsgefühl* refers to the human pull toward community, empathy, and interdependence. For clients who feel suicidal, increasing social interest in general, and engaging in service to others in particular, can reduce self-rumination (Lantz, 1981). Shifting from self-interest to interest in others—and specifically focusing on acts of kindness toward others—is linked to increased happiness and well-being (Curry et al., 2018; Rowland & Curry, 2019; see Wellness Practice 6.1 for information on positive psychology).

Wellness Practice 6.1
Intentional Acts of Kindness

Anne Herbert (Herbert & Pavel, 1982) is credited with popularizing the phrase "Practice random kindness and senseless acts of beauty." Herbert wrote out her random kindness maxim on a placemat in a restaurant in Sausalito, California, as a wordplay response to "random acts of violence and senseless acts of cruelty" (see Wikipedia, 2020).

The idea of unpremeditated, random kindness is appealing, but deliberate kindness is more powerful. As Aristotle posited, deliberate kindness can contribute to the development of moral virtues. Rather than being kind when it strikes your fancy, this assignment is about planned, intentional kindness.

(continued)

Wellness Practice 6.1
Intentional Acts of Kindness (*continued*)

> Intentionally engaging in kind and caring acts gives you greater personal agency. Instead of being stuck with a script someone else wrote, you author your own lines in every life scene. You exert your will; plan ahead; and creatively, consciously, and consistently act in kind, thoughtful ways.
>
> Intentional kindness is a mental discipline. Sometimes a stranger will provide you with an opportunity to be kind. You pay for the groceries in the checkout line. You notice someone dropped something and you pick it up. You hold open a door. Metaphorically or literally, you scoop the poop of someone else's dog. If you set your intention and plan kindness whenever the opportunity arises, even spontaneous acts will reflect your deeper values and character.
>
> Maybe you would like to be intentionally kind to a friend, a parent, or a sibling; this requires thought and the ability to step outside yourself and into another's world. Rather than offering up something you would like yourself, you can deepen your kindness behaviors by contemplating what your friend, parent, or sibling would appreciate. Set a goal to do one, two, or three kind acts every day, whether for strangers or loved ones. Notice your own emotional reactions to being kind. Engaging in acts of kindness can make people happier and lead to more satisfying lives (Lyubomirsky, 2007).
>
> Despite your best efforts, sometimes you will fail to demonstrate kindness. That's OK. This assignment is for you to notice and reflect on your successful kind actions. Ignore the missed opportunities; only count your successes. Also, drop any expectations you might have for how others should respond to your kindnesses. Your goal is to intentionally engage in kind actions without a worry over how others respond. Throughout the week, write notes to yourself about how you feel about engaging in this experience. Implementing and monitoring an intentional acts of kindness activity can make for productive homework for clients with interpersonal struggles.

Social interest (especially kindness) is so robustly related to happiness that Christopher Peterson, a renowned happiness researcher, claimed he could deliver a whole lecture on positive psychology in 5 seconds. He said,

Sometimes when I give a talk, I tell the audience, if you really don't want to listen to me for the next hour, listen to me for 5 seconds, because I'll tell you what positive psychology is all about. *Other people matter* [emphasis added]. Period. I'm done with my talk. (UM News Service, 2011)

Social disconnection or unmet needs for belonging can trigger suicidality. Joiner labeled this suicide factor "failed belongingness." Many different life experiences result in failed belongingness or unwanted social disconnection. Examples include the following:

- The death of a loved one
- Chronic racism or sexism
- Rejection by a parent
- Separation or divorce
- Romantic breakups or sexual rejection
- Relocation, social transitions (e.g., graduations), unemployment, and forced social isolation (e.g., social distancing and shelter-in-place policies)

Complexities inherent in relationships make it difficult to find a single recipe for social belonging. Individual clients may show mixed social signals—pulling for greater intimacy while simultaneously rejecting intimacy. This push/pull of intimacy versus autonomy is a common internal struggle that plays out in interpersonal relationships (Scarf, 1987).

When clients hold collectivist, individualist, or multicultural orientations, defining optimal belongingness becomes even more complex. Clients may have cultural identities that conflict with dominant individualist social norms and values. Clients themselves may be unclear or ambivalent about what they want from social relationships. Our point is not to disparage individualist, collectivist, or other approaches to social connection. Instead, we want to emphasize that every client has unique social needs and preferences and that understanding your client's unique needs, challenges, and strengths is key to excellent counseling.

Monitoring the quality and fit of your therapeutic alliance with clients is one method of individualizing counseling and addressing your clients' interpersonal needs and preferences. For all clients, and especially clients who are suicidal, tending to the therapeutic relationship is essential (Jobes, 2016; Norcross & Lambert, 2018).

Interpersonal Loss and Grief
Interpersonal loss and the grief that ensues is a variant of Joiner's (2005) failed belongingness. In the midst of loss, some clients fear that resolving their grief dishonors the beloved person who died. Working with clients to create ways to honor their loved one is important. At the same time, your clients may need support as they are "renegotiating the continuing bond" and working on accepting the loss they are experiencing (Rubin, 2012, p. 20).

Loss is a ubiquitous human experience. Loss occurs when loved ones die; when romantic relationships or friendships end; when families come apart; when employment ends; and when individuals lose physical, social, spiritual, or other significant, meaningful activities or abilities. To the extent that they involve unmet wishes for social connection, all forms of interpersonal loss can trigger a sense of failed belongingness. Romantic relationship breakups thwart wishes for connection and cause acute distress; this distress can quickly spiral downward, activating core cognitive beliefs of being unlovable and destined to a life of isolation and loneliness.

Perceived burdensomeness also plays out with loss. Clients who are physically ill or incapacitated may experience themselves as a burden. Statements like, "Everyone would be better off without me" communicate perceived burdensomeness. When clients who have long valued their independence suddenly have physical or mental limitations or impairments (or unemployment), they may conclude that death is preferable to living dependent on others.

Social Skill Deficits
Although social media is ostensibly about social connection, for many it interferes with meaningful social relationships. Greater use of social media platforms such as Facebook and Instagram is linked to increased depression and diminished well-being (Tromholt, 2016). More research is needed, but as of this writing, little evidence suggests that social media connections adequately replace face-to-face interpersonal relationship connections (Chow & Wan, 2017).

Social media can shrink social connection, but many other obstacles to healthy interpersonal relationships exist. For example, social skill deficits such as extreme shyness, poor hygiene, impaired listening skills, or lack of empathy interfere with satisfying relationships. Also, racist attitudes and harsh judgments of others create interpersonal tension and deprive people of reciprocal, thriving relationships.

Several social skills are useful for clients who desire meaningful social connection. These include (a) conversational skills, (b) social problem-solving or conflict management skills, (c) skills for evaluating whether potential friends and romantic partners are trustworthy, (d) skills for obtaining and maintaining employment, and (e) nonjudgmental listening skills. The preceding list of positive social skills (e.g., role playing and homework assignments) can be important for helping clients attain interpersonal treatment goals.

Repeating Dysfunctional Relationship Patterns
Human relationships begin at birth and continue through childhood, adolescence, and adulthood. As psychoanalytic and attachment theorists emphasize, distinct relationship patterns are established in childhood and continue in predictable ways throughout adulthood (Ainsworth et al., 1978). In many cases, repeating interpersonal relationship patterns include patterns that are healthy and functional. However, clients often get stuck in repeating dysfunctional interpersonal relationships that contribute to unhappiness, depression, and suicidality (K. M. Nelson et al., 2019). Many individuals, in particular youth, report that relationships characterized by secure attachment helped them recover from suicidal crises (Bostik & Everall, 2007).

Professional counseling is a relationship, and interpersonal interventions are at the heart of counseling process and outcome. Case examples featured in this chapter focus on how counselors can work with clients to identify and achieve realistic interpersonal goals.

Interventions in the Interpersonal Dimension

As with all seven life dimensions, zeroing in on interpersonal relationship dynamics has an artificial, reductionist feel. Relationships are ubiquitous to human functioning and influence every other dimension. However, as you will see in the following assessment and intervention tasks, focusing primarily on relationships is particularly meaningful to clients who are suicidal.

Assessing and Improving the Client's Social Universe

Many different formal and informal methods of assessing social support are available. If you are inclined toward standardized questionnaires, the Multidimensional Scale of Perceived Social Support (Zimet et al., 1988) is a 12-item scale with good psychometrics that provides an efficient glimpse into your clients' perceived social support in romantic, friendship, and familial domains (Dahlem et al., 1991). This straightforward measure is easily used in the spirit of therapeutic assessment.

In the following case, Clark, a 35-year-old gay cisgender male, describes his closest relationships as toxic, which prompts the counselor to use an interactive and informal method of assessing Clark's social universe. Although familial, religious, and interpersonal rejection are risk factors for suicide in general, rejection is especially salient for individuals who are suicidal and who identify as lesbian, gay, bisexual, transgender, queer, or questioning (or other sexual and gender minorities; LGBTQ+; Ahuja et al., 2015). For LGBTQ+ clients, rejections of sexual identity can trigger self-doubt, distress, feelings of isolation/alienation, and self-hate; these reactions can exacerbate suicidal thoughts and impulses.

Treatment for LGBTQ+ clients requires, at a minimum, acceptance and affirmation of sexual identity (Bigner & Wetchler, 2012; M. Luke et al., 2017). LGBTQ+ clients need positivity and affirmation. Affirming sexual diversity as a natural and valid way of being in the world will lead to better outcomes.

Identifying and Modifying Toxic Relationships
Clark begins his session by describing current frustrations. He says, "Nobody understands me" and "I have no one to turn to." These statements are a common way for clients to express emotionally painful interpersonal disconnection.

Clark also articulates his physical agitation by saying, "I don't know what to do." Two days previously he purchased a construction razor blade at a hardware store as part of a suicide plan. In the session, he says that somehow the blade did not function, and his suicide attempt failed. Clark's initial presentation includes high distress, agitation, social isolation, and the belief that his life is meaningless. He reports increased alcohol use and an intention to die. Clark's risk of suicide is extremely high.

Given the breadth of Clark's suicide symptoms, it would be reasonable to proceed with a comprehensive assessment, goal setting, and treatment planning to address his pain across all seven life dimensions. However, Clark's most palpable source of distress is in the interpersonal dimension.

Clark is very verbal and tends to ramble from one complaint to another. To address this, the counselor uses a less verbal process, a visual and practical activity, to provide focus and to explore Clark's interpersonal relationships. Like many suicide-related clinical procedures, the social universe activity is used as both assessment and intervention.

Counselor: You started feeling suicidal at around age 15, and you've been hospitalized a few times, once at 15 and then at some point after that.

Clark: Within the past year or so. I've been in the hospital a few times.

Counselor: What was going on just before your recent hospitalization?

Clark: The people I was hanging out with used me. I started hanging out with them a few years ago. They're a gay couple. I thought I could find some sort of identity or something. I give everything I have to them, and they're still not interested. I try so hard to feel validated. But they just take me down and I feel used. It's toxic.

Counselor: This sounds very painful. It makes me think we should talk more about your relationships and how they're affecting you. Is that OK with you?

Clark: OK.

Counselor: I'm drawing a circle in the middle of this paper. This circle is you. In your life you probably have people who are more and less validating. I'm wondering, if this is the universe of Clark, who are the people you get more validation from and who do you get less validation from? I'll draw them around you.

Clark: I honestly don't know if there's anyone who gives me any sort of validation.

Counselor: OK. Who's the least validating, the worst of all? Who's really toxic?

Clark: Brad.

Counselor: OK. I'll put Brad here. I'm putting the word *toxic* in here because you used it before and he sounds so invalidating that it's toxic.

Clark: Uh-huh.

Clark's initial response to the social universe activity is characteristic of depressed clients. When the counselor asks who is most validating, Clark comes up empty. He says, "I honestly don't know if there's anyone who gives me any sort of validation."

The counselor's response to Clark's negative disclosure is similar to the protocol for working with hopelessness (see Chapter 5). Instead of continuing a search for positive relationships (i.e., "Who are the people you get more validation from?"), the counselor switches to a negatively worded question ("Who's the least validating, the worst of all? Who's really toxic?"). Switching to the negative is purposeful: Identifying the most toxic person resonates with what Clark is feeling. If Clark can name the most toxic person in his social universe, there is a chance he can work up to identifying people who are less toxic. Once less toxic people are identified, Clark and his counselor can plan how he can protect himself from toxic people and spend more time with less toxic (supportive and validating) people.

The session continues:

Counselor: OK. Who's also toxic but less toxic than Brad?
Clark: Bill.
Counselor: OK. So somebody named Bill. And is that the couple?
Clark: Yeah.
Counselor: And so the two of them, they're ranking as the most toxic.
Clark: Right.
Counselor: If you look around, is there anybody in your universe who's neutral or who you would put as neutral or as less toxic than Brad and Bill?
Clark: Debbie.
Counselor: OK. So Debbie is on the less toxic end.
Clark: Right.
Counselor: Anybody else who's more in that neutral category?
Clark: My brother maybe.
Counselor: OK. Your brother. Is he the least toxic of your family?
Clark: It's between him and my dad, but I don't really talk to my brother that much.

After focusing on the most toxic person and someone who is slightly less toxic, Clark identifies people who are less toxic. Together, Clark and his counselor use this information to validate Clark's experiences and build new relationship plans. Reflective questions can help determine what directions clients might want to go with their relationships. For example, you could ask, "What changes in your relationships does this map of your social universe make you think about?" and "As we look at goals for our work together, how about we move toxic people further away and move the neutral or more validating people closer?"

Engaging in the social universe activity can accomplish several objectives. First, as a visual approach, mapping a social universe transforms vague social dynamics into visible relationship patterns.

Clients can quickly see who is close to (and distant from) them in their social universe. Second, asking "Who is supportive to you?" and "Who is unhealthy or toxic?" acts as a gentle confrontation, shedding light on how current relationships are affecting clients. Third, because insight enhances motivation, the activity becomes empowering. Clients feel energy to work on moving emotionally closer to supportive people and putting distance between them and unhealthy influences. If clients are stuck living with toxic people, the question can turn to emotional coping: "How can you protect yourself from the unhealthy, toxic, or dismissive behaviors you're likely to experience?"

Reducing the time he spends with people who treat him poorly will decrease negativity in Clark's life. But treatment can also focus on the creation of new positive social relationships, communication skills training, and social anxiety management. Overall, the social universe activity—as well as other approaches to assessment—can help you identify goals and formulate homework tasks that move clients toward their social and interpersonal goals (see Table 6.1).

As you listen to your clients describe their failed sense of belonging, be sure to notice strengths. You might make observations like "You keep trying to figure out how to relate. That takes guts." Or, "You're very insightful as you talk about how your relationships affect you. That's a skill that will help you as you begin to turn things around."

Working With Clients Following Romantic Relationship Breakups

Pain from romantic breakups can trigger despair and suicidality. Zoe, a 21-year-old cisgender heterosexual person, had been dating

TABLE 6.1
Treatment Plan for Clark—Interpersonal Dimension

Problem	Goals and Strengths[a]	Interventions/Plan
1. Clark spends most of his time with people whom he finds toxic.	1. Decrease time spent with interpersonally toxic people.	1. Identify socially validating people and contact them for positive social time.
2. Clark has very few relationships, if any, that feel validating to him.	2. Increase time spent with interpersonally validating people.	2. Identify steps needed to protect Clark psychologically from toxic relationships.
3. Clark is unclear how to meet new people who will affirm his sexual identity.	3. Clark will socialize in settings that affirm his sexual identity.	3. Role-play social skills in anticipation of entering new social groups.
4. Clark feels anxious about new social contacts.	4. Clark will learn relaxation and self-soothing skills.	4. Practice relaxation skills for new social situations.

[a]Clark has several interpersonal strengths: He is interested in interpersonal relationships, is sensitive to how he feels in relationships, and appears ready for reciprocal intimacy.

Mario for 3 months when they moved in together. After cohabitating for 6 months, she became pregnant. They got married after the birth of their first child, Zade. The birth of their second child, Teena, was a year later. Zoe was happy as a mom and in her marriage. She was living her fairytale story.

Not long after Teena's birth, cracks began forming in the marriage. Zoe was preoccupied with being a mom, and Mario felt neglected. He complained, but Zoe was exhausted by the day's end. She thought Mario was being childish. One evening, her frustration burst out. She yelled, "Mario, you need to get your shit together and man up! I can't take care of three children!"

Mario was already pulling away, but Zoe's anger hit him in a vulnerable place. His self-appraisal was positive. He had been working and trying to be the best dad possible, but that was not good enough. He pulled away more. He got together with his old drinking buddies. They expressed sympathy for him being married to a crazy, selfish bitch. Eventually he hooked up with another woman who ended up pregnant. Mario announced to Zoe that he wanted a divorce. A month later, he was starting over with a new family.

When Zoe arrived for counseling, she was emotionally devastated. Her fairytale life was shattered. She was not financially prepared for Mario's exit. She could not stop thinking about Mario being with another woman. She felt trapped with two toddlers and impossible finances. Eventually she had to move in with her mother, which made her feel like a complete failure.

In counseling, Zoe confessed to nearly constant suicidal ideation. She had a plan for how she could kill herself with her mother's medications. She wanted to "put an end to" her pain and remove her "loser-self" from her children's lives.

With her counselor, Zoe cycled from self-blame to castigating Mario and then back to self-condemnation. She said, "I should have seen this coming." She viewed herself as failing Mario and her children. The counselor was unable to convince Zoe to step back from her emotional storm and look at the situation more rationally. After three sessions, they were still talking about the same issues.

> *Zoe:* I can't believe Mario left. I don't know what I did wrong. I need real answers. I failed him and my children. I can't go on without answers.
>
> *Counselor:* This feels familiar. You've said before how you wish you could know what Mario really thinks. And we've talked about how he never opened up much when you were married. Now, as a coparent, he seems like a brick wall. Is that right?

Zoe: Yes. But if I could get him alone, I think I could make him answer my questions.
Counselor: What would you ask him?
Zoe: I'd ask, "Why don't you love me anymore?"
Counselor: Can I give you some direct feedback?
Zoe: OK.
Counselor: You've been focusing on how Mario would answer this question. But we can't control him. What if he never answers your question? What if you have to move forward with your life without his answer?
Zoe: I don't think I can.
Counselor: What if we found someone else to answer that question? What if we found someone who knows you better than Mario? We could ask that question and more.
Zoe: Who? Do you mean my mom? She doesn't really know me.
Counselor: No. I don't mean your mom. I mean you. You know yourself better than Mario does. You're the best authority on you. We should tap into your wisdom.
Zoe: [*looking a tiny bit intrigued*] Well, maybe. Weird idea, but maybe.

Zoe's counselor convinced her to put her suicidal impulses on hold and make a commitment to exploring her self-evaluations. The counselor used the classic Gestalt empty chair technique to shift the focus away from Mario. They explored what Zoe had learned about herself from the marriage and what she was still learning. When Zoe recognized how alone she felt, she and her counselor searched for and found an online single-parent support group. Not only was Zoe able to begin answering her own questions, but she also found the online single-parent community to be a big part of her healing and recovery.

Zoe had been emotionally hooked on getting answers from Mario. Wanting answers about why relationships fail is common, but wanting answers from an ex violates the first rule of goal setting: Your goals should be within your control. The empty chair technique and support group helped refocus Zoe's energy away from Mario, and, as a result, Zoe felt greater control over her life. Also, being in the single-parent support group gave Zoe a chance to help others in their pain. She was able to benefit from the empowering force of *Gemeinschaftsgefühl*.

Social Skills Training and Related Interventions

Social isolation kills. This statement is dramatic, but it is also true. Not only does social connection increase happiness, but it also increases the life span (Holt-Lunstad et al., 2010). If you want to live longer, surround yourself with healthy and positive social, romantic, and family relationships (Bono, 2018). Of course, this is easier said than done. Two obstacles that interfere with relationship formation are communication skill deficits and social anxiety.

Focusing on social communication skills and reducing social anxiety can be empowering to clients. Most people want skills to help them cope more effectively with challenging interpersonal situations. In theory, teaching and learning social skills and anxiety management skills is straightforward. Traditional evidence-based treatments include components like (a) identifying skill deficits, (b) role-modeling or demonstrating effective skills, (c) role-playing challenging social scenarios, (d) providing feedback, and (e) repeatedly practicing effective social and self-management skills (Cooper & Widdows, 2008; Hofmann, 2020).

Although the materials are available, evidence based, and straightforward, the actual practice of teaching and learning social and anxiety management skills can be quite complex. As in the following case example, when clients experience harassment or bullying or are living in pathologically oppressive families or communities, singling them out for training can feel like blaming the victim. For example, in school settings, minority students can become targets for bullying. Although social skills training and anxiety management are appropriate interventions, they should be framed as supportive and empowering and combined with interventions that address larger systemic problems (see Chapter 10 for more information on systemic factors and suicide).

Externalizing the Cyberbullying Problem

Elijah was a 14-year-old biracial (Black and Latinx) boy who exhibited characteristics of sexual fluidity and identified as queer. He often visited the school counselor's office, usually in considerable distress. Elijah complained of not fitting into his body; he also felt he did not fit into his school. He had occasional close relationships with peers but was also consistently targeted by school bullies. In response to the bullying, Elijah experienced intermittent passive suicidal ideation (e.g., "Sometimes I wish I were dead" and "I'd like to go to sleep and not wake up").

Over a weekend in early spring, Elijah was a victim of cyberbullying harassment and outing. Outing occurs when cyberbullies share private information to publicly humiliate a victim. Elijah had talked with a friend about his sexual feelings toward another male student. For unknown reasons, Elijah's friend went online and outed

Elijah. Elijah was horrified and humiliated. On Sunday evening, Elijah tried to hang himself. His mother found him sobbing in his room with rope burns on his neck.

On Monday morning, Elijah's mother called in sick and took Elijah to an urgent care clinic, where he was referred to a mental health professional (MHP) for an emergency evaluation. MHPs traditionally follow a psychiatrically oriented medical model and ask a series of questions that can seem designed to pin the diagnosis (or pathology) on the patient. Fortunately, Elijah's MHP was trained in a strengths-based approach to working with patients with suicidal ideation. Drawing from narrative and solution-focused therapy approaches, the MHP used questions to separate and externalize the problem from the patient.

The MHP met with Elijah and his mother. After initial small talk, the MHP asked, "Elijah, can I ask some questions about your mood?" Elijah consented. The MHP administered the mood rating scale with a suicide floor (see Chapter 3). Elijah's responses included the following:

Present mood = "Negative 10. I'd kill myself if I could because my life at school is over."
Worst mood ever = "Last night my mood was negative infinity."
Best mood ever = "An 8. I got high with some friends last weekend."
Usual average mood = "A 5. Maybe."

After the initial mood assessment, the MHP listened, gathered more details about what happened over the weekend, and eventually asked, "Elijah, do you mind if I share with you what I'm thinking?" Elijah said, "Go ahead. I don't care." The MHP followed with, "Elijah, what happened to you was terrible and unfair. It wasn't your fault. Sadly, there are people in the world who are unhappy and disturbed. They get off on hurting others. This past weekend, and it sounds like for about a year, they've been targeting you. But I hope you know, if it wasn't you, it would have been someone else. I know that doesn't help, and I'm sure you still feel horrible about what happened. My point is that for whatever twisted reason, they wanted to hurt someone, so they hurt you. But their behavior was about them and their problems; it wasn't really about you and who you are."

Expecting and fearing that he would be labeled as having a mental problem, Elijah experienced immediate relief. His reaction was to sob . . . and then feel embarrassed about sobbing. In response, the MHP provided additional reassurance, telling Elijah that it was natural to cry about being treated so badly. Then, after more reassurance and validation, the MHP engaged Elijah in making a goal list. They agreed on the following:

- Elijah would be assigned to a counselor at the mental health center; the MHP promised to find a counselor for Elijah who liked working with sexually diverse teens.
- Because the school's climate was unhealthy, Elijah did not need to return to school immediately. Having time away from the toxic school environment was perfectly acceptable.
- Elijah, his mom, and their assigned counselor would evaluate whether returning to that particular school would be safe. Educational alternatives would be identified.
- They would contact the school counselor, the principal, and possibly the school superintendent to ask what could be done to improve the school climate and protect students from harassment and bullying. They would also find out what Elijah needed to do to keep up academically.
- There would be serious conversations about whether Elijah should take a break from social media. Initial options included changing his online identity or taking a 30-day social media break, but additional alternatives would be identified and discussed.
- As a teen, Elijah had important social needs. Alternative social activities would be an important part of Elijah beginning to feel normal again. The MHP recommended a local day treatment program with multiple counseling groups every day. Elijah agreed to try the day treatment program for 1 week.
- Both Elijah and his mother agreed to read about and locate gay-friendly youth and family organizations, such as the Genders & Sexualities Alliance Network and PFLAG.

In addition to helping Elijah by externalizing the problem, the MHP emphasized, "Even though none of this is your fault, most people in your situation benefit from working on their own skills. For example, I want you and your counselor to work on skills that you can use at school and online to protect yourself from bullies. I also want you to work on a thing we call *self-regulation*. That means you and your counselor will work on skills for calming yourself down, for relaxing, and for coping with situations that make you want to freak out. We have two big goals. One is to change your situation as much as we can to stop the bullying. You can do that with your new counselor and possibly through your school and alternatives to school, like the day treatment center. The other big goal is to get you stronger emotionally. If you're stronger, then you'll have a menu of options for handling these assholes and options for calming yourself down when the going gets tough. How does that sound to you?"

The case of Elijah illustrates several principles for working with youth who are suicidal. Most important, by definition, young people experiencing suicidality are emotionally and psychologically fragile. They have typically been exposed to traumatic and/or oppressive incidents at home and/or at school. As a consequence, mental health providers need to provide a safe, nonpathologizing haven. Narrative strategies, such as externalizing the problem, are especially useful. When counselors normalize a youth's experiences and emotional reactions and push problems outside of the self, the young client is able to partner with the provider in a supportive, problem-solving process. Although skills training strategies for individual clients can be helpful, skills training should be framed as a supportive method for adding to client strengths rather than a remediation activity for dealing with implied deficits. Learning to handle difficult interactions can be framed as an advanced skill that is sometimes needed in an unjust world.

Working From a Collectivist Interpersonal Perspective

Clients from diverse cultural backgrounds may present with collectivist social dynamics. Understanding and working from collectivist perspectives can be difficult for individualist counselors because such counselors may think in terms of self-development, whereas collectivist clients may value community and family goals and not believe in focusing on the self. For clients with collectivist values, even simple and common counseling language around personal goal setting may feel like a poor fit (Sue et al., 2019).

Embracing Normal Cultural Variation

Mutual goal setting is an evidence-based counseling activity (Tryon et al., 2018). Goal setting is not just a counseling norm, it is expected. Individual goal setting may not resonate with clients with collectivist social values. Instead, factors related to suicidality (e.g., shame, failure, addiction, loss) may be viewed as familial, tribal, or cultural and not as components of the self. Some clients with collectivist values may chafe at the mention of individual goals; alternatively, they may fall silent. If your client has a collectivist orientation, and if, during an initial session, you push for individual goal setting, you may mislabel your client as resistant or cause a relational rupture. Collectivist orientations are a normal cultural variant and require counselors to reconceptualize client problem identification, treatment goals, and interventions. We explore cultural variations on goal setting and interpersonal values in the case of Matthew.

Matthew is a 28-year-old Lakota Sioux cisgender heterosexual male and an Iraqi war veteran. He is returning to college after two tours of duty in the Middle East. Matthew reports excessive alcohol use. He also has sleep problems associated with posttraumatic stress disorder. He grudgingly admits to suicidality.

Listening for and Summarizing Important Cultural Values

Early in the first session, Matthew talks about his cultural identity and values.

Counselor: What are some things that would be good for me to know about you?

Matthew: I'm Lakota. I come from a small reservation. It was a comfortable life growing up. I didn't know different. I remember sitting with my family watching the war. We wanted to help bring honor to our tribe. So I signed up for the Army at 17.

Counselor: [*nodding*] OK.

Matthew: It was a big deal. We had a big honor gathering for me, big sendoff, and it was pretty great and I felt good. I deployed to Iraq when I was 18. I felt like I was doing something. I didn't get to talk to my family much, and I didn't know what was going on at home. I had a fiancée when I left. Life was great. Eventually it was time to come home. My family was in disarray. My grandma had died. I didn't get to go to her funeral. They didn't even tell me.

Counselor: After the big celebration you went away and then didn't even know much of what was happening at home.

Matthew: Yeah. It tore me up. My fiancée left me for one of my best friends. That was the shock of my life.

Counselor: You were on kind of a high and feeling good at 17, you got a big sendoff from your tribe, from your family, and you go to Iraq. And you get back, and things are a mess and your fiancée had left you.

Matthew: Yeah. Meth hit our reservation hard. I had family members on meth and in prison. The world changed, I guess. I started drinking. Wasn't sure who I was anymore. I was feeling down and kept drinking. Culturally we don't talk about feelings. A lot of shame comes from it. You're supposed to just deal with it.

Counselor: I hear a couple of cultural pieces. One is that sense of honor of serving that reflects well on your tribe. And then another cultural thing is that it can be shameful to express emotions, maybe emotions like sadness.

Matthew: Yeah, I guess I could describe it as shame. Like I feel guilty talking about it because we're supposed to be men.

Several challenges emerge early in this session. Matthew's language ("tore me up" and "shock of my life") and the fact that he is facing shameful feelings by coming for counseling suggest he is in substantial distress. One dilemma facing the counselor is how to talk about Matthew's painful emotional experiences without getting too focused on emotions and triggering shame. Using words like *torn up* and *shock* might be better than *hurt* or *sad*.

Counselor: So being here in counseling is a big step for you. I'm honored that you told me about your cultural values. I'm going to do my best to track all those things. If you think I'm not getting it from your cultural perspective, I'd love you to tell me. But I don't want to put all that on you. So I'll check in every once in a while to see if I'm understanding things. Is that OK with you?

Matthew: Yeah, that's fine.

When working across cultures, a big challenge is to make an interpersonal connection and build trust quickly. Without connection and trust, clients may not return for a second session.

Collectivist Goal Setting

After Matthew shares that he is feeling suicidal, the counselor focuses in on what brings Matthew up and what brings him down. There is a discussion of goals, and Matthew makes it clear that he does not set personal goals for himself.

Matthew: Sometimes I avoid calling home because talking to family members who are on meth makes me mad. That's a trigger because the first thing they ask for is money.

Counselor: So that brings you down.

Matthew: Yeah. I want to feel connected, but they just care about their next high.

Counselor: But connection to family seems important to you. Is there a time or a person who would be better for you to call? I'm brainstorming because if you're already feeling down, and they take you down further, that could be a dangerous spot.

Matthew: Yeah, I could call my niece. I've done that and we talk about school, and she tells me what she's doing in school.

Counselor: And that's a more positive experience?

Matthew: Yeah, definitely. I'm at college. I hope my niece will use me as a role model.

Counselor: That's more of an up, talking with your niece and being a role model.

Matthew: Definitely.

Counselor: Any other situations that trigger you and get you into a suicidal place?

Matthew: When I do bad in school and I feel like a failure. I feel like I'm not going to be able to accomplish my goal of helping out my community.

Counselor: And so one goal for you is to do well in school.

Matthew: No. It's not like that. We don't set goals for ourselves. I want to help my community.

Counselor: OK. What I said wasn't quite right. It's not a goal you'd set for yourself but a goal to do something honorable for your community and family. Is that it?

Matthew: Yeah. Exactly.

Counselor: OK. Good. Thanks for telling me that. I like how you and your tribe think about goals.

Matthew: Yeah, another thing that takes me down is that I have no family here. Nobody understands. Nobody can pick me up. Then the hopeless feeling comes in because I don't know who to turn to, can't call home, can't go home. It's a nine-and-a-half-hour drive. That's a lot of money. I can't just drive there and back.

Counselor: One thing we can do here is talk. It's not a substitute for family, but maybe it's better than not talking. I hope we can honor your style, which, I think, is to not just vent or feel bad about a bad grade but focus on what you can do to be a success for your niece and your community. Would that be an OK way to talk about it?

Matthew: That would be good.

To reach goal consensus, the counselor focuses on Matthew's school performance, but Matthew makes it clear that he does not set personal goals. Rather than forcing Matthew into individualist goal setting, the counselor respects Matthew's way of being and reconceptualizes the goal to fit Matthew. The counselor also talks about using future sessions for problem-solving, partly because Matthew has made it clear that talking directly about emotions is shameful to him and his people. This case illustrates how to use collectivist language and counseling procedures that honor the client's cultural values.

Identifying and Creating Functional Relationship Patterns

Psychotherapists historically dealt with repeating maladaptive relationship patterns through psychoanalytic or psychodynamic approaches. The message was something like this: "Through psychotherapy we will go through the long and arduous process of identifying dysfunctional relationship patterns that you've been unconsciously repeating since childhood. As you gain insight into these patterns, we'll work to change them."

Although there is nothing inherently wrong with psychodynamic approaches, the model implies internalized, unconscious psychopathology. The underlying premise is that unconscious impulses might be dangerous or destructive and that pathological impulses need to be uncovered and modified. For some clients, psychodynamic ideas can feel threatening. The uncovering and expressive qualities of depth work can be destabilizing for clients, especially clients who are struggling with suicidality.

Many clients experiencing suicidality are already inclined toward negative labeling of the self; they typically hold core beliefs of inadequacy or defectiveness. Using free association to drill into unconscious destructive patterns and achieve insight runs the risk of activating self-deprecating beliefs. We recall examples of this from the 1970s and 1980s: After being hospitalized following severe suicide attempts, patients were sometimes labeled, in retrospect, as having been poor candidates for psychoanalysis. This labeling was a convenient way to blame patients for having been exposed to inappropriate and likely damaging treatments.

Although counseling should focus on helping clients modify their repetitive unhealthy relationship patterns, we prefer using a strengths-based approach with clients who are suicidal. Within the positive psychotherapy discipline, multiple evidence-based approaches are available for intentionally practicing positive relationship patterns (see Rashid & Seligman, 2018, and the following list). Although integrating routine positive psychology assignments into daily life will not magically fix less than optimal relationship patterns, positive or strengths-oriented homework assignments can improve mood, disrupt negative relational spiraling, and improve relational problem-solving (Seligman et al., 2006).

The following assignments are summarized from Seligman et al. (2006) and Rashid and Seligman (2018):

1. *Active-constructive responses.* Clients practice responding in constructive ways to the positive news that others report to them.
2. *Family tree of strengths.* Clients use information from the past and present to create a family tree of strengths, including strengths of children. Clients are coached to provide positive feedback to other family members.
3. *The forgiveness letter.* Clients write a letter of forgiveness to a person who has hurt them in some way. The letter includes the hurtful act, emotional responses, and an openness to forgiving the offending person. The letter may or may not be sent.
4. *The gratitude letter.* Clients write and deliver (through whatever modality is preferred) a letter of thanks or gratitude to someone toward whom the client feels a debt of gratitude (see Wellness Practice 9.1 in Chapter 9 for a gratitude assignment).

Although taking a deep dive into the origins of your clients' repeating dysfunctional relationship patterns makes for good counseling in some situations, when working with clients who are suicidal we recommend a laser-like focus on constructing new and healthy relationship patterns.

Concluding Comments

Interpersonal relationships are central to health and well-being. In your work with clients or students who are suicidal, you are likely to notice many different relationship dynamics that contribute to their distress. Although most of the strategies described in this chapter are technical, remember that the ways in which you interact with your clients are also powerful tools for exerting positive interpersonal influence.

Practitioner Guidance and Key Points to Remember

In this chapter we described four key interpersonal issues to address in counseling: (a) social disconnection, (b) interpersonal loss and grief, (c) social skill deficits, and (d) repeating dysfunctional relationship patterns. Interventions in the interpersonal dimension include the following:

- Assess your client's social universe as a method for identifying relationships that are toxic or emotionally painful and relationships that are vitalizing.
- When working with clients following romantic relationship breakups, help clients learn what they can from the old relationships and focus on gaining support and gratification from current relationships.
- Focus on developing and refining social skills that enable clients to initiate and sustain positive new relationships.
- When working with youth or adults who are experiencing bullying or cyberbullying, externalize the problem and avoid pathologizing or blaming the victim for being bullied.
- Remember to accept and affirm collectivist interpersonal perspectives as normal cultural variations. Also, modify basic counseling language and concepts, including goal setting, to fit with collectivist cultural values.
- Listen for and summarize cultural values that are important to your clients.
- Use positive psychology methods for identifying and creating functional relationship patterns.

Chapter 7

The Physical Dimension

Integrating awareness of the body into your work with clients who are suicidal can be daunting. The physical body includes the brain, spinal cord, organs, tissues, tendons, muscles, bones, blood, cells, and a multitude of chemicals, all of which are traveling through the brain and body while simultaneously and sequentially engaging in various molecular, electrical, and possibly magical life-sustaining activities. To some extent, physical bodies are genetically predetermined, but physical traits can also be altered by surgery, aging, accidents, nutrition, disease, and drugs.

Aerobic or cardiovascular exercise, yoga, psychoactive substances, sleep, and many other behaviors directly affect brain structure and function—and are implicated in suicide risk and treatment. The opposite is equally true: Brain structure and function unarguably affect behaviors, and some brains are, albeit only slightly, predisposed toward suicide. With all this as a backdrop, welcome to the complex, intricate, and sometimes confusing physical dimension.

Working in the Physical Dimension

Human brains are the physical source from which all cognition, emotion, and behavior flow. At least in part, suicidal thoughts and behaviors are always physical phenomena. All seven dimensions overlap and interact, but the boundaries between the physical and behavioral (see Chapter 9) dimensions are especially permeable because of the reciprocal relationship between human activity and physical development. Your clients' lived experiences and physical movements are constantly shaping their physical bodies as well as their neurophysiological structure and performance (Chaouloff, 1997; Millon & Shors, 2019).

As an aside, we should note that most of what passes for neuroscience in the popular media (e.g., "You can rewire your brain" or "Low serotonin is linked to depression") are gross oversimplifications that make real neuroscientists shudder (Lilienfeld et al., 2015). For instance, here is an excerpt from a journal article that examined how MAOA-uVNTR and 5-HTTLPR (two common serotonergic polymorphisms) combine with early and later life stressors to account for individual variations in self-control. The authors wrote, "Our findings highlight the need to study the etiology of self-control from both developmental and biological perspectives by demonstrating that molecular genetic variation related to serotonergic function interacts with distal stressors to increase reactivity to proximal stressors" (Boisvert et al., 2018, p. 98).

Boisvert and colleagues (2018) seem to be repeating a common message from diverse scientific disciplines. That is, nature and nurture are deeply integrated—even at the genetic, molecular, and neurosynaptic levels (see also Chaouloff et al., 1999).

What does this brief glimpse into neuroscientists' musings about serotonin, stress, and experience imply as we consider treatments for suicide? Assessment, expectations, and treatments for clients and students who are suicidal need to be individualized. Individualizing treatments means finding the best path forward for each unique person with whom we are working. In this chapter, we consider how counselors attend to the physical dimension and integrate it into suicide assessment and treatment.

Key Physical Issues to Address

Most counselors and mental health professionals do not have backgrounds in medical science, neuroscience, or exercise physiology. Nevertheless, assessing physical symptoms and recommending, monitoring, and using physical interventions are within the broad domain of counseling and psychotherapy. Key physical areas to assess and address include the following:

- Biogenetics and medical treatments
- Physical movement or exercise
- Agitation, arousal, and anxiety
- Trauma, nightmares, and insomnia

Biogenetics and Medical Treatments

Family studies, including limited adoption and twin studies, indicate that "suicidal behavior runs in families" (Brent et al., 1996, p. 1145). To date, estimates of how much suicide risk is genetically driven versus environmentally driven are largely based on research studies with limited external validity. In general, genes appear to play a small and limited role in death by suicide: "Genetic epidemiology studies suggest that genetic contribution is quantitatively somewhat weaker than the environmental one" (Brezo et al., 2008, p. 179). Nevertheless, when the siblings, parents, grandparents, or other relatives of clients (and counselors) die by suicide, many questions are triggered, including the following:

- Am I genetically predisposed to suicide?
- How much does having a parent die by suicide increase my risk?
- Does suicide run in families because of genetics or because suicidal behaviors have been modeled?
- Can I control my genetic predisposition toward depression or suicide?

Joiner (2005) wrote about his father's suicide and how it contributed to his interest in understanding suicide on a deeper level. He also recognized, based on his own experiences, how having someone in your family die by suicide creates angst and anxiety. Joiner described how he talks with clients about genetic predispositions and suicide:

> A family history of suicide appears to contribute about a two fold increase in risk—a little more if there are multiple, close relatives who have died by suicide; a little less if there are relatively few and distant relatives. This rule of thumb can be very useful to people who have lost a loved one to suicide. In fact, I have had visits and calls from people around the United States about this very question.
>
> Usually, the call or visit is from the wife of a man who has died by suicide, wanting to know the genetic risk to her children. Anecdotes like the family mentioned by Menninger in which five of seven siblings died by suicide can make people understandably anxious. It is often reassuring for people to hear that the risk for any given person walking down the street is 1 out of 10,000, or .0001. A child whose dad has died by suicide has a risk that is around 2 out of 10,000, or .0002—no higher than 5 out of 10,000, or .0005, in any event. The fact that I am a surviving child of a dad who died by suicide adds credibility, I think, to the reassurance. (p. 174)

When clients are anxious about their genetic risk (or the risk for their children), conveying Joiner's credible reassurance is a good first step. However, fear is not easily sated through rational argument. If rational argument calmed fears, everyone would be more frightened of walking on sidewalks and driving cars than flying in airplanes. To generalize from the words of the great psychoanalyst Frieda Fromm-Reichmann, in addition to rational arguments "the patient needs an experience, not an explanation" (quoted in May, 1983, p. 158).

Medical treatments for suicidality have mixed outcomes. Antidepressant medications are the most common medical intervention for treating clients with suicidal ideation or behavior. Unfortunately, antidepressants have been documented as potentially decreasing and increasing suicidality. Increases in suicidality in response to the use of SSRIs have been especially concerning among youth and young adults. As a consequence, in 2007 the U.S. Food and Drug Administration mandated a black box warning to accompany all SSRI antidepressants. The label reads,

> Antidepressants increased the risk compared to placebo of suicidal thinking and behavior (suicidality) in children, adolescents, and young adults in short-term studies of Major Depressive Disorder (MDD) and other psychiatric disorders. Patients of all ages who are started on antidepressant therapy should be monitored appropriately and observed closely for clinical worsening, suicidality, or unusual changes in behavior. Families and caregivers should be advised of the need for close observation and communication with the prescriber.

Researchers continue to report that clients are more likely to attempt or complete suicide within approximately 30 days after starting a new psychotropic medication (Katz et al., 2018).

Counselors are likely to work with many clients who are taking psychotropic medications. As nonprescribing professionals, counselors have a limited role in recommending or advising against treatment with medication. However, given that the first 30 days of beginning a new psychotropic medication can increase suicide risk, one clear role for counselors is to engage in ongoing communication with prescribers regarding clients' responses to medications. Specifically, if clients are experiencing increases in physical agitation (e.g., akathisia) or reporting strange or violent thoughts, counselors should inform the medication prescriber (J. Sommers-Flanagan & Campbell, 2009).

Physical Movement or Exercise

If clients struggling with suicide need an experience to counter their fears and lift their moods, physical exercise may be the best place to start. The general benefits of exercise are legion. Bono (2018) put it this way:

> These findings suggest a very simple premise: engaging in vigorous exercise regularly carries benefits for you. Yes, you. It doesn't matter where you are from or what external circumstances are unique to your life, exercise will make you happier. . . . You don't need specialized shoes or equipment or to sign up for a 10K or expensive spin class. . . . Just about any activity that gets your heart rate elevated will work. It's about finding something that you enjoy and that is realistic for you. (pp. 51–52)

The benefits of exercise include the following:

- Increased happiness (Bono, 2018)
- Improved sleep (C. L. Davidson et al., 2013)
- Improved sexual functioning (Hoffman et al., 2009)
- Increased vigor (energy) and decreased fatigue (Puetz et al., 2008; Shors et al., 2014)
- Decreased depression (Szuhany & Otto, 2019)
- Improved memory, executive functioning, and problem-solving (Khatri et al., 2001)

You might think that all this information about exercise being beneficial is true for the general population, but you may doubt that it works for clients who are depressed and suicidal. Well, it is time to put those doubts aside. Exercise, all by itself, is an effective treatment for a vast array of depressive problems, including postpartum depression (Özkan et al., 2020), clinical depression in adults and youth (Babyak et al., 2000; Hughes et al., 2013; Nasstasia et al., 2019), and suicidality among veterans (C. L. Davidson et al., 2013), to name a few.

In one of the first direct comparisons of exercise versus an antidepressant medication for treating depression, the findings surprised even the researchers. After 4 months of treatment with sertraline (i.e., Zoloft) only, Zoloft plus exercise, or exercise only, more than 60% of patients in all three groups no longer met the diagnostic criteria for depression. Although the fact that exercise is equivalent to antidepressant medications is good news, the better news came later. Ten months after initiating treatment, patients in the exercise-only group had the highest recovery rates—even better than those for Zoloft plus exercise (see Figure 7.1). Although it is impossible to know why exercise-only had better outcomes than Zoloft plus exercise, Bono (2018) speculated that exercise by itself increased self-efficacy; participants in the exercise-only group may have attributed their positive mood changes directly to their own behavior, consequently increasing their beliefs that they had made a difference in their own lives. Overall, not only is exercise an excellent prescription for a healthier and happier life within the general population, but it is also well established as an effective treatment for clinical depression.

Another important question involves the crossroads of exercise and genetic predisposition for depression. For many years, mental health professionals believed that if clients have a genetic predisposition for depression, treatment with medication might be required. More recently, knowledge of epigenetics (i.e., how environmental factors trigger specific genetic responses) combined with research on depression and physical exercise has shaken the premise that pharmaceutical interventions are required for so-called biological depressions (K. W. Choi et al., 2019).

To test the interaction of physical exercise with polygenic risk for depression, K. W. Choi and colleagues (2019) generated polygenic

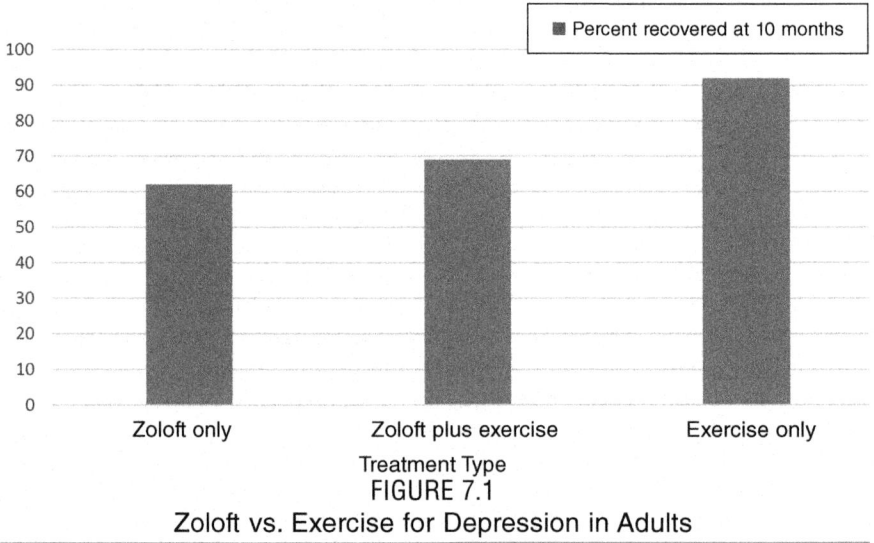

FIGURE 7.1
Zoloft vs. Exercise for Depression in Adults

Note. Figure created from data originally published by Babyak et al. (2000).

risk scores for 7,968 European Americans. They found that virtually any form of measurable exercise, including higher intensity aerobic exercise (e.g., running and cycling) and lower intensity stretching (e.g., yoga), conferred significant benefits on individuals classified as having low, intermediate, or high polygenic risk for depression; with just 3.2 hours per week of exercise, individuals with polygenic risk for depression reduced their risk to that of individuals with no polygenic risk for depression. They concluded,

> Providing people with specific knowledge that a modifiable factor such as physical activity can exert protective effects above and beyond the influence of one's genetic makeup can enrich counseling efforts and potentially motivate shifts in lifestyle behavior to improve mental health. (pp. 112–113)

Without question, mental health professionals should integrate regular physical exercise into client treatment plans. Not only is exercise powerful medicine for depression, but as a therapeutic intervention, applied consistently and in moderation, exercise also has minimal side effects. Exercise is arguably the first-line treatment of choice for youth, college students, veterans, the elderly, stroke victims, and other individuals at risk for depression and suicide.

Agitation, Arousal, and Anxiety

Suicide researchers use the words *arousal* or *agitation* to describe increased heart rate, respiration, and subjective characteristics of individuals who feel mounting internal pressure to act. When clients say, "I don't know what to do," they are often speaking of their internal pressure to "Do something!" Combined with excruciating distress, problem-solving impairments, and social disconnection, agitation adds substantially to suicide risk (Ribeiro et al., 2014). Trauma, insomnia, drug withdrawal, initiating or terminating the use of antidepressant medication (i.e., in particular, SSRIs), and many other factors increase arousal and contribute to suicidality (Healy, 2009; Ribeiro et al., 2014). In the following excerpt, Matthew (the 28-year-old Lakota Sioux client from Chapter 6) describes a mix of excruciating pain, social disconnection, and agitation—much of which can be tracked back to a traumatic war experience:

> Every time I go to sleep, I remember one time in Iraq, we were sitting there, and Al-Qaeda blew up a whole city block. Every building came down. We were trying to help. You had kids with missing arms and missing eyes and moms with no legs and crying, screaming. We

were trying to help. At the same time, people are shooting at us. My friend's yelling, "Why the fuck are we here? This isn't what we're here for!" Yeah, I remember a mom with a missing leg trying to carry her helpless child in her arms, and the child was dead. Every time I go to sleep, I remember that kid helpless laying there. And so I'm not sleeping much, I'm doing a lot of drinking still. I don't know what to do anymore.

Matthew's description lays out multiple ways in which trauma affects physical sensory experiences, sleep, and impulses to do something. Having endured all of these experiences, it is not surprising that Matthew engages in behaviors that escalate his suicide risk. These may include social isolation, alcohol consumption for desensitization, and impulsive behaviors to discharge the arousal or agitation from his body.

Anxiety is not a powerful predictor of suicide. However, among youth and adults who are experiencing depression, adding anxiety, panic—or any extra source of personal distress—exacerbates overall distress and increases suicidality (Fawcett et al., 1993). Anxiety is a particularly troubling source of distress, partly because virtually every pharmaceutical agent with antianxiety effects (primarily the benzodiazepines) also has substantial addictive potential and is contraindicated for long-term use (Frances, 2014, 2016).

Trauma, Nightmares, and Insomnia

Trauma is the root of many emotional and behavioral problems, including suicidality (Read et al., 2001). Renowned psychologist Donald Meichenbaum reflected on his 35-plus years of working with and consulting on suicide:

> In reviewing my clinical notes from . . . suicidal patients and the consultations that I have conducted over the course of my years of clinical work, the one thing that they all had in common was a history of victimization, including combat exposure (my first clinical case), sexual abuse, and surviving the Holocaust. (Meichenbaum, 2006, p. 334)

Meichenbaum is not alone in his observations. In one research study of 200 clients, child sexual abuse was a better predictor of suicidality than depression (Read et al., 2001). Similarly, data from the National Comorbidity Survey ($n = 5,877$) showed that men who were sexually abused as children were 4 to 11 times more likely to attempt suicide; women who experienced child sexual abuse had a

2 to 4 times higher likelihood of attempting suicide (Molnar et al., 2001). Also, in the original Adverse Childhood Experiences Study, Felitti and colleagues (1998) estimated that individuals who reported four or more adverse childhood experiences had a concomitant 4 to 12 times increase in their likelihood of experiencing alcohol/drug abuse, depression, and suicide attempts.

Trauma is an external event that manifests through physical, emotional, behavioral, and psychological symptoms. Perhaps the most pernicious physical effect of trauma is sleep disturbance. Following trauma, many individuals become sleep avoidant because sleep brings horrific nightmares filled with frightening images and scenarios that stimulate physical hyperarousal (Krakow & Zadra, 2010). As sleep loss accumulates, other suicide-related symptoms increase, including distress, agitation, impaired problem-solving, spiritual/existential disorientation, and moral injury. Like Matthew, many clients turn to substances to deal with flashbacks, numb their emotions, and dull their consciousness. Although posttraumatic stress disorder often triggers insomnia, insomnia is also an independent risk factor for suicide; insomnia is an important treatment target regardless of trauma history (Bernert et al., 2014).

Interventions in the Physical Dimension

Most approaches to counseling and psychotherapy are intellectual and verbal. However, early on, psychoanalysts wrote about physical, muscular, and movement-based manifestations of psychopathology and healing. Adler (1931/1958) wrote, "To a certain degree, every emotion finds some bodily expression. The individual will show his [sic] emotion in some visible form; perhaps in posture and attitude, perhaps in the face, perhaps in the trembling of his legs and knees" (pp. 40–41).

Many contemporary mental health providers are dissatisfied with the overly educational quality of cognitive behavior therapy and are actively integrating body awareness and physical movement into their counseling approaches (Levine, 2010; van der Kolk, 2014; van der Kolk et al., 2007). At the same time, there has been a greater emphasis on neuroscience and brain structure in the development of new treatments (Field & Ghoston, 2020; C. Luke, 2020).

For the most part, whether explicitly weaving the body and neuroscientific hypotheses into mental health treatments improves outcomes remains unknown. Of the preceding efforts, only eye-movement desensitization and reprocessing (EMDR) and physical exercise have supporting empirical research (P. R. Davidson & Parker, 2001). However, to the extent that you can integrate the body into treatment plans while at the same time staying within professional ethical guidelines, clients likely stand to benefit—even if your integration of the physical only consists of motivating your clients to engage in a few hours a week of physical exercise.

Physical Exercise for Depression, Anxiety, and Suicidality

Exercise is an evidence-based treatment for depression. That is the good news. The bad news is that getting clients who are depressed and anxious to exercise is exceedingly difficult. Convincing clients that exercise is beneficial is not the problem; the problem is motivation.

Simon Says . . . Exercise

Simon, a 17-year-old cisgender male high school student, was referred for counseling because of intermittent explosive behaviors, including threats of suicide and suicidal ideation. Simon's suicidal talk was short lived. He would suddenly shout, "I'm going to kill myself!" Typically, within minutes, Simon calmed down, retracted his suicidal statements, and said he did not want to die.

Simon was diagnosed with autism spectrum disorder (previously Asperger's disorder). His parents and school personnel viewed his suicide threats as his way of communicating discontent regarding changes in structure and routine. Simon was also socially isolated and sometimes ostracized at school. Although Simon usually appeared oblivious to his social status at school, he occasionally expressed acute awareness of how he did not fit in with other students. Simon was referred for counseling because (a) his threats needed to be taken seriously, and (b) he needed to learn socially acceptable alternatives for expressing his frustration.

Simon was not the least bit interested in counseling. He made his case: "Counseling is stupid. Besides, I'm not suicidal." To get Simon to counseling, his parents told him they were going for pizza. Once they got Simon in the car, they told him they would not get pizza until they all went for family counseling. Simon protested. His parents held firm. Upon arriving at the counselor's office, Simon greeted the counselor with, "My parents are liars. I'm only here for pizza. When will we be done?"

After a rough start, Simon repeated his core reasons for opposing counseling, saying, "Counseling is stupid. Besides, I'm not suicidal." The counselor responded with the following:

I don't know you at all, but I can agree with you on both those points. Counseling is stupid. And, for now, I believe what you're saying about not being suicidal. How about this? Let's not do counseling. Let's just meet a few times. I'll be your consultant. I don't want to be your counselor. I'll consult with you on a plan to accomplish three things:

1. Get your parents to stop lying.
2. Get you to stop doing whatever you're doing to make people think you're suicidal.
3. Make a new and interesting plan—one that involves computer games—so that you can start having more fun in your life than you're having right now.

To his parents' surprise, Simon agreed to see the "consultant."

The challenge for Simon's counselor was to frame their sessions in ways that Simon found acceptable. Having worked with youth like Simon previously, the counselor implemented a plan for several short (30-minute), game-based individual sessions. After 1 month, Simon was transferred into a broadly evidence-based after-school autism spectrum computer-based gaming and exercise group. The group used principles from recent research on computer games for youth on the autism spectrum combined with a 12-week exercise-based protocol. Details included the following:

- Participants could earn money and time to participate in a combination exercise and Pokémon group.
- Individual screenings were conducted in which prospective participants had to agree to cooperate with the rules and treat other group members with respect.
- To earn money and participate in the Pokémon group, participants agreed to (a) cooperate, (b) wear a heart monitor, and (c) complete 40-minute activity routines at least three times weekly.
- The activity routines could be Wii Sports or Wii Fit, Jazzercise, jogging, weight training, yoga, cycling, swimming, or an agreed-on alternative physical activity.
- Upon arriving at group, all participants had to take turns verbally reporting on how they did on their activity routines.
- For 100% compliance, participants received $25; 90% compliance, $20; 80% compliance, $15; and 70% compliance, $10 (money for compensating participants was provided by parents).

- Group facilitators coached participants on providing encouraging comments and positive feedback to one another.
- Students practiced how to express frustration and disappointment using appropriate feeling words. Verbal encouragement and reinforcement were provided for appropriate language use along with sugar-free candies. In cases when students were frustrated or disappointed, they were coached to use nonthreatening feeling words (instead of things like "I'm going to kill myself!").

The group format described here follows the protocol from a research study called Depressed Adolescents Treated With Exercise. The study, which included youth diagnosed with major depression, used physical exercise and an exercise monitoring device as the primary intervention. After 12 weeks of treatment, the exercise group ($n = 16$) had a 100% response rate, and 100% remission was maintained at weeks 26 and 52. In addition to the study protocol, computer gaming was integrated into this simulation because of its documented value in working with youth diagnosed with autism spectrum disorder (Bittner et al., 2017; Yu et al., 2018). (See Wellness Practice 7.1 for more behavioral change suggestions.)

Wellness Practice 7.1
Creating New Habits 101

Dr. B. J. Fogg of Stanford University runs a lab on behavior change. In an article for *Time*, Fogg (2019) wrote, "In my own research, I found that habits can form very quickly, often in just a few days, as long as people have a strong positive emotion connected to the new behavior" (para. 4).

In our Art and Science of Happiness course at the University of Montana, we introduced 50-plus students to Fogg's article and other information about how to start new habits. Many students successfully created new habits. Here is a first-person account:

> Something I worked on this semester was running more often. To pair it with something I enjoy, I only listened to R&B music on my jogs. Other times, I listened to other types of music, but when running I listened to my favorite music. Immediate rewards after the behavior helped cement it. After the gym, I always went to the coffee shop with kind baristas, good music, and turmeric lattes.

(continued)

Wellness Practice 7.1
Creating New Habits 101 (continued)

> The three steps I incorporated into my life for habit formation were (a) reflect on what behaviors I want to implement, (b) find ways to pair my favorite stimulus with that behavior, and (c) structure in rewards immediately following the behavior. With this system, I've successfully added new habits to my life that help me be a healthier person. I even floss daily now!
>
> In addition to this student's wisdom, here are a few more tips:
>
> - *Make short-term (very short-term) goals.* Many people fail at change because they aim for big changes (e.g., lose 20 pounds) and grow discouraged. Instead of big goals and delayed reinforcement, use small goals that lead toward bigger goals. Then celebrate the small goals several times a day.
> - *Make a clear and realistic plan.* Read, consult, and gather information before developing habit-changing plans. Most people are not good at creating practical plans with realistic goals. Before launching your behavior change project, make a good plan that fits your life situation.
> - *Go public.* Commit yourself to changing by telling friends, family, or other important and supportive witnesses.
> - *Manage self-talk.* Keep in mind that all success includes many failures. When possible, substitute positive, affirming, and encouraging self-talk for your negative judgments.
> - *Celebrate immediately and uniquely.* Even very small celebrations (e.g., saying "Yesssss!" under your breath or doing a personal fist pump) can give your brain the positive reinforcement (or dopamine surge) it needs.
>
> For more information on forming positive habits, check out Dr. B. J. Fogg's (2019) Time article "Better Control of Your Emotions Will Help You Create Better Habits" or listen to the December 30, 2019, *Hidden Brain* episode "Creatures of Habit: How Habits Shape Who We Are—And Who We Become" at https://www.npr.org/transcripts/787160734.

Medication Consultation With a Younger Client

The base rate for suicide among preteen clients is extremely low (less than 1 per 100,000). Although this fact is reassuring, by no means does it imply that you should ignore or minimize the seriousness of suicidality in younger children. In fact, when younger clients or students have thoughts of death or suicide, it often signals high distress associated with a trauma history. In one recent study of 337,135 youth, sexual abuse exhibited the strongest link to suicidality (although many other forms of trauma were also positively correlated with suicide attempts; Angelakis et al., 2020).

Given the infrequency of suicide among prepubertal youth, the principles of assessment and treatment with young clients who are suicidal are still developing. Assessment and treatment generally includes the family, and longer term contacts are likely because early-onset suicidality tends to predict later suicidality (Pfeffer, 2006). Unlike assessments with teenagers and adults, it is appropriate to ask, "Do you have thoughts of hurting yourself?" instead of always asking directly about suicide. In addition, human figure drawings, play, and other projective assessment techniques may be helpful with children who are less verbal (Zalsman et al., 2000).

Although family-based interventions are first-line treatments, sometimes families are less than optimally cooperative, and other times medical consultation and treatment is needed to address acute and disturbing symptoms. Group home treatment, partial hospitalization, and other intensive approaches to treatment may be necessary. The following case illustrates some of the dynamics of treating children who are suicidal.

Max was an 11-year-old biracial boy (Black and Latinx) whose father had been deported to Guatemala 1 year prior to his referral for mental health counseling. In the past 2 weeks, Max had become increasingly agitated and paranoid. He had been exposed to news of increased racial violence in his neighborhood. Max began clinging excessively to his mother, sleeping with her at night, and refusing to leave the family home. At his intake interview, Max and his mother reported that Max was not sleeping or eating, that he intermittently was unable to speak, and he had begun seeing visions telling him that it was his turn to die. Max stated that he needed to kill himself to make his visions go away.

Diagnostically speaking, Max had symptoms consistent with anxiety and depressive disorders and possibly trauma, but there was also the possibility that Max was in the early (prodromal) stage of schizophrenia. Given the intensity of Max's symptoms, the counselor initiated treatment but also made an urgent referral to a local psychiatrist.

After meeting with Max, the psychiatrist discussed the case with Max's counselor. Although there was evidence of the onset of a psychotic episode, both the counselor and psychiatrist puzzled over Max's visual hallucinations because exclusively auditory hallucinations are more common in the prodromal phase of schizophrenia. Max also had no identifiable family history of psychotic disorders. As a consequence, the psychiatrist took a conservative approach to treatment, prescribing a very low dose of an antipsychotic with sedating properties to help stabilize Max's sleep. The plan also included twice-weekly counseling and further assessment for potential trauma. As Max's treatment unfolded, he admitted that although his fears were related to a wide array of factors (i.e., deportation, neighborhood violence, his father's well-being), he also had been jumped and physically attacked in his neighborhood and had been threatened to stay silent. After 2 weeks of a combination of increased sleep, stabilized eating patterns, supportive counseling, and initiation of a neighborhood safety plan (with his older brother's support), Max's visions and suicidality vanished.

Max continued to see his psychiatrist (once monthly) for 6 months, at which time he was tapered off of his medications. He continued in treatment with his counselor (once weekly) for more than 2 years. Max continued to be vulnerable to anxiety and experienced occasional relapses. During the relapses, the counselor worked with the psychiatrist on medication management and provided ongoing feedback on Max's responses to the medication. The counselor also worked with Max's school to make sure Max had ongoing supportive counseling and educational planning going forward.

Self-Regulation and Anxiety Management

In Chapter 4 we described emotional regulation as part of dialectical behavior therapy (Linehan, 1993). Using dialectical behavior therapy, practitioners guide clients toward practicing emotional awareness and mindfulness strategies. *Self-regulation* and *anxiety management* are broader terms that often involve teaching physical self-regulation skills designed to reduce heart rate, blood pressure, and respiration and activate the parasympathetic nervous system.

Physical Self-Regulation

All approaches to anxiety management, relaxation, and self-regulation flow from Mary Cover Jones's (1924a, 1924b) original research from the 1920s. Working with small children, Jones demonstrated that young children suffering from intense fear could replace their fear responses with calmness through counterconditioning. Although Jones used food items as a counterconditioning stimulus, in 1938,

Edmund Jacobson wrote about progressive muscle relaxation (PMR) as a physical counterconditioning tool. Jacobson provided detailed procedures for PMR.

We describe the historical and theoretical context of self-regulation because counterconditioning is at the heart of virtually every anxiety reduction approach. Whether you are using EMDR, somatic experiencing therapy, person-centered therapy, diaphragmatic breathing, clinical hypnosis, or psychodynamic psychotherapy, if your goal is to reduce anxiety, you will be using counterconditioning. Here is how it works.

First, you identify an aversive stimulus that triggers unwanted physical, emotional, and cognitive responses. The triggering stimulus might be a person, a memory, a location, an activity, or specific social or performance situations. For many clients who are suicidal, not only is the aversive triggering stimulus one of the preceding factors, but it also has merged with the self. When clients think of themselves (and their life situation), they often feel negatively aroused, agitated, and as if something is terribly wrong with them or their situation.

Traditionally, you might use diaphragmatic breathing or PMR as a counterconditioning stimulus. First, you would train your client to self-regulate using breathing or PMR, and then you would begin initiating a process of in vivo or imaginal exposure. Over time, with support and practice, repeated pairing of the triggering stimulus with a calming stimulus results in reduced anxiety and greater perceived control over the fearful, negative, or aversive response. Jones (1924a) put it this way: "By the method of direct conditioning we associated the fear-object with a craving-object, and replaced the fear by a positive response" (p. 390).

Although some theorists debate the specifics (Hayes, 2004), good counseling nearly always involves pairing a positive, calming, and soothing stimulus (e.g., you, your voice, your office, supportive comments, active and nonjudgmental listening) with stimuli that initiate a fear, anxiety, anger, or discomfort response. With clients who are suicidal, the pairing might be the client's feelings of shame and self-revulsion with your soothing acceptance, kindness, supportive psychoeducational activities, teaching of mindfulness strategies, or whatever nontriggering and soothing counseling techniques you use. In many ways, pairing a soothing stimulus will be incidental (as when you are listening with acceptance). Other times, the pairing will be more explicit (as when you are practicing diaphragmatic breathing, meditation, or PMR).

Triggering stimuli vary for each client. The optimal self-regulation stimulus (or strategy) also varies from one client to the next. These variations in triggers and optimal self-regulation stimuli make it necessary for counselors and clients to work together with an experimental mindset to find the best path toward calmness and self-regulation (see Case Vignette 7.1).

Strategies for Dealing With Insomnia and Nightmares

Insomnia and nightmares contribute directly to client distress in general and suicidal distress in particular. In this section, we use a case example to illustrate how counselors can begin with a less personal issue (insomnia); use empathy, psychoeducation, and curiosity to track insomnia symptoms; eventually arrive at nightmares; and then inquire about trauma. Focusing first on insomnia, then on nightmares, and later on trauma can help counselors form an

---

Case Vignette 7.1
Using Mindfulness With a Veteran With a Mild Traumatic Brain Injury

Raymond was a Black American cisgender heterosexual veteran who had experienced a mild traumatic brain injury while stationed in Afghanistan. Seven months after being discharged, he was diagnosed with major depression. His symptoms also included intermittent attentional impairments, impulsive behaviors, and chronic suicidal ideation.

Given recent research supporting mindfulness-based interventions for treating depression in clients with traumatic brain injury, Raymond's counselor offered to experiment with him using a modified mindfulness-based stress reduction approach (Kabat-Zinn, 1990; Ozen et al., 2016). To address memory problems, the counselor provided oral and written versions of each activity and assignment, practiced mindfulness with Raymond, repeated procedures as needed, and gave Raymond a concrete tactile stimulus (a rabbit's foot) to promote emotional soothing and link to nonjudgmental mindfulness mental states (Azulay et al., 2013).

After 12 weeks of treatment, Raymond's depressive symptoms were in partial remission. He reported no suicidal ideation and bragged that his ability to concentrate had improved so much that he was able to resume playing games with his children. Raymond indicated that he regularly used his rabbit's foot to initiate a calm and mindful state.

alliance with clients who are initially reluctant to talk about death images and trauma experiences.

Focusing on Insomnia

Miguel is a 19-year-old cisgender heterosexual Latino male working on vocational skills in a Job Corps program. He arrives for his first session in dusty work clothes and stares at the counselor through squinted eyes; it is difficult to tell whether Miguel is squinting to protect his eyes from masonry dust or to communicate distrust. However, because he has been referred by a physician for insomnia, he also might just be sleepy.

> *Counselor:* Hey Miguel. Thanks for coming in. The doctor sent me a note. She said you're having trouble sleeping.
> *Miguel:* Yeah. I don't sleep.
> *Counselor:* That sucks. Working all day when you're not sleeping well must be rough.
> *Miguel:* Yeah. But I'm fine. That's how it is.

To start, Miguel minimizes his distress. Whether you are working with Alzheimer's patients covering their memory deficits or 5-year-olds who get caught lying, minimizing is a common strategy. When clients say, "I'm fine" or "It is what it is," they may be minimizing.

But Miguel is not fine. For many reasons (e.g., pride, shame, or age and ethnicity differences), he is reluctant to open up. However, given Miguel's history of being in a gang and his estranged relationship with his parents, the expectation that he should quickly trust and confide in a White male adult stranger is not appropriate.

Rather than pursuing anything personal, the counselor communicates empathy and interest in Miguel's insomnia experiences.

> *Counselor:* Not being able to sleep can make for very long nights. What do you think makes it so hard for you sleep?
> *Miguel:* I don't know. I just don't sleep.

When asked directly, Miguel declines to describe his sleep problems. Rather than continue with questioning, the counselor fills the room with words (i.e., psychoeducation). Psychoeducation is a good option because sitting in silence is socially painful and because multicultural experts recommend that counselors speak openly when working with clients from historically oppressed cultural groups (Sue et al., 2019). The reasoning is that if counselors are open and transparent, culturally diverse clients can evaluate them before sharing more about themselves. As Miguel's counselor talks, Miguel can decide, based on what he hears, whether his counselor is safe, trustworthy, and credible.

> *Counselor:* Miguel, there are three main types of insomnia. There's initial insomnia—that's when it takes a long time, maybe an hour or more, to get to sleep. They call that *difficulty falling asleep*. There's terminal insomnia—that's when you fall asleep pretty well and sleep until maybe 3 a.m. and then wake up and can't get back to sleep. They call that *early morning awakening*. Then there's intermittent insomnia—that's like being a light sleeper who wakes up over and over all night. They call that *choppy sleep*. Which of those fits for you?
> *Miguel:* I got all three. I can't get to sleep. I can't stay asleep. I can't get back to sleep.
> *Counselor:* That's sounds terrible. It's like a triple dose of bad sleep.

As Miguel begins opening up, he says, "I haven't slept in a week." Although it is obvious that 0 minutes of sleep over a week is not accurate, for Miguel it feels like he has not slept in a week, and that is what is important.

Exploring Nightmares

After Miguel yawns, the counselor asks permission to share his thoughts.

> *Counselor:* Miguel, if you don't mind, I'd like to tell you what I'm thinking. Is that OK?
> *Miguel:* Sure. Fine.
> *Counselor:* When someone says they're having as much trouble sleeping as you're having, there are usually two main reasons. The first is nightmares. Have you been having nightmares?
> *Miguel:* Shit yeah. Like every night. When I fall asleep, nightmares start.
> *Counselor:* OK. Thanks. I'm pretty sure I can help you with nightmares. We can probably make them happen less often and be less bad in just a few meetings.

The counselor's confidence is based on previous successful experiences, including using a nightmare treatment protocol that has empirical support (imagery rehearsal therapy; Krakow & Zadra, 2010). Although evidence-based treatments are not effective for all clients, they can establish credibility and instill hope. Nevertheless, Miguel does not immediately experience hope.

> *Miguel:* Yeah. But these aren't normal nightmares.
> *Counselor:* What's been happening?
> *Miguel:* I keep having this dream where I'm sticking a gun in my mouth. People are all around me with their voices and shit telling me, "Pull the trigger." Then I wake up, but I can't get it out of my head all day. What the hell is that all about?"
> *Counselor:* That's a great question.

When the counselor says, "That's a great question," his goal is to start a discussion about all the reasons why someone (Miguel, in this case) might have a gun-in-the-mouth dream. If Miguel and his counselor can brainstorm different explanations and possible meanings for the dream images, it is less likely that Miguel will interpret his dream as a sign that he should die by suicide. What is important, we tell our clients, is to look at many different possible meanings the unconscious or God or the Great Spirit or the universe or indigestion might be sending to the dreamer. To help clients expand their thinking and loosen up on their conclusions about their dream's meaning, we have used statements like the following: "You may be right. Your dream might be about you dying or killing yourself. But our goal is to listen to the message your brain sent you and be open to what it might mean. It's perfectly normal to think your dream was about you dying by suicide—but that's not necessarily true. That's not the way the brain and dreams usually work."

Some counselors use self-disclosure about dreams or nightmares they have had themselves. Others offer hypothetical or historical dream examples. Either way, normalizing nightmares helps clients become more comfortable talking about their bad dreams and nightmares.

Asking About Trauma

You may have a form to screen clients for a trauma history. However, more often than not, you need to ask directly about trauma, just like you need to ask directly about suicidality. In many cases, as discussed in Chapter 3, it may be beneficial to wait and ask about trauma until the second or third session or until there is a logical opportunity. Although insomnia and nightmares do not always signal trauma, when they coexist, they provide an avenue to ask about trauma.

> *Counselor:* Miguel, I'd like to ask a personal question. Would that be OK?
> *Miguel:* OK.
> *Counselor:* Almost always, when people have nightmares about guns and death, it means they've been through some bad, traumatic experiences. When you've been through something bad or terrible, nightmares get stuck in your head and get on a sort of repeating cycle. Is that true for you?
> *Miguel:* Yeah. I went through some bad shit back in Denver.
> *Counselor:* I'm guessing that bad shit is stuck in your brain and one way it comes out is through nightmares.
> *Miguel:* Yeah. Probably.

Even when clients know their trauma experiences are causing their nightmares, they can still be reluctant to talk about the details. Physical and emotional discomfort associated with trauma is something clients often want to avoid. To reassure clients, you can tell them about specific evidence-based approaches—approaches that do not require detailed recounting of trauma or nightmare experiences. Two examples include EMDR (Shapiro, 2001) and imagery rehearsal therapy (Krakow & Zadra, 2010).

> *Miguel:* If I talk about the nightmares, they get more real. I have enough trouble keeping them out of my head now.
> *Counselor:* That's a good point. But right now your dreams are so bad that you're barely sleeping. It's worth trying to work through them. How about this? I've got a simple protocol for working with nightmares. You don't even have to talk about the details of your nightmares. I think we should try it and watch to see if your dreams get better, worse, or stay the same. What do you think?
> *Miguel:* I guess maybe my nightmares can't get much worse.

Evidence-Based Trauma Treatments

In Miguel's case, the first step was to get him to talk about his insomnia, nightmares, and trauma. Without details about his experiences, there is no chance to dig in and start treatment.

The scenario with Miguel illustrates one method for getting clients to open up about trauma. Other clinical situations may be different. We have had Native American clients who were having dreams (or not having dreams, but wishing for them), and we needed to begin counseling by seeking better understanding of the role and meaning of dreams in their particular tribal culture.

Counselors who work with clients who are suicidal should obtain training for treating insomnia, nightmares, and trauma. Depending on your clients' age, their symptoms, their culture, the treatment setting, and your preference, several different evidence-based treatments may be effective for treating trauma. The following bulleted list includes treatments recommended by the American Psychological Association (2017), the VA/DoD Clinical Practice Guideline Working Group (2017), or both (Watkins et al., 2018):

- Cognitive processing therapy (Resick et al., 2017)
- EMDR (Shapiro, 2001)
- Narrative exposure therapy (Schauer et al., 2011)
- Prolonged exposure (Foa et al., 2007)
- Trauma-focused cognitive behavior therapy (Cohen et al., 2012)

Although the preceding list includes scientifically supported approaches to treating trauma, you may prefer other approaches, many of which are suitable for treating trauma (body-centered therapies, narrative exposure therapy for children [KID-NET], etc.).

Specific treatments for insomnia and nightmares are also essential for reducing arousal and agitation. Evidence-based treatments for insomnia and nightmares include the following:

- Cognitive behavior therapy for insomnia (Cunningham & Shapiro, 2018)
- Imagery rehearsal therapy (Krakow & Zadra, 2010)

Targeting trauma symptoms in general, and physical symptoms in particular (e.g., arousal, insomnia, nightmares), can be crucial to your treatment plan. Addressing physical symptoms in your treatment instills hope and provides near-term symptom relief (see Table 7.1).

TABLE 7.1
Treatment Plan for Miguel—Physical Dimension

Problem	Goals and Strengths[a]	Interventions/Plan
1. Miguel reports initial, intermittent, and terminal insomnia.	1. Miguel will use sleep hygiene, relaxation, and other CBT-I skills to improve his sleep.	1. Introduce Miguel to sleep hygiene, PMR, and mindfulness meditation to reduce arousal.
2. Miguel reports disturbing nightmares with images of suicide and death.	2. Miguel will actively manage his disturbing dream images.	2. Initiate imagery rehearsal therapy with Miguel and begin homework assignments related to nightmare reduction.

Note. CBT-I = cognitive behavior therapy for insomnia; PMR = progressive muscle relaxation.
[a]Strengths: Miguel is very articulate regarding his dream experiences. After initial reluctance, Miguel becomes engaged in the counseling process.

Concluding Comments

Physical symptoms and physical or medical treatments are an important consideration when working with clients who are suicidal. Although consultation with medical providers is always recommended, when physical symptoms are present, medical treatments become increasingly more appropriate. Ongoing communication between medical and nonmedical providers is indispensable.

Practitioner Guidance and Key Points to Remember

In this chapter we described four key physical issues to address in counseling: (a) biogenetics and medical treatments; (b) physical movement or exercise; (c) agitation, arousal, and anxiety; and (d) trauma, nightmares, and insomnia. Interventions in the physical dimension include the following:

- Encourage and support physical exercise as a first-line treatment for depression, anxiety, and suicidality. Getting clients to initiate and maintain exercise may require creative incentives.
- Help clients develop new physical routines and habits.
- Consult with physicians regarding medical treatments.
- Teach clients self-regulation and anxiety management skills, including a variety of physical self-regulation tools.
- Teach clients strategies for dealing with insomnia and nightmares. Providing clients with psychoeducation on insomnia can provide a good entry point for exploring nightmares and asking about trauma.
- Recommend or implement evidence-based trauma treatments.

Chapter 8

The Cultural-Spiritual Dimension

Humans seek meaning. If you doubt this, try hanging out with a happy 4-year-old who has discovered that annoying three-letter word *why*. Like the song that never ends, the question "Why?" goes on forever. Parents often resort to "Because I said so," but persistent children follow up with, "But why? Why do you say so?"

Being curious and wondering why are normal human mental states that vary with age and context. Most young children focus on immediate explanations for why things are the way they are. In adolescence, cognitive development and other factors sometimes contribute to a shift in thinking to questions like "What's the point of life?" or "Why should I keep on living?" For individuals, the question of whether to continue living may come and go with more or less force throughout the life span. The natural human need and capacity for meaning bring the cultural-spiritual dimension front and center.

When, in the course of living, meaning breaks down or disappears, the value of life comes into question. Camus (1955) wrote,

> There is but one truly serious philosophical problem, and that is suicide. Judging whether life is or is not worth living amounts to answering the fundamental question of philosophy. All the rest—whether or not the world has three dimensions, whether the mind has nine or twelve categories—comes afterwards. (p. 11)

The question of meaning gets to the heart of human consciousness. Some, like Viktor Frankl, suggest that meaning is something we search for, that it exists outside the human mind. Others, like Simone de Beauvoir, argue that humans are meaning makers, taking in stimuli through the senses and constructing meanings. Either way, or somewhere in the middle, meaning matters, whether out there or personally and socially constructed (for a description of the differences between constructionism and social constructionism, see J. Sommers-Flanagan, 2015a).

For many, a meaningless life is not worth living. But if life has meaning—even a vague, illusive, difficult to articulate, intermittent meaning that is harder to catch than a butterfly—the will to live continues. Meaning is not an all-or-nothing proposition, and meaningfulness is not exclusively spiritual. Clients with collectivist cultural perspectives usually view meaning as not only spiritual but also derived from family and community (Sue et al., 2019). The ideas of how much meaning is enough to make life worth living or which particular experiences confer meaning are individual matters. In this chapter we focus on counseling methods and interactions that can contribute to meaning and motivation for life in people who are feeling suicidal.

Working in the Cultural-Spiritual Dimension

Many clients find comfort, identity, and solace in their cultural and spiritual beliefs and practices. Others are tormented by the same beliefs and practices, convinced they are sinners or failures in the eyes of their cultures, communities, or deities. Sometimes people decide to remove themselves from religious or cultural communities because of oppression, abuse, or a crisis of faith. The cultural-spiritual dimension includes complex, powerful, multidimensional beliefs, values, and practices that protect individuals from suicide. These same factors can increase suicide risk or have little bearing on suicidality (Lawrence et al., 2016).

Although spiritual and religious beliefs confer meaning, some clients hold secular beliefs with equal meaning and power. Clients with few connections to specific cultural or religious traditions still experience joy and ecstasy when acting on deeply held values. We have worked with clients who have no links to traditional cultural and spiritual ways of being but who are profoundly uplifted or driven to despair when their values related to specific prosocial human enterprises, such as social justice, climate change, animal rights, and/or political positions, are violated or vindicated (Kistler et al., 2017).

Key Cultural-Spiritual Issues to Address

At the risk of oversimplification, in this chapter we boil everything down to three main cultural-spiritual factors. These factors can contribute to or buffer clients from suicidality:

- Religious or spiritual disconnection and connection
- Meaninglessness and meaning fulfillment
- Cultural disconnection, dislocation, and acculturative stress

Next, we briefly discuss these key issues. Later in the chapter we identify interventions and provide cases that illustrate methods for working with cultural and spiritual issues.

Religious or Spiritual Disconnection and Connection
Religiosity and frequency of church attendance generally function as protective factors against suicide, but some studies show no protective relationship (Lawrence et al., 2016). Research on whether integrating religion and spirituality into treatment facilitates recovery from suicidal crises is also mixed (Plöderl et al., 2020). To make matters more confusing, occasionally religiosity, church attendance, and integrating spirituality into treatment are linked to "less optimal outcomes" (Plöderl et al., 2020, p. 95). In particular, religiosity appears to function as a risk factor for sexually diverse youth (Shearer et al., 2018). Because religion and spirituality have unique influences on suicidality, you should approach religion and spirituality carefully, nonjudgmentally, and with openness to each client's personal beliefs and experiences (Johnson, 2013).

Many religions consider suicide sinful. The notion that anyone who dies by suicide will be damned to hell might serve as a protective factor for some clients, but it also causes great shame, thus making suicidal ideation more difficult to openly disclose and talk about constructively. Although there is no scientific evidence regarding whether death by suicide results in going to hell, we strongly believe that struggling with thoughts about suicide is a normal part of the human experience and that talking about suicidal thoughts can help.

Telling clients to resist or turn off their suicidal thoughts can backfire. Directly discussing suicidal thoughts is more likely to help clients understand the meaning of their thoughts and actively pursue health and wellness. One exception to this general rule: For clients who hold strong cultural, religious, or personal beliefs against suicide, openly talking about suicidal ideation might increase shame. If this is the case, two options are reasonable:

1. Agree to talk with your clients about suicide without directly using the word *suicide*. One strategy is to focus on factors that increase your clients' reasons for living or enthusiasm for life. You can initially touch on suicide (as you must) but then refocus on wellness and positive psychology and agree to monitor suicidality using words that are acceptable to your clients.
2. Help your clients see the robust rationale for talking about suicide as a means of preventing suicide. If religious clients understand that talking about suicide will reduce the probability of suicide, they may experience less shame.

Clients who want to stay connected or reconnect to religious communities can benefit from your support as they pursue this direction. Clients who need to disconnect from or replace their religious community will also benefit from your empathy and acceptance. Decisions about your clients' religious beliefs are not yours to make, but you can help them weigh the religious pros and cons, facilitate their decision-making, and offer compassion when emotional pain emerges.

Meaningless and Meaning Fulfillment
Prominent existentialists emphasize that meaningfulness is linked to the will to live and meaninglessness contributes to the wish to die. As Friedrich Nietzsche noted (as paraphrased by Frankl, 1962), people who have a "why" to live can bear most any "how." The alternative statement might be "People who believe they have no reason to live may be especially prone to suicidality." Either direction, it is clear that—whether you are working with veterans, clients with eating disorders, or any other population—meaning confers resilience, whereas meaninglessness increases vulnerability to suicide (Corona et al., 2019; Marco et al., 2019).

Meaninglessness can be fleeting or chronic. Meaninglessness or existential nihilism can be triggered by interpersonal losses (e.g., the death of a loved one) or other significant losses or upheavals (e.g., job loss). Losing loved ones to suicide can trigger suicidal ideation in survivors (Sands et al., 2011). When exploring meaning, you may need to align with your clients' perceptions that life has no meaning while simultaneously working to engage clients on other fronts so that possibly meaning can reemerge from one of the other dimensions.

Cultural Disconnection, Dislocation, and Acculturative Stress
Cultural sensitivity, humility, and competence have become de rigueur in counseling, as they should be. However, like nearly everything about counseling, being culturally sensitive and humble is harder than it seems. Instead of making assumptions or judgments about clients' cultural or intersectional identities, culturally sensitive counselors are aware of and bracket their biases and values (Kocet & Herlihy, 2014). This means that no matter your biases, you listen and inquire with a warm, interested, and receptive attitude.

Cultural disconnection, dislocation, and accumulated acculturative stress can trigger suicidal thoughts and impulses. Major disconnections and dislocations, such as "the immigration experience and economic disadvantage such as poverty or low social status, education, or income [have] been linked to increased suicide risk" (Chu et al., 2017, p. 1353). Minor cultural disconnection and dislocation also confers risk. For example, collectivist, tribal, and family values among Asian American and Native American college students can contribute to distress around academic performance.

Cultural identity is not limited to racial or ethnic origins. People form identities and join communities with others for a myriad of reasons—religion, political beliefs, military status, disabilities, sexualities, occupation, giftedness, music, athletics, sciences, and much more. As writers, thinkers, activists, and many others have noted, one way to think about multiple identities is through intersectionality (Crenshaw, 1989, 1991). Cultural, racial, ethnic, class, gender, and sexual identities are rarely singular. For many or most clients, multiple identities intersect and manifest at different times and in different situations.

Micro- and macroaggressions can accumulate and increase the burden of stress and illness among specific populations. In particular, Black Americans, Native Americans, and individuals who identify as lesbian, gay, bisexual, transgender, queer, or questioning (or other sexual and gender minorities; LGBTQ+) are at greater risk for disease and illness due to systemic discrimination and oppression (Flentje et al., 2019; Ginicola et al., 2017; Indian Health Service, 2019; Nobles et al., 2016). Perceived inclusion in or exclusion from larger social or spiritual groups can powerfully affect self-image and can increase or decrease emotional distress. Sometimes clients may disavow who they really are and play along with social rules to avoid discrimination. Listening closely for systemic discrimination is an important part of clinical assessment and treatment planning.

Many individuals enter the helping professions intending to support and advocate for oppressed populations. In so doing, you should be prepared to work with people whose perspective is at odds with yours. For example, it is not unusual for some White, Christian males to feel oppressed by terms like *White fragility* and *White privilege*. You may not immediately understand where they are coming from, because, from an external perspective, White, Christian males have substantial advantage. If you use logic to explain to them the definitions of privilege and fragility, you are unlikely to convince them that their subjective distress is irrational. Instead, returning to empathy and listening for what hurts and how you can help creates a reasonable culturally sensitive foundation. One reminder to take everyone's pain seriously is the fact that, ironically, privileged White males (along with Native American and Alaska Native young adults) generally die by suicide at the highest rates in the United States (see Chapter 3; Curtin & Hedegaard, 2019). Although cultural oppression contributes to stress, illness, and suicide—and requires therapeutic advocacy—culturally sanctioned and socially constructed power and privilege offers no protection from suicide.

Interventions in the Cultural-Spiritual Dimension

For nearly a century, mental health professionals have mostly ignored or pathologized clients' cultural identities and spiritual/religious issues. Nevertheless, cultural and spiritual realities still held power. When conducting assessments, developing treatment plans, or intervening with clients, the big question is this: Do your clients' religious, spiritual, and cultural values, practices, and experiences contribute to emotional and psychological distress or provide emotional comfort and relief?

Opening the Door to Spiritual and Religious Discussions

Clients who have issues with religion are often willing to talk about their issues and may do so with intensity and passion. Asking directly or inviting input is essential, because if you do not know where your clients stand on religious issues, you cannot understand how religion or spirituality might work to support counseling or to increase distress. Starting with an open question along with a normalizing frame is recommended: "We haven't talked much about religion or spirituality. I know sometimes religion or spirituality can be a positive force in life and sometimes it can be negative. How is it for you?"

Clients may be willing to talk about their religious beliefs, experiences, and practices, or they may be defensive and reluctant. If, as in the preceding example, you ask an open question, you may get an uncensored response. One potential challenge is accepting your clients' spiritual strengths or wounds without judgment. Emotional topics—such as abortion, capital punishment, immigration, racism, tolerance, LGBTQ+ concerns, sexual infidelity, women's roles, and the right to suicide—can cause you to flinch with judgment. Nevertheless, your approach is to collaborate with your client to explore their spirituality "rather than rejecting the client's beliefs and imposing an alternative that [you deem] superior" (Cashwell & Young, 2020, p. 3).

Clients who are suicidal may be sensitive to and anticipate your judgment. If clients expect you to judge them, they are also probably expecting judgment from others outside counseling. From a psychodynamic or interpersonal perspective, your clients' expectations of judgment may represent transference; using a psychoanalytic model, you might let those transference reactions build for later interpretation. However, if you are operating from a practical (and strengths-based) perspective, you will be active and directive in expressing acceptance, avoiding judgment, and providing affirmation or validation. You can do this with four steps:

1. *Use nondirective listening skills to show acceptance:* "I hear you saying you've felt hurt and wounded by religious judgments in the past."
2. *Express empathy for the expectation of judgment:* "When you've been judged like you have, it's normal to expect judgment from almost everyone, including me."
3. *Provide reasonable reassurance:* "My goal in our work is to be accepting of you and your values and beliefs."
4. *Offer an invitation for ongoing feedback:* "If I say or do something that feels uncomfortable, or if you feel judged by me, I hope you'll tell me and we can talk about it, because that's not the sort of counselor I want to be with you."

Exploring Intersectionality

Working with intersectionality in counseling requires an attitude of openness and affirmation and a willingness to partner with clients to explore identity issues that may be deep and emotional. In some cases, clients may not be fully aware of how their multiple identities contribute to their suicidal distress or provide them with strength and resilience. Clinical work around multiple racial, ethnic, sexual, gender, ability, and other identities is complex; counselor respect and sensitivity when exploring these issues is essential.

The Multicultural and Social Justice Counseling Competencies (Ratts et al., 2016) identify four developmental domains that lead to multicultural competence:

1. Counselor self-awareness
2. Client worldview
3. The counseling relationship
4. Counseling and advocacy interventions

Speaking specifically to intersectionality, Ali and Lee (2019) articulated the complexity and challenge of achieving competency: "Counselors who exhibit cultural competency must be able to examine their own identity components, analyze the spectrum of privilege to marginalization for each domain, and assess how their identities interact with one another" (p. 512). Developing the awareness that Ali and Lee recommend is a tall order for counselors.

Developing an awareness of intersectionality can be a similarly tall order for clients, requiring reflection, contemplation, and exploration. Given this challenge, using visual activities (e.g., a colorable pie chart to explore identities within individuals; Ali & Lee, 2019) can help make abstract intersectional identities clearer. For example, while exploring "What are the biggest parts of you and your identity?" counselors and clients can articulate several identities, accompanying values, and proportional significance. In addition, counselors can explore questions like, "In what situations does your identity of being a transgender person increase your feelings of being strong and well?" and, "In what situations does your identity of being a transgender person cause you distress and activate suicidal thoughts?" Exploring where, when, and how strength and suicidality emerge in connection with core identities can facilitate treatment planning (e.g., "How can we increase the frequency, power, and influence of the times when your Asian identity adds to your strength and resiliency?").

One method we have used with success is to use a large gingerbread person to label and color different internalized and intersectional identities. In that way, we and our clients can collaboratively explore what situational or systemic factors cause pain to specific parts of the self (see Adames et al., 2018, and Ali & Lee, 2019, for more information about purposeful and creative exploration of intersectionalities; see Figure 8.1).

You can also learn more about your clients' intersectional views of themselves with a reassuring query like, "People belong to many different groups. We're born into some, choose some, and sometimes just end up in some. I'm wondering how you define yourself." If your client needs more specifics, you could add, "I mean, when you think of yourself, what labels do you use?"

Dealing With Moral Injury: A Case Example

In recent years, language around military trauma has shifted from a narrow focus on posttraumatic stress disorder (PTSD) to a more holistic definition that includes moral injury (Litz et al., 2009). *Moral injury* is defined as "a syndrome of shame, self-handicapping, anger, and demoralization that occurs when deeply held beliefs and expectations about moral and ethical conduct are transgressed" (Gray et al., 2017, p. 383). Suicidality is a by-product of moral injury (Bryan et al., 2018).

As a group, military veterans have one of the highest suicide rates in the United States. Young veterans are at particularly high

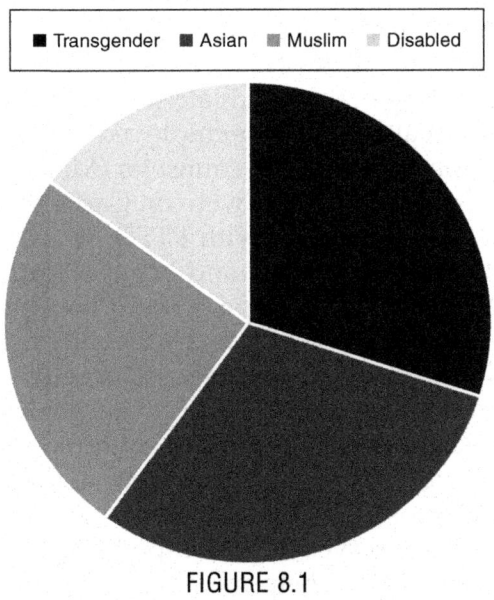

FIGURE 8.1
Intersectional Identities

risk, at more than 3 times the overall national average (44.5/100,000; U.S. Department of Veterans Affairs, 2019). This rate is equal to or higher than rates for other high-risk groups, such as Native American young adults and older White males. Focusing on the spiritual fallout from military combat as a distinct part of PTSD can complement traditional treatments for military veterans who are experiencing suicidality.

Spiritual, religious, and philosophical knowledge is foundational for understanding moral injury. As a strengths-based provider who is open to treating the whole person (including spirituality and moral injury), you may need to look beyond mainstream approaches to treating suicidality in veterans. Alternative health care methods, spiritual direction, and indigenous treatment approaches may be useful. We use the case of Carl to illustrate how counselors might integrate alternative or indigenous treatments within a traditional medical system.

Incorporating Indigenous and Alternative Treatments
Carl Flores was a 22-year-old, single, biracial, cisgender, heterosexual Army veteran. He received an honorable discharge after 4 years of service, including three tours of duty in Afghanistan. Carl experienced two firefights, one of which ended in him shooting and killing three enemy combatants. Upon returning to civilian life, Carl was seen for psychiatric and neuropsychological assessments through a Veterans Affairs hospital outpatient clinic. The hospital used an integrated behavioral health (IBH) model. During Carl's second psychiatric appointment, the psychiatrist introduced him to Mitch, a licensed mental health counselor employed at the clinic. Together, the psychiatrist, the mental health counselor (Mitch), a clinical social worker, and a neuropsychologist were on Carl's IBH team.

Initially Carl was diagnosed with PTSD, was given a prescription for an SSRI antidepressant, and began cognitive processing therapy with Mitch. (Cognitive processing therapy is a cognitive behavioral approach to treating trauma frequently used with military veterans.) Carl's neuropsychological assessment was clean. After 3 months of treatment with medication and cognitive processing therapy, Carl acknowledged improvement but remained agitated, interpersonally oversensitive, intermittently suicidal, and, in his words, "spiritually lost." Carl stated, "I can't shake the feeling that I'm a bad man who deserves to get jumped and killed. There must be something else that can help me." Carl also told Mitch that he wanted to discontinue the medications. Carl and Mitch discussed alternative treatments, and Mitch consulted with Carl's IBH team; all team members, including the psychiatrist, agreed that Carl would taper and discontinue his medication contingent on his continuing in supportive counseling, weekly progress updates from the counselor to the team, and engagement in alternative therapies. Mitch's job included closely monitoring Carl's depression, suicidal ideation, and PTSD symptoms. Carl completed a checklist every week, discussed his symptoms with Mitch, and described his responses to the therapeutic activities.

The alternative treatments for Carl included a weekly drop-in yoga and mindfulness meditation group at a local vet center. Mitch also told Carl, "We've got a small group of guys who have found peace and calm up on the Salish-Kootenai reservation. They're joining some Native American veterans and doing some indigenous ceremonial stuff. Several guys have said they're really liking the sweat lodge experience. It's different. But if you're interested, I can connect you with the Native American vet who's organizing this."

After 3 months of alternative treatments, Carl's scores on the symptom checklist were virtually 0. Each week he faithfully met with his counselor and reported, much to his amazement, that yoga and meditation offered him concrete coping skills while his sweat lodge experiences made him feel "more spiritually centered than ever." Consistent with empirical research on treatment for moral injury, Carl was able to use the indigenous sweat lodge experience to begin forgiving himself for moral transgressions he had committed during his deployments (Wortmann et al., 2017). Ongoing interprofessional communication regarding progress made possible Carl's transition away from traditional medically oriented treatments.

For Carl, the traditional treatment strategies were modestly helpful but limited. In his debrief at the end of counseling, he described the alternative treatments as profound. He believed the alternative treatments gave him new perspectives, vitality, inner peacefulness, and hope beyond what he had imagined possible. Carl became a staunch advocate for alternative treatments through his vet center. Eventually he completed his bachelor's degree and enrolled in a master's program so he could become a professional helper.

Addressing Religious Excommunication or Exile

Religions can condemn, excommunicate, and exile people for many reasons. One common example of religious alienation or exile occurs when people are judged based on sexuality. When religious authorities or communities condemn LGBTQ+ individuals as sinners, the fallout can go in several directions: The LGBTQ+ person may feel anger toward religious authority and move toward rejecting religion; the person may feel doubt, shame, and anger toward the self and move toward self-rejection or shame; or the person may seek input from other sources to cope with the disturbing judgment.

Religious or spiritual ostracism is emotionally painful and destabilizing. To regain balance and perspective, clients may need to break away from church or religious membership. Later they may return. Other times, the break is permanent. Permanent breaks may be painful but also may be a relief. If you are working with clients who have experienced religious or spiritual ostracism, you will want to weave methods for helping them cope with their emotional reactions into the treatment plan. These methods may include increased social support (the interpersonal dimension), self-regulation skills training (the emotional and physical dimensions), and spiritual consultation or direction. If their previous faith connection was strong, excommunication may destabilize their personal identity. Supporting clients as they reconstruct their identity and pursue religious acceptance or grace is essential (see Case Vignette 8.1).

Working With Loss, Religion, and Passive Suicidal Ideation: A Case Example

Clients who are religious and suicidal sometimes become passively suicidal. They feel suicidal, but their religious beliefs stop them from actively considering suicide. We use the case of Jane, a 66-year-old White, cisgender, heterosexual woman, to illustrate how counselors can navigate passive suicidality and guide clients toward reengaging in life.

Jane came to counseling after the death of her second husband. Having experienced substantial grief after her first husband's tragic death, Jane was not motivated to do grief work a second time. She bluntly stated, "I've been through this before."

Although easy to engage, Jane showed little motivation for change. The counselor asked, "What gives you hope?" "What makes you laugh?" "With whom do you enjoy spending time?" and "What do you do for fun?" Jane responded blandly, "I love my friends, but I'm tired of being the person they're trying to cheer up. I'm tired of being the third wheel."

Case Vignette 8.1
Gay, Gray, and a New Identity

Don was a 53-year-old recently divorced, religious, and mostly closeted gay man who agreed to see a counselor on the recommendation of his friend, Ramon. Don had turned to Ramon because Ramon was one of the few openly gay people Don knew. After years of suspicion, Don's wife discovered his other life and initiated divorce proceedings. She was not vindictive and did not out Don to the couple's church family. She just told Don that she was tired of living a lie.

Ramon recommended a counselor who was a well-known ally to the LGBTQ+ community. Ramon thought that Don might be most comfortable with a nonjudgmental heterosexual male counselor. Here is a snippet of the counselor's initial interactions with Don.

> *Don:* Nancy divorced me. It was finalized last month. I can't attend church anymore. Being there is too painful. Nancy said we were living a lie. But I don't know how else to live. I'm too old. Old and gray. I might rather die than face this. Ramon said you'd understand.
>
> *Counselor:* You've been through a lot, Don. Lots of loss. Lots of questions about life. I'll do my best to understand you and your situation. My first thought is that it took guts to come talk to me, especially if you're wondering if you even want to live.
>
> *Don:* Thanks. You seem like a good guy, but I need to check. Am I safe talking with you?
>
> *Counselor:* [*sensing how new it was for Don to verbalize his sexual orientation*] Of course. What you say here stays here. Don, I can tell you've learned to be very careful. Counseling is a safe place to talk about whatever attractions you may have. What you say here is confidential. But if you're actively suicidal, we'll need to talk about how you can be safe. I already respect your willingness to come in and your caution and thoughtfulness.

If you have worked with older clients who have been long closeted, you will recognize why Don was more concerned about a confidentiality breach regarding his sexuality than he was about his suicidality. In response to this initial encounter and the counselor's acceptance and reassurance, Don visibly relaxed and was able to begin counseling in earnest, exploring his suicidality along with new losses and opportunities in his life.

Exploring Religion and Suicidality
Along with grief symptoms, Jane spoke longingly of the "joy" of dying and moving on. She wished to go to sleep and not wake up. When Jane said she believed death would be joyful, it was easy for the counselor to make a bridge to asking about her religious beliefs.

Counselor: I don't know if you have religious or spiritual beliefs. If you do, I'm wondering how they fit in with you feeling that it might be joyful to pass on.
Jane: Well, it's conflicting there. I believe in heaven. And I'm Catholic. I have almost a childlike belief that you really do meet up with people you love when you get there. My dad and my husbands will be there waiting at the gate. I've always enjoyed that scenario. I don't try to probe it intellectually because I don't want to not have that scenario in my mind.

Jane was clear that she did not want to analyze or alter her beliefs. If the counselor had tried questioning her religious beliefs, there would have been a good chance Jane would not have returned for a second session. While discussing religion, Jane explained that Catholics do not believe in suicide. Despite her Catholic suicide prohibitions, Jane enjoyed the image of "floating up" to Saint Peter at the Pearly Gates. Jane's religious beliefs mostly contributed comfort and had an inhibiting effect on her suicidality.

Using an Existential 6-Months-to-Live Question
After exploring Jane's religious beliefs, the counselor used an existential 6-months-to-live intervention inspired by Yalom's (1980) work with terminally ill cancer patients.

Counselor: I just thought of an interesting line of questioning. Do you mind if I just go ahead and ask you?
Jane: Sure. Of course.
Counselor: What if you had 6 months to live? What would you want to do? What would be the most meaningful way that you could live that last 6 months?
Jane: Now that's a neat thought. That could get me excited. Like I'm planning for the short term, not trying to figure out how I'm going to live for another 25 years with a heavy heart. I would probably travel some.
Counselor: Where would you go?

Jane: Oh, Italy, Greece, Mississippi, Louisiana, listen to Cajun music. I can think of a million places. Just the thought makes me a little excited.
Counselor: Yeah, I can see that.
Jane: Along the way, I'd connect with friends I haven't seen in a while. Rather than just relying on friends around here to bolster me up, I'd reconnect with folks whom I cherish but don't see regularly.
Counselor: So if you had 6 months to live, you'd connect with friends who are around, travel, and reconnect with friends you've lost touch with.
Jane: Yes! I can even imagine it being fun.

Once Jane began focusing on her final 6 months, several things happened. Her mood lifted. She began talking about meaningful ways to spend her time. As she answered, the counselor used solution-focused questions to draw Jane out about what exactly she would do, whom she would see, and other important details (Murphy, 2015). Jane's affect brightened and she displayed increased energy and motivation.

After a few minutes, Jane moved past talking about traveling and focused on activities she could immediately start doing in her life, like art. She said, "I've been thinking about doing art during retirement, but the art I pictured myself making was vibrant, and because I don't feel vibrant, that doesn't seem right. But maybe taking art lessons would open that creativity faucet a tiny bit. Maybe vibrant colors could be a way to express grief."

For Jane, traditional grief work sounded unpleasant. Although her religious beliefs provided comfort, she still experienced passive suicidal ideation. Instead of focusing on improving her affect, increasing her religious activities, or countering her suicidal thoughts, the existential 6-months-to-live question refocused Jane on meaning and pleasure in the short term. The 6-months-to-live intervention is not a great fit for every client, but it moved Jane away from resigning herself to, in her words, "soldiering on toward death" (for Jane's treatment plan, see Table 8.1).

Exploring, Framing, and Enhancing Meaning

In *Love's Executioner*, Irvin Yalom (1989) described a simple activity that evokes deep emotions. He has clients pair up and repeatedly ask each other, "What do you want?" He wrote,

TABLE 8.1
Treatment Plan for Jane—Cultural-Spiritual Dimension

Problem	Goals and Strengths[a]	Interventions/Plan
1. Jane is grieving and passively suicidal.	1. Jane will reengage in positive life activities.	1. Jane will use art to express her grief.
2. Jane is unable to identify meaningful activities in her life.	2. Jane will identify meaningful activities and begin engaging in them.	2. Have Jane explore the 6-months-to-live question and generate activities she wants to experience.

[a]Strengths: Jane has a strong religious identity that provides her with emotional stability.

They call out to those who are forever lost—dead or absent parents, spouses, children, friends: "I want to see you again." "I want your love." "I want to know you're proud of me." "I want you to know I love you and how sorry I am I never told you." "I want you back—I am so lonely." "I want the childhood I never had." "I want to be healthy—to be young again. I want to be loved, to be respected. I want my life to mean something. I want to accomplish something. I want to matter, to be important, to be remembered." (p. i)

Longing for connection, meaning, love, and forgiveness is central to being human. No one wants to be irrelevant. Everyone wants a purpose.

This general longing for connection and meaning is universal but also cultural and individual (Sue et al., 2019). Exploring, framing, and enhancing meaning in clients' lives requires collaboratively translating the culturally universal to the culturally and individually specific. Like Yalom's exercise, it involves finding ways to ask, "What do you want?" Undoubtedly, some clients will answer that question in ways that are unrealistic or in ways we cannot understand. If so, you can continue the exploration and seek mutual understanding (e.g., "I hear you saying you'd like your father to be alive again. Thanks. I'm writing that down. I want to learn more about you, so let's keep going. What else do you want in your life?").

For Asian clients, Wubbolding (2000) recommended using less directive questioning about existential wants. He suggested asking, "What are you looking for?" or "Would that be a minus or a plus?" (p. 181). Wubbolding's guidance illustrates subtle ways to modify language and questioning to interact with culturally diverse clients.

Meaning seeking and meaning making are lifelong human enterprises. Instead of arguing with clients who claim life has no meaning, consider noting the strength required to explore meaninglessness. Professional training and credentials will not shield you from these profound questions. When clients doubt the meaning of life, we as counselors may start questioning the meaning of life as well.

In a professional video, Yalom (Yalom & Yalom, 2019) worked with a young woman whose grandmother had recently died. The death affected the young woman in profound ways. She no longer saw any point in living, because it all ends anyway. Among other gentle observations and queries, Yalom used the example of going to a party. "Parties are fun, but they wouldn't be fun if they never ended, would they?" The young woman found this statement illuminating and comforting.

Many existentially oriented philosophers point out that death is what gives life meaning. As Tibetan Buddhist Sogyal Rinpoche wrote, "Death is like a mirror in which the true meaning of life is reflected" (see Lagacé, 2020). When people have suicidal thoughts because of a dearth of meaning, they may find the mirror blank. Counselors cannot fill in the mirror, or create meaning, but they can help pinpoint problems and provide encouragement in the meaning-seeking process.

Both Don and Jane had strong religious beliefs. Jane's Catholicism pushed her in two directions: She viewed death as joyful but suicide as forbidden. It is interesting that Jane did not mention anything religious in response to the 6-months-to-live question. Perhaps this was because she was already at peace with her religious views. With her faith foundation intact, when faced with 6 months to live, she focused on interpersonal and creative meaning experiences.

In contrast, Don's home congregation was an evangelical Protestant denomination that takes a hard line on sexual diversity and suicide. After working in counseling for many months, Don's counselor reflected on Don's longing for meaningful, spiritual connection and growth. The counselor urged Don to consider how to honor this deep longing. Don decided to try attending an open and inclusive congregation. He even convinced Nancy, his former wife, to attend with him occasionally; it is there that he met a man who later became a life partner (for another look at loss, see Case Vignette 8.2).

Asking and Learning About Cultural Perspectives on Suicide: A Case Example

In previous chapters, we described Matthew, a 28-year-old member of the Lakota Sioux tribe. In the following exchange, Matthew's counselor learned more about how the Lakota Sioux culture views suicide:

Case Vignette 8.2
Loss and Possible Replacement

The saying "Nature abhors a vacuum" is relevant to meaning. Sources of meaning can suddenly disappear; emptiness and pain follow. Consider this condensed exchange between a counselor and a 55-year-old single Latinx woman:

> *Maria:* I took care of my mother for 10 years. Her death makes me feel like I don't matter. Watching her die was painful. If life means nothing in the end, to me, it means nothing now.
>
> *Counselor:* That's a huge loss Maria. Losing your mom has swung the spotlight on heavy questions. Like, what's the meaning of life?
>
> *Maria:* I don't know. People get old and die. That's it. What's the point?
>
> *Counselor:* Maria, you have courage. It's hard to look at death and meaning. I'm impressed. I bet that courage shows itself in other parts of your life. Do you see yourself that way? Courageous?
>
> *Maria:* Not really. But maybe. I guess I face things.
>
> *Counselor:* So I wonder what it would be like for you to use that courage to create something new in your life. Something to hold onto while you sort things out.
>
> *Maria:* New? Like what?
>
> *Counselor:* I'm not sure. What just came into your mind when I said "something new"?
>
> *Maria:* [*looking a little shy*] A dog.
>
> *Counselor:* [*smiling*] A dog?
>
> *Maria:* Mom was allergic. I wanted a dog, but we couldn't have one. Now that she's gone, I don't know. Dogs are work. But I think I'd love a puppy.
>
> *Counselor:* Yeah, it is hard to know whether something new in your life would be nice or not. Dogs are a hassle. But you can realistically weigh the pros and the cons of having a dog now without worrying about your mom's allergies.

In this abbreviated exchange, the counselor was listening for strengths that might have led Maria toward meaningful activities. The counselor did not try to convince Maria that life was meaningful; she gently pushed Maria to contemplate small things to reconstruct meaning.

Counselor: As you talk about suicide, I find myself wondering what suicide means to you and your tribe. I know for some cultures, suicide is dishonorable or immoral, but I don't know how it's viewed in your culture. Do you mind sharing that?

Matthew: No problem. One way we look at it is that we've had a lot of our rights taken from us. That's one thing you can't take from us. Our life is ours to give to the Creator, to Wakan Tanka, our God. So when it's our time, it's our choice.

Counselor: So it comes down to preserving the right to choose?

Matthew: I was probably 9 years old when my best friend committed suicide. And it brings the community together. We had a big honoring, a big feast for his family and for him. There were many days of celebrating. It brings the family back together. I had another friend do it after that because he couldn't graduate high school, and he wanted his family to come back together, so he committed suicide. He just felt like it was going to bring his family back together.

Matthew openly shared his tribe's beliefs about suicide. Afterward, he described a childhood filled with loss and suicide. He shared that some people on his reservation see suicide as a means of bringing families together. Later he shared his anger about that view. Eventually he and his counselor talked about alternative (and better) methods of Matthew bringing family and community together, including ways Matthew could reduce suicide in his community.

Reconnection, Reconciliation, or Reconstruction

T. S. Eliot (1943) wrote, "We shall not cease from exploration, and the end of all our exploring will be to arrive where we started and know the place for the first time" (p. 47). One reason people consider suicide is that they believe they no longer fit in their families or social circles. The suicidal impulse may be one of despair or one of anger over exclusion or intolerance. One way to reduce suicidality is to help clients return to relationships of value. Sometimes there is no way back, or going back would be dangerous or destructive. Nevertheless, using insight-oriented therapeutic approaches that prompt clients to look back on old relationships from new perspectives can clarify whether returning and knowing a place for the first time is a viable option.

Forgiveness

Forgiveness has powerful therapeutic potential (Enright & Fitzgibbons, 2015). Both interpersonal and spiritual forgiveness have been described as having a salutary influence on suicidality (Sansone et al., 2013). When clients forgive themselves and others, their suicidal thoughts and impulses sometimes fade away (Webb et al., 2015).

Tiffany was a White, cisgender, heterosexual woman in her mid-20s. Her personal history included volatile relationships and significant trauma. She joined a progressive church in her neighborhood and found a sense of belonging. She built a few close friendships for the first time in years and began dating a man she had met there. When he broke off the relationship, by her own description she went "totally ballistic." She stalked him, sent endless texts to mutual friends, and refused to let go. When he threatened a restraining order, she threatened to kill herself. In response, she reported that church got "cold" and people avoided contact with her. Pastor Cheryl intervened, suggesting that Tiffany see a counselor.

The counselor sensed Tiffany's longing to repair her church relationships. Using protocols from dialectical behavior therapy and educational materials on forgiveness (Enright, 2019), Tiffany's counselor helped her improve her interpersonal skills, reduce her expectations and demands, and seek forgiveness and reconnection. After 2 months of work, with Tiffany's permission, her counselor invited Pastor Cheryl to a counseling session. Tiffany rejoined her church community. With support, she accepted that her former boyfriend had moved on and was dating someone else.

In some cases, you may want to obtain your client's consent to contact reputable clergy and engage them in client care and safety planning. In other cases, there may be support groups to replace religious or spiritual groups that your client identifies as unhealthy. The religious and spiritual dimension overlaps significantly with the interpersonal dimension; your counseling efforts might involve actively helping clients find a new and supportive spiritual or religious community or empowering them to locate one on their own.

Reconstructing Spiritual Community Connections

Sometimes reconciliation, reconnection, and forgiveness are impractical or impossible. In the case of Don, the best option was to move on to a new and more supportive community and a more forgiving religious or spiritual doctrine. Experimenting with different church communities can be frightening; the support of a counselor can be essential.

Helping Clients Seek Higher Causes

The question of whether one has or has not lived a well-lived life can occur to anyone at any age, but it is likely more salient to people approaching or well into retirement age. Erik Erikson referred to this eighth (and final) stage as *ego integrity versus despair*. Suicide statistics reflect this dichotomy: Men older than age 65 die by suicide at the highest rate of all demographic groups. Although aging can bring wisdom and life satisfaction, it also involves decline and loss. As one of our clients said, "I didn't know the golden years simply meant I'd have more gold in my mouth than enamel." This particular 60-something client was struggling with many physical, mental, and social changes and challenges, not the least of which involved extensive dental care.

At age 93, Joan Erikson moved beyond Erik Erikson's final stage and wrote about the ninth stage of psychosocial development (Erikson & Erikson, 1998). She noted that as individuals reach their 80s, they begin losing physical and cognitive functioning along with social relationships. These losses activate a replaying of the previous eight stages of psychosocial development. Essentially, aging triggers regression across all psychosocial stages and life dimensions, eventually taking the elderly back to basic issues of trust versus mistrust. Joan Erikson believed that the resolution of this final stage centered on hope and on developing a basic trust in "the blessings" of life (p. 113).

As Joan Erikson noted, aging brings a panoply of developmental challenges. Such was the case for a 72-year-old Black cisgender heterosexual male named Duke, who came in for what he referred to as "grief counseling." Duke's granddaughter, Liz, died by suicide at age 17. Her death was linked to severe high school bullying. Duke was a Vietnam veteran and retired school principal. Joslyn, Duke's wife of 45 years, had died prior to Liz's suicide. Living alone, Duke ruminated on regrets that he had not somehow intervened to prevent Liz's death.

> *Counselor:* Tell me about what you'd like to accomplish in counseling, Duke.
>
> *Duke:* Relief, I guess. Thank God my wife didn't live to see this. She died from breast cancer 6 years ago. I'm not over that, exactly, but this thing with Liz. I don't know if I can keep going. I should have seen this coming.
>
> *Counselor:* Duke, this may be a tough question, but, for you, what would relief look like?
>
> *Duke:* You mean besides cashing it in myself?

At this point, the counselor realized a suicide inquiry/assessment was necessary and loosely followed the protocol from Chapter 3, collaboratively exploring Duke's suicidal thoughts, impulses, plans, hopes, and reasons for living. Duke did not have an active suicide plan and agreed to inform his counselor if that changed. In subsequent counseling sessions they continued to examine what relief would look like for Duke.

Counselor: In some ways, you'd be relieved if you didn't wake up every morning with regrets and didn't keep seeing people who look like Liz because it reminds you of losing her.

Duke: Yeah, but I don't want to forget her. I want to make up for failing her. I want to kill those racist bastards who bullied her.

Counselor: Sometimes revenge feels like it would bring relief.

Duke: Right. Do you blame me? How would you feel?

Counselor: Probably a lot like you. And no, I don't blame you. As I listen, I feel a little revenge impulse too. That said, I want to help you find the best way forward. I'm not sure revenge would provide lasting relief. I don't know. Maybe revenge is an answer, but maybe not.

Duke: You probably won't believe this, but I was reading about forgiveness. This guy had a daughter [who] was raped and killed, and he . . . [*Duke tears up a bit*] He actually started visiting the rapist in prison. He started some kind of educational thing.

Counselor: Your emotions around that story make me think we should talk more about what you're feeling. [*Note that the counselor is familiar with research on forgiveness in grief and recovery, but she stifles her enthusiasm and tries to stay neutral. The counselor wants Duke to decide about and lead the potential process of exploring forgiveness.*]

Duke: I feel like I'm a long way from doing anything remotely like that.

Counselor: That's a ways out. But something about it brings up emotion for you.

Duke: Yeah. I don't have much to lose. I'm sliding into the sunset. I don't want to be angry and bitter all the time. That makes me feel like ending it all. But that's no solution.

Duke continued counseling for more than a year. During the last few months, he reconnected with other retired school personnel. Together, they started an after-school tutoring program for students in need of safe shelter and supervision. Duke felt his volunteer work had a chance of preventing youth from becoming bullies as well as protecting youth from bullying. He said, "If I can just save one kid from getting bullied, now that would mean something."

Not all clients will be as eager to work, explore, and change as Duke. His case illustrates how growth following traumatic loss exists as a counterpoint to deterioration, discouragement, and suicide (Black et al., 2020; Martinčeková & Klatt, 2017).

Taking Baby Steps Toward Meaning

Many years ago, Gary, a graduate supervisee, was working with Annie, a depressed and impulse-ridden client who, at age 23, was still living with her mother. Annie discussed suicidal thoughts openly, almost manipulatively, but did not present as acutely suicidal. During their fifth session, Annie reported that her mother was drinking again and had lost another job. She suddenly stood up and stomped out of the building, shouting, "I can't deal with this anymore! Nothing matters! Nothing changes! Nothing!" Gary was uncertain of what to do. He could not remember any classes about what to do when clients who are passively suicidal abruptly leave a counseling session. What should he do? Call the police? Call us? Would Annie hurt herself?

Gary followed Annie out the door and down the sidewalk to see if he could get her to come back and finish their session. It was early spring, and there was still snow on the ground. Annie saw Gary following her. She paused and began kicking at the snow on the lawn. Gary approached cautiously. "There's no hope. Nothing changes," she said, breaking down in tears.

Gary had an inspiration. He knelt in the slushy snow, scraped it back, and uncovered the light green grass of early spring. "Look, Annie," he said with a gentle calmness he did not feel on the inside. "Things do change, but also, in a good way, some things don't change." Annie stared at Gary, kneeling in the snow, pointing at the uncovered earth. She squinted at the patch of green. "Yeah," she agreed finally. "Things change and they don't." Annie accompanied Gary back into the building, and they finished their session. See Wellness Practice 8.1 for your best possible self activity.

Wellness Practice 8.1
Your Best Possible Self

Some people see the glass half full. Others see the glass half empty. Still others just drink and savor the water without getting hung up on how much is in the glass. Obviously, there are many other responses, because some people spill the water, others find a permanent water source, and others skip the water and drink the wine or pop open a beer.

Reducing people to two personality types never works, but it never gets old either. The wellness practice for this chapter is an optimism activity developed by Dr. Laura King called Your Best Possible Self. Regardless of your spiritual or cultural values, practicing optimism is probably a good thing.

According to research, writing about your best possible self shows long-term health benefits, increases life satisfaction, increases positive affect, increases optimism, and improves your overall sense of well-being (Layous et al., 2013). Various versions of this activity are all over the internet, but here is what we advise:

- Spend 10 minutes a day for four consecutive days writing a narrative description of your best possible future self.
- Pick a point in the future and write about what you will be doing/thinking. Try to capture a vision of you being your most successful self or having accomplished your life goals.

This activity is very similar to the Adlerian Future Autobiography. Alfred Adler was often ahead of most people in his thinking, so we are not surprised that he advocated envisioning a positive future many decades ago. Undoubtedly, Adler saw the glass half full, sipped and savored his share, and then shared it with his community. We should all be more like Adler.

Concluding Comments

Humans automatically orient toward asking why. If clear answers are not forthcoming, rather than drop the topic, most people seek or create answers to their deeper questions. As a professional counselor, you should prepare yourself to partner with clients to ask and seek answers to life's big questions. There are many ways in which meaning, spirituality, religion, and culture—or the lack thereof—move clients toward or away from suicide. Your job is to identify and develop your clients' cultural and spiritual wellness.

Practitioner Guidance and Key Points to Remember

The depth and breadth of cultural-spiritual concerns that can come up in counseling is extensive. In this chapter, we described three key cultural-spiritual issues to address in counseling: (a) religious or spiritual disconnection and connection; (b) meaninglessness and meaning fulfillment; and (c) cultural disconnection, dislocation, and acculturative stress.

Interventions in the interpersonal dimension include the following:

- Use nondirective listening skills, acceptance, empathy, reassurance, and an invitation for feedback to open the door to talking about spirituality and religion in counseling.
- Be gentle, be collaborative, and use guidance from the Multicultural and Social Justice Counseling Competencies when exploring intersectionality and other deeply emotional identity issues.
- Consider using an IBH model and incorporating indigenous and alternative treatment approaches when working with clients who have experienced moral injury.
- When it is present, address religious excommunication.
- When clients have passive suicidal ideation and seem unmotivated to reengage in life, using an existential 6-months-to-live question may facilitate spiritual, religious, and meaning exploration.
- Partner with clients to explore and better understand their diverse cultural perspectives on suicide.
- When helping clients reconnect and reconcile with others from a religious community, consider forgiveness and new spiritual communities.
- Helping clients focus on higher causes can facilitate movement away from anger or preoccupation with loss.
- When clients are especially nihilistic, finding meaning in small things can be the best place to start.
- The positive psychology intervention Your Best Possible Self may be useful for instilling hope and optimism in you or your clients.

Chapter 9

The Behavioral Dimension

The behavioral dimension is the realm of action. Maybe you should sit down and let that sink in. Sitting down is a behavior. Letting something sink in is more cognitive. However, as we have noted before, the dimensions of being human are mostly distinct while at the same time endlessly entangled.

Research and practice in suicide prevention, assessment, and treatment tend to focus on suicidal ideation (Klonsky & May, 2014). Most risk factors in suicide prevention and treatment are linked to ideation. Klonsky and May (2014) wrote, "It may come as a surprise to some that so many oft-cited risk factors for suicide [i.e., mental disorders, hopelessness, and impulsivity] are in fact predictors of suicide ideation not predictors of the progression from ideation to attempt" (p. 3).

The work of Klonsky, May, and others (Joiner, 2005; O'Connor, 2011) supports a shift toward focusing on what moves (literally) clients past the suicidal thinking stage and into suicidal action. In this chapter, we explore the behavioral dimension of suicidality—a focus that Klonsky, as well as B. F. Skinner, would appreciate.

Working in the Behavioral Dimension

When times are difficult and life feels intolerable, many people think about suicide as an alternative to life. But most individuals, despite intense emotional and psychological pain, do not act on their suicidal thoughts. In fact, people often cling to life even in the face of great pain. Philosophers, suicidologists, and evolutionary biologists all point to the likelihood that humans are genetically predisposed toward survival (Glasser, 1998).

For a variety of biological, psychological, and environmental reasons, it is usually easier to get people to experiment with new behaviors than it is to get them to stop engaging in their old, habitual behaviors. As children, you may have been repeatedly told, "Don't smoke," "Don't drink," "Don't date that person," and "Don't you dare miss your curfew again." But often those admonitions did not stick. Given how difficult it is to successfully get people to comply with prohibitions makes the "Don't act on suicidal impulses" goal of this chapter an arduous task.

This chapter is less about telling people what not to do and more about helping them identify and act on alternative behaviors. Our aim is to stay primarily strengths based, helping clients flood their personal lives with positive behaviors. We will review and describe methods for building healthy behavior patterns, developing positive safety plans, and more.

Key Behavioral Issues to Address

The empirical research is thin, but several near-term predictors of suicidal behavior have been identified. These include (a) active suicide planning or intent, (b) dispositional pain insensitivity and acquired suicide capability, (c) impulsivity, and (d) access to lethal means (Joiner, 2005; Klonsky & May, 2015; O'Connor, 2011).

Suicide Planning or Intent

Suicidal ideation is common—especially among clients and students who are experiencing depressive symptoms, but nearly everyone who thinks about suicide chooses not to act on their thoughts.

Suicide planning is a step closer to action. When clients have suicide plans, their ideas have taken shape into potential behaviors. Clients who have plans that include greater specificity, greater lethality, more accessibility, and less chance of being prevented are typically at higher risk. Nevertheless, most clients who have suicide plans do not act on them.

Suicidal intent—although still in the realm of thought—implies the enactment of a plan. Suicidal intent is especially disturbing when it is associated with repeated suicide attempts or the rehearsal of specific suicide methods. Mentally rehearsing or physically practicing suicidal behaviors makes the manifestation of those behaviors more likely. However, when intent is high, planning and rehearsing may not be required; given an opportunity, clients with extremely high intent may spontaneously and impulsively jump from moving cars, dash into heavy traffic, throw themselves into bodies of water, or find whatever means they can to end their lives.

Clients with high suicidal intent sometimes require hospitalization and may need to be on safety watch. Pulling clients back from the edge of suicide and modifying their intent is frightening but potentially gratifying. If you work with clients who have extremely high intent, remember to focus on your own safety and find support for potential vicarious traumatization.

Suicide Desensitization or Acquired Capability

Some individuals are unusually fearless and sensation seeking from birth. O'Connor (2011) referred to this as having *dispositional pain insensitivity*. In contrast, other individuals, born with normal pain sensitivity and a normal aversion to death, can over time achieve what Joiner (2005) called *acquired capability*; this process is also called *suicide desensitization*. Joiner wrote, "The capability to act on (suicidal) desire is acquired over time through exposure to painful and provocative events" (p. 3).

The predisposition to fearlessness and a high pain tolerance likely have biogenetic roots (Klonsky & May, 2015). In such cases, psychosocial therapeutic strategies are limited. Identifying high-risk and high-vulnerability situations and activities and then working collaboratively with clients on appropriate coping strategies may be the best treatment option.

Clients who have acquired capability have become desensitized to suicide over time (Joiner, 2005). Desensitization can be unintentional or intentional. Repeated trauma or exposure to chronic physical pain can produce desensitization. Alternatively, self-mutilation and substance abuse and dependence are intentional behaviors that produce numbness and can reduce fear of pain and suicide.

Impulsivity

Clients who are highly impulsive tend to act suddenly, without planning, and without reflective contemplation. Impulsivity can be examined as a trait: Individuals who display a pattern of acting without planning and who do so across time and different circumstances have trait impulsivity. Impulsivity can also be situationally triggered; ingesting alcohol, being around certain people, or being in particular situations can magnify impulsivity.

Clients diagnosed with bipolar disorder, borderline personality disorder, and substance use disorders are more inclined toward impulsive behavior patterns and suicide. Effective treatments for impulsivity are limited. Some possibilities include (a) dialectical behavior therapy (Linehan, 1993), (b) lithium (Cipriani et al., 2013), and (c) individual or group treatment for substance abuse (López-Goñi et al., 2018).

Access to Lethal Means

Easy availability of lethal means increases suicide risk. Firearms are far and away the most lethal suicide method. Although firearms can quickly become a politicized issue, access to firearms unarguably magnifies suicide risk (Anestis & Houtsma, 2018). Other common and lethal suicide methods include poisoning (using pills or carbon monoxide) and suffocation/asphyxiation. Reducing access to lethal means or enhancing firearms safety are common strategies that reduce immediate suicide potential (Runyan et al., 2015).

Interventions in the Behavioral Dimension

Several approaches to counseling minimize cognition, instead focusing primarily on behavior change. These approaches include (a) behavioral activation for depression, (b) acceptance and commitment therapy, and (c) reality therapy. The common theme across these approaches is the emphasis on identifying behaviors that are valued, adaptive, or pleasant and then making plans to regularly engage in these activities. The behavioral theory of depression posits that if clients increase their valued, adaptive, and pleasant behaviors, they will obtain increased positive reinforcement from the world, which will lead to greater personal satisfaction, improved health, and positive moods. The following interventions are practical manifestations of the behavioral theory of depression.

Reasons for Living

For decades, suicide research mostly focused on psychopathology. In 1983, Linehan shifted the focus when she developed the Reasons for Living (RFL) inventory. Following Viktor Frankl's thinking, Linehan believed that studying individuals who experience profound distress and yet continue to embrace life could provide information about how clients can bear excruciating emotional distress and hope-depleting life circumstances.

The RFL includes 48 items; there is also an RFL for older adults (RFL-OA) with 69 items. Both instruments have good psychometric properties and include positive items linked to happiness, hope, and meaning as well as negatively worded items focusing on moral objections, fears of suicide, and social disapproval.

Developing a Personalized Version of the RFL
Emily was a 50-year-old lesbian woman and single mother living with her 11-year-old daughter, Gracie. She presented as anxious and depressed. She reported having lost trust in herself after discovering that her life partner had betrayed her. Emily acknowledged frequent and intense suicidal ideation along with intermittent suicidal intent ("Yes, I want to kill myself") and a specific and lethal plan (i.e., using her handgun). Emily also described a reason for living.

> *Emily:* I don't trust the decisions I make at work. I don't trust myself. I don't want to make mistakes with Gracie. She deserves a better mom and a better life. I'm ready to die, but I can't do it without hurting Gracie.
> *Counselor:* You're feeling miserable, you don't trust yourself, and I think you're saying that, if not for Gracie, you'd go ahead and kill yourself.
> *Emily:* I think I would.
> *Counselor:* And so you've got one reason to live.
> *Emily:* But that's all I've got.

The fact that Emily had a reason to live was good news, but when parents head down the behavioral track toward suicide and focus on children as their sole reason for living, they are vulnerable to engaging in murder-suicide. One immediate goal with Emily was to validate Gracie as a great reason for living while also expanding Emily's reasons for living beyond Gracie.

Using a collaborative approach, the counselor used Linehan's RFL to expand Emily's reasons for living. She introduced the RFL items, discussed them with Emily, and offered Emily a chance to critique and improve the RFL items. Although Emily resonated with a few items on the RFL, she labeled many of the items "stupid" and "too dramatic." As a person who took pride in her work, Emily was annoyed about the lack of work-related items on the RFL. The counselor thanked Emily for her insight and offered an assignment: "How about you take this questionnaire home and revise it. You can delete items and create new ones. I'm interested in you developing your own personal Reasons for Living inventory." At her next session, Emily unveiled a new questionnaire: She called it the "RFL-Emily." The RFL-Emily included Gracie but also much more.

Behavioral Activation

Behavioral activation evolved from Aaron Beck's cognitive therapy for depression (A. T. Beck, Rush, et al., 1979). Originally, as a part of cognitive therapy for depression, Beck and his colleagues included a component called *activity scheduling*. Later, N. S. Jacobson and colleagues (1996) renamed activity scheduling *behavioral activation* and compared its efficacy to that of other treatments for depression. Somewhat surprisingly, Jacobson found that behavioral activation—as a free-standing treatment—was as effective as other cognitive treatments in alleviating depression.

Behavioral activation focuses almost exclusively on increasing the rate of clients' pleasant activities. To make the process easier, Hindman (2018) of the Beck Institute recommended that practitioners "focus on valued or meaningful activities instead of, or in addition to pleasurable activities" (para. 3). Hindman pointed out that because depressed clients have trouble identifying pleasurable behaviors and often do not immediately feel pleasure in response to behavioral homework, orienting clients toward their values makes for a better starting place. Hindman recommended the following:

> We can obtain the client's values by listing different value categories and then asking the client to rate the strength of each category from 0 (not valuing it at all) to 10 (the most they can value something). The categories we include are work, self-education/learning, volunteering, intimacy, family, friendship, religion/spirituality, entertainment/recreation, and health/fitness. (para. 3)

Managing client expectations is crucial to behavioral activation. Initially, most clients report experiencing no pleasure when engaging in pleasurable activities. Reassuring clients that it may take a month or two before behavioral activation takes effect and then using progress monitoring—watching closely for the emergence of positive emotions—helps clients have more realistic expectations.

Countering Suicide Desensitization

Desensitization to suicide is challenging to understand and address in counseling. The most direct method for addressing desensitization is to partner with clients to develop a list of activities to avoid that might facilitate desensitizing behaviors. Such a list might include the following:

- No drinking or using drugs when alone
- No being alone after using drugs or alcohol
- No engaging in suicide rehearsal behaviors (e.g., progressive cutting, practice poisoning, Russian roulette)
- No careless storage of lethal suicide methods

The problem with generating a list of prohibitions is that it might be polarizing and ignite reactance. The key to using a list of prohibitions is to engage your client in the process and then brainstorm some alternative highly stimulating positive behaviors. For example, adding skydiving as a substitute for drug use and volunteer firefighting for Russian roulette can orient clients toward positive fearlessness. Although a list of prohibitions might be useful, when clients are regularly using methods (e.g., alcohol, drugs, cutting, suicide rehearsal) that increase desensitization and fearlessness, counselors may need to pursue hospitalization or engage family, friends, or other supportive people to assist with lethal means restriction and safety planning.

Addictions Treatment

One prominent theoretical perspective on suicide is that suicide involves a behavioral escape from the self or from failure (Baumeister, 1990). Examples of suicide as an escape behavior include suicides that occur following highly publicized failures, exceptionally shameful behaviors, or legal sentences to death or imprisonment.

Addiction is another behavior pattern that clients use to escape from painful realities. Drug abuse and addiction also create shame, especially when clients are repeatedly making efforts at recovery and repeatedly failing. When suicides occur in the context of drug addiction, they might have been efforts to escape from facing the reality of addiction. Individuals who are in recovery and then relapse may be at heightened risk for suicide.

Addiction and suicide are often linked. However, addiction alone is not strongly associated with suicide. In contrast, addiction plus another diagnosable mental disorder (e.g., major depression, bipolar disorder, attention-deficit/hyperactivity disorder, or a personality disorder) confers significantly greater risk (Penney et al., 2012). Clients who are addicted to two or more substances or who have gambling problems along with their substance addictions are also more prone to suicide (Simoneau et al., 2017).

Acceptance, social support, and forgiveness are central components of addiction treatment (Webb et al., 2015). Many individuals with substance problems find great comfort in the acceptance, interpersonal support, and spiritual meaning associated with 12-step programs, but, as is always the case, one treatment approach does not fit everyone. If you are working with clients who are suicidal and have addiction issues, you need to closely collaborate with your clients to determine the best fit for alcohol, drug, or other addiction treatments (see Case Vignette 9.1).

Lethal Means Restriction (Safety)

Firearm availability or easy access to other lethal means is significantly linked to death by suicide (Bryan & Rudd, 2018). Access to lethal means is especially important because acute suicidal crises tend to be brief. If guns, razor blades, pills, or other means are not

Case Vignette 9.1
Outdoor Addiction Treatment

James was working as an addictions counselor at a residential vocational training center. Part of his employment duties involved engaging 16- to 24-year-olds in group counseling. Although he directed his students toward Alcoholics Anonymous and Narcotics Anonymous programs, James also used overnight outdoor retreats as a reward for residents who were making good progress.

James and his group members were buoyant regarding their overnight adventures. He regularly took them into the mountains, where they camped and challenged one another to hike long distances. James also used mindfulness, gratitude, and savoring activities during the outdoor retreats. Specifically, group members meditated together around the campfire, engaged in group savoring of the magnificent outdoor scenery, and practiced mutual reminiscing during the weeks between their overnight trips.

At an exit interview, Phillip, a 23-year-old Latino resident, shared his belief that participating in the outdoor program had rescued him from substance addiction and suicidal thoughts. He stated, "When we were outside together, hiking and talking, my shame melted away. The highs I used to get from drugs were replaced with new and better highs from being outside. James taught me about something better than drugs—something I can use to maintain my recovery for the rest of my life."

immediately accessible, the crisis may pass without an attempt occurring. Summarizing pertinent research, Bryan and Rudd (2018) noted the following:

> The final decision regarding the suicide attempt method typically occurs approximately 2 hours prior to the attempt, the final decision regarding the location of the attempt typically occurs approximately 30 minutes prior to the attempt, and the final decision to act typically occurs approximately 5 minutes prior to the attempt. (p. 143)

Given that intense suicidal impulses usually pass quickly, limiting easy access to lethal means may be one of the most effective interventions available.

Bryan and colleagues (2011) published an article on how to engage clients who are suicidal in means-restriction counseling. As they noted, mental health professionals are expected to talk with clients about locking up and removing lethal means for suicide. However, little practical advice on how to do so is available (other than articles by Britton et al., 2016, and Bryan et al., 2011).

Early in her session with her counselor, 15-year-old Sophia (introduced in Chapter 4) made it clear that she knew where her father kept the family's guns. Although the counselor did not feel the need to immediately respond to her statement, as they worked on a collaborative safety plan later in the session lethal means restriction came up for discussion:

> *Counselor:* Sophia, we need to talk about a big issue that's related to your safety. Is it OK with you if I just bring it up right now?
> *Sophia:* Yeah.
> *Counselor:* When people are suicidal, guns are the most dangerous thing to have in the house. Because my biggest goal is to keep you safe, we need to talk about how to lock up the guns or get them out of the house.
> *Sophia:* My dad will completely freak about that.
> *Counselor:* That's OK. Lots of people have strong feelings about keeping guns in their homes. Don't worry about talking with your dad, because I can do that. I want to keep you safe but also respect your dad's rights.
> *Sophia:* Yeah. No way am I bringing that up.

Sophia's reluctance to bring up gun safety with her father was natural. Her clear statement "No way am I bringing that up" meant that bringing up gun safety was the counselor's responsibility—as it should be.

Although phone conversations about gun safety with parents or family members may be helpful, we prefer a face-to-face contact if possible. In our experience, the best approach is to be direct, straightforward, and matter of fact. The core message is that because suicidal impulses often briefly escalate but then subside, all highly lethal methods should be locked away or removed.

Bryan and colleagues (2011) recommended presenting options for restricting firearms access. They presented options such as completely removing the means from the home by disposing of it or giving it to a supportive person. They noted that you can also have clients lock up the means and give the key to a supportive person or dismantle the firearm and give a critical piece to a supportive person (pp. 341–342).

Discussing firearms during counseling sessions can result in instant escalation and polarization. Preparing for firearms discussions with clients can smooth out the process. We recommend the following:

- Be prepared to talk about firearm safety. Talking directly about firearm safety is one of the most effective methods you have of reducing risk.
- Keep a laser focus on safety; avoid using the word *restriction*. Your discussion is not about restrictions on firearms or gun rights. Your discussion is about safety.
- If it feels helpful, say, "I support your Second Amendment rights." Conversations about firearms in the context of suicide prevention do not need to be political.
- As needed, state unequivocally, "I want to respect your right to own your guns . . . *and* I want you [or your daughter] to be safe and to live a long and fulfilling life."
- Brainstorm different methods for enhancing safety. Recognize that there are two general approaches to gun safety: (a) removing firearms from the premises and (b) creating obstacles to the impulsive use of firearms during a suicidal crisis (e.g., trigger locks, gun safes). Although removing guns is the safest alternative, creating obstacles is a reasonable alternative. You may want to conduct your brainstorming with the parent, client, essential support person, or all of the above.

- Remember that because there is no single perfect safety solution, and because nearly everyone is more agreeable if they participate in a decision-making process, less directive procedures like Socratic questioning and motivational interviewing are recommended.

If you would rather not be boldly direct about gun safety, consider using Socratic questions to help clients come to their own conclusions. Bryan and Rudd recommended questions such as "What do you think about someone having access to guns when they're really upset and are suicidal?" "What might be some benefits of temporarily limiting your access to firearms?" "If complete removal of the guns is not possible, what are some other options for practicing good gun safety while you're going through this treatment?" and "What do you think about putting together a plan for this?" (2018, p. 148).

Motivational interviewing is a less directive method for discussing firearms safety. Keeping in mind the core principle of motivational interviewing—that clients should be the ones making the case for change—clinicians can use open-ended questions, reflections, affirmation, and other technical strategies to increase firearms safety (Miller & Rollnick, 2013). The following short exchange is excerpted from an extended case example in which a veteran has refused to remove his firearms, so the clinician is using motivational interviewing to elicit talk around adding obstacles to enhance safety (see Britton et al., 2016, pp. 56–58, for the full case example):

Clinician: Would it be ok for me to share a little bit about what I know about gun safety? (asking for permission)

Veteran: Sure, go ahead.

Clinician: Basically, the greater number of barriers you have in the way, the safer you are. Suicidal thoughts and desires can be extremely intense, but they are often intense for short periods of time. The more barriers you have, the more likely it is that you start thinking about your family, your grandkids, and proving that the people who tried to take your guns away were wrong. So putting barriers in the way makes a lot of sense. What do you think about that? (giving information, open question)

Veteran: I think I can do that. What do you suggest? (Britton et al., 2016, p. 56)

The Safety Planning Intervention (SPI)

Obtaining a commitment-to-treatment statement from clients is a core component of counseling for suicide prevention. These statements go by various names, including *commitment to intervention, crisis response plan, safety plan,* and *safety planning intervention* (Bryan & Rudd, 2018; Stanley & Brown, 2012). Safety or crisis response plans detail what clients will do—when in a suicidal crisis—to manage their suicidal impulses and prevent suicidal acts from occurring. Safety or crisis plans also include ways for clients to access emergency support after hours (such as calling the National Suicide Prevention Lifeline at 1-800-273-TALK or similar emergency crisis numbers or textlines).

Stanley and Brown (2012) developed a brief treatment protocol called the *SPI*. The SPI is a cognitive behavioral approach often used in hospital emergency rooms, inpatient and outpatient settings, and schools. It includes a written form with six parts:

1. *Unique suicide warning signs.* Unique warning signs include an internal or environmental sign that suicidality has increased and safety measures need to be taken. Ask, "What are the signs, in yourself or in your environment, that will be a warning that tells you that you need to do something to keep yourself safe?"
2. *Personal coping strategies.* Coping strategies are activities clients can use to distract themselves from escalating suicidal thoughts or impulses. Ask, "What can you do in the moment to distract yourself from or cope with suicidal thoughts and feelings?"
3. *Social contacts and settings that are distracting.* Social contacts and settings include places to go and people to be with that distract or dampen suicidal impulses. Ask, "Who could you be with to stay safe? Where's a safe place you can go?"
4. *Family/friends and other people whom I can ask help.* With your clients, generate a list of names of people from whom they can directly ask for help. Ask, "Who can you turn to and ask for help if you're in crisis?"
5. *Mental health professionals or agencies I can contact for help.* A list of emergency contact numbers that the client is willing and able to contact is included in the safety plan. Ask, "Who should be put on your professional contact list?"
6. *How can I make my environment safe?* Making the environment safe involves reducing the potential use of lethal means. Ask, "What do we need to lock up or store so that you can't kill yourself in an impulsive moment?" (This list and the descriptions are adapted from Stanley & Brown, 2012.)

The sixth treatment component, reducing lethal means, is not addressed until the other five components of the safety plan have been completed. Component 6 may require assistance from family members or friends, depending on the situation. The whole safety plan, including lethal means management, should be included in your professional documentation.

In the following excerpts, the counselor is discussing a safety plan with a 21-year-old, White, cisgender female college senior named Kayla. Kayla is attending a large state university and living off campus in a small apartment. In this case, Kayla is socially distancing in compliance with state stay-at-home orders; the session is conducted remotely via an online video-based platform that is compliant with the Health Insurance Portability and Accountability Act of 1996 (e.g., Doxy.me, SimplePractice).

The Opening and Unique Suicide Warning Signs

Counselor: Kayla, I'm putting your name on the top of this form. It's called a *safety planning form*. Some very smart people made up this form to help people stay safe. There are six questions. We're supposed to fill it out together. If you hate it when we're done, we can toss it in the trash. OK?

Kayla: OK. That's possible.

Counselor: That would be fine. Here's the first question. I'm just going to read them to you. Then you answer, I'll write down your answers, and then we'll talk about your answer. What are the signs, in yourself or in your environment, that will be a warning that tells you that you need to do something to keep yourself safe?

Kayla: I just like feel a wave of sadness and defeat. Like my life means nothing. Like I'm a damaged, bad person who should die.

Counselor: OK. A wave of sadness and defeat. How will you know that wave has come? What do you feel in your body or think in your brain?

Kayla: I feel a physical ache. I think about being abused. I think horrible thoughts.

Counselor: I'm writing down, "Wave of sadness and defeat; and physical ache; and thoughts of being damaged, bad, and abused." Those are all signs that you should follow this safety plan.

Kayla: Also, being home alone at night.

In this initial exchange, the counselor empowers Kayla to reject the plan if she wants to. Offering to let Kayla reject the plan probably makes it more likely for her to take ownership of the plan. If Kayla ends up rejecting the plan, that information becomes part of the overall assessment and guides treatment decision-making.

Kayla immediately engages in the process. Specifically, her trauma-based thoughts of being damaged and bad could be fruitful therapeutic grist for cognitive processing therapy or eye-movement desensitization and reprocessing, both of which address trauma and focus on beliefs about the self. However, when using the SPI, it is best to stay focused on the SPI and save the deeper therapeutic content for later. The counselor can (and should) say, "For now, we're working on this plan. But later on, if you want, we can start working on your feelings of being damaged and bad."

Personal Coping Strategies

Counselor: What can you do in the moment to cope with suicidal thoughts and feelings?

Kayla: Look. I could cut myself to feel better, but nobody wants me to do that.

Counselor: I'm sure it's true that people don't want you cutting. I also think it's true that people would rather have you cut yourself than kill yourself. If cutting keeps you alive, we should put it in the plan, at least for now.

Kayla: I think it should be there then.

Counselor: OK. So cutting goes on here as a method for calming or soothing yourself. Have I got that right?

Kayla: Yeah. It calms me down when I'm upset.

Counselor: What else could calm you down or distract you from suicidal thoughts?

Kayla: I could listen to music or call a friend.

Counselor: Great. I'm writing those ideas into the plan right now.

Brainstorming coping responses is similar to other processes discussed in Chapter 5 (problem-solving and alternatives to suicide). One key principle is to accept all responses before evaluating them later. In the preceding interaction, the counselor accepts that cutting might be a viable (even if not preferred) short-term coping strategy and then continues to nudge Kayla to generate additional coping ideas. Although cutting is not addressed in this case example, after the safety plan is developed, therapeutic conversations about cutting and alternatives to cutting should become a part of ongoing counseling (see Kress & Hoffman, 2008; Stargell et al., 2017).

Social Contacts and Settings That Are Distracting
Counselor: I'm wondering about those times when you're alone. Who could you be with to stay safe? Even if it's only for you to distract yourself?
Kayla: I have a friend named Monroe. He's crazy. He's always happy. Sometimes he annoys me, but he's a good distraction.
Counselor: Monroe sounds like a great distraction. He's in the plan. Are you able to see him in person, or would you do FaceTime or a Zoom call?
Kayla: He lives in the apartment building and we could meet up outside.
Counselor: That sounds great. Who else?
Kayla: I can always call my parents, but when I do, I feel like a failure. I'm an adult.
Counselor: If you're feeling suicidal, would your parents want you to call?
Kayla: Yeah.
Counselor: OK then. Let's put your parents down. We can talk more later about how calling them might make you feel.

The counselor does a good job of getting Kayla to be specific about how she could connect with Monroe. Overall, Kayla does not have an extensive social support network. Expanding that network will likely become an important goal for counseling.

Family/Friends and Other People Whom I Can Ask Help
Counselor: This question is similar to the last one, but a little different. Instead of people who are distracting, now I'm wondering who you can turn to if you're in crisis.
Kayla: Monroe wouldn't be the right person for that.
Counselor: Not Monroe. But who would be right for that?
Kayla: My parents, I guess. And my aunt, Sarah. She's always been there for me. I could call her if I need to. And my grandma.
Counselor: Good. That's four. Your mom, your dad, your aunt Sarah, and your grandma. Are they around here, or would you call or text them?
Kayla: My parents and aunt live close by, but we'd probably just FaceTime because they're older; I don't want them to get COVID. My grandma lives in Minnesota.

While generating lists, it is useful to draw clients into being even more specific than illustrated in this exchange. For example, as Kayla identifies people to call, it is good practice to get specific about texting or calling, where the person might be, and what to do if there is no answer. Role-playing a call or text can be useful, because rehearsing behaviors makes them more likely to occur.

Mental Health Professionals or Agencies I Can Contact for Help
Counselor: How about professionals or agencies that you can call if you're in a crisis?
Kayla: I don't have anyone.
Counselor: Wait. You need to put me here. I should be on the list. I can be available for short calls Sunday through Thursday evenings up until 9 p.m.
Kayla: OK.
Counselor: And there's 911, right? You can always call 911. In an emergency, that's what you do. There's also a number for texting if you're in crisis. I'm going to write that number down too. You don't have to call or text any number, but it's good to have these resources available just in case you do want professional help during a crisis. The other thing to remember about calling or texting hotlines is that you may get someone you don't like or don't connect with. If that happens, keep trying, but also jot down a few notes so you can tell me about it.

In the preceding exchange, the counselor offers what seems to be a limited crisis option. Whether you provide a personal contact number is up to you. Whatever you do, spell it out in your informed consent and have boundaries around the times when communications with you are acceptable. Because calling hotlines may or may not feel helpful, empowering Kayla to critique her hotline experience and then report it to the counselor might increase her willingness to call.

How Can I Make My Environment Safe?
Counselor: This last question has to do with how you can make your environment safe. We've talked about various things, like how you can cope and who you can call. Now we need to talk about whether there's anything dangerous in your home, anything that could be used to kill yourself if you were suddenly suicidal.

Kayla: Yeah. Well I bought a handgun last year. That's how I would do it.

Counselor: Right. Thanks for telling me about the gun. Can I just tell you what I'm thinking right now?

Kayla: Sure.

Counselor: With guns and suicide, there are two good options. One is for you to give it to someone for now, until you're feeling better. The other is for you to safely store the gun or get a trigger lock. I'm just being totally honest with you about this. The reason we should get your gun locked up or given to your parents or someone else is because most of the time, people are intensely suicidal for only 5 or 10 or maybe 30 minutes. During that intense time, people can do things they later regret. Most people who make a suicide attempt don't make another attempt. It's usually a one-time thing. My main goal is for you to be safe.

Kayla: But I'm not planning to use the gun or anything.

Counselor: Right. That's great. But let's say your aunt Sarah was suicidal and she had a gun. Would you be willing to keep it for her if it made her safer?

Kayla: Of course I would.

Counselor: So whether it's you or your aunt Sarah, we want to make sure suicide doesn't happen because of one terrible moment.

The preceding is an example of psychoeducation around suicidality and safety planning. If you have a good rapport and connection with your client, the psychoeducation is likely to be well received. If your rapport and connection is less good, then you will need to either work on the relationship or take a more directive and authoritative role to promote your client's safety.

Counselor: Alright. I've written down your ideas for the safety plan. Now I'm going to scan it and send it to you through our secure portal. As we've already discussed, we're going to make a bigger plan for your counseling. But in the meantime, we need to keep you safe so we can do the counseling. Right now you've got this safety plan you can use, and we can revise it if we need to. OK?

Kayla: OK.

Counselor: Kayla, thank you very much for working with me on this safety plan. I think we made a good plan together.
Kayla: Me too. I guess I won't throw it in the trash.
Counselor: You're pretty funny.

Becoming Directive and Responsible

When clients are a clear danger to themselves, it is your responsibility to intervene and provide protection. Sometimes, despite our strong preference for working collaboratively with clients, we as counselors need to take a directive role. You may have to tell clients what to do, where to go, and whom to call.

Linehan (1993) discussed several directive dialectical behavior therapy approaches to reducing suicidal behaviors. She advocated

- emphatically instructing the client not to die by suicide,
- repeatedly informing the client that suicide is not a good solution and a better one will be found, and
- giving advice and telling clients what to do when or if they are frozen and unable to construct a positive action plan.

Linehan's tips give you a feeling for how directive you may need to be when working with clients who are suicidal.

Clients with active suicide plans, with high intent, and who have been rehearsing their suicide method may not respond to outpatient counseling interventions. You will still begin your intervention process with an effort to make a relational connection, you will still offer invitations for collaboration, and you will still engage your client in safety planning. However, if your efforts to engage and develop a collaborative safety plan fail, you may need to consider hospitalization. Even then, framing hospitalization as a logical alternative is recommended:

Counselor: We've been talking about how to keep you safe and we've made a safety plan, but I hear you saying you're not interested in enacting the safety plan. I'd like to offer one more alternative. Can I share another idea with you?
Client: Sure. Whatever.
Counselor: According to almost all the research, including stories from people who have jumped off the Golden Gate Bridge and survived, suicidal feelings tend to come in waves and then subside. You're right in the middle of a big suicide wave, and

so you can't imagine anything but killing yourself. What we need to do is keep you safe until your big wave of suicidal feelings gets smaller. Hospitals are good for that. We can get you in a hospital and then see whether the suicidal feelings get smaller or go away.
Client: My suicidal feelings won't go away. I know that.
Counselor: OK. You may be right. But I still vote for the hospital now. I figure if it doesn't work, you can always kill yourself later, after you get out. I'm just being honest with you. Let's take some time to see if this wave will pass.

In this example, the counselor is pushing for hospitalization. The client is pushing back. To get more leverage, the counselor openly tells the client that he can kill himself later, after the hospitalization. This is not perfect verbiage, but it is consistent with recommendations from evidence-based approaches (Jobes, 2016; Linehan, 1993). During crisis management, counselors may need to stall for more time, mostly because more time is the best available option. In the end, the counselor may need to call 911 or have someone transport the client to the hospital.

Civil commitment is the process through which individuals are hospitalized involuntarily. Although the details vary from state to state, individuals must have a diagnosable mental disorder and pose a risk of harm (to self or others) to qualify for civil commitment and involuntary hospitalization. Knowing the civil commitment law and process in your state is essential. The Substance Abuse and Mental Health Services Administration (SAMHSA) has a document describing the history and legal principles underlying civil commitment (see SAMSHA, 2019). We are grateful to SAMHSA for this resource and encourage you to explore gratitude for yourself and your clients in Wellness Practice 9.1.

Concluding Comments

The main goal of suicide assessment, treatment, and prevention is to stop people from engaging in suicidal behaviors. However, because getting people to stop thinking and stop acting on suicidal impulses is arguably more difficult than getting people to engage in alternative behaviors, teaching, directing, and encouraging positive, health-affirming alternative behaviors were the main focus of this chapter.

Wellness Practice 9.1
Expressing Gratitude

Although nearly everyone experiences gratitude, most people do not intentionally create time and space to express it. Expressing gratitude is a smart thing for several reasons. First, expressing gratitude reminds you of the positive things you are grateful for. Second, saying thanks often feels good. Third, expressing gratitude can make others feel good. Fourth, practicing gratitude regularly improves mood and well-being. Overall, expressing gratitude makes for a nice, positive, happiness-creating loop.

When depression, pandemics, or other challenging situations strike, it can be tempting to focus on negative experiences and forget about gratitude. Although negative experiences are real and compelling, dwelling on the negative is unhelpful. If you are feeling sad, depressed, or unhappy, now is the time to use your brain to force yourself to think and behave with positivity.

Try the following steps:

1. Identify someone toward whom you feel or have felt appreciation and gratitude. You may have plenty of options, or it may take a while to think of someone. You may want to pick someone toward whom you have not yet expressed enough gratitude.
2. Write a gratitude note to the person you have chosen. Include in the note why you feel gratitude. Also include other specifics as well as words that best express your sincere heartfelt feelings.
3. Find a way to express your feelings directly to the target of your gratitude. You can read the note in person, read it over the phone, or send it in whatever way you find best.

As with acts of kindness, it is wise to drop all expectations for how the recipient of your gratitude should or will respond. Instead, focus on doing the best job you can of expressing the gratitude that you sincerely feel and accept whatever response or nonresponse you get.

If you feel inspired, repeat this gratitude experiment a second or third time. You may find gratitude begets gratitude.

Practitioner Guidance and Key Points to Remember

In this chapter we described four key behavioral issues to address in counseling: (a) active suicide planning or intent, (b) dispositional pain insensitivity and acquired suicide capability, (c) impulsivity, and (d) access to lethal means. Interventions in the behavioral dimension include the following:

- Assist clients in focusing on their reasons for living; this might include working with clients to develop their own personalized version of the RFL.
- Teach clients how to engage in behavioral activation.
- Counter suicide desensitization through brainstormed lists of prohibitions accompanied by highly stimulating behavioral alternatives.
- Provide treatment for addictions.
- Engage clients and parents of clients in developing methods for restricting access to lethal suicide means, especially firearms.
- Implement a safety planning intervention.
- Become directive and refer clients for higher levels of care as needed.
- Practice expressing gratitude and encourage your clients to do so as well.

Chapter 10

The Contextual Dimension

Suicide is a human phenomenon that has occured across cultures, age groups, genders, races, religions, and socioeconomic groups and throughout history (Minois, 1999). In the preceding chapters, using the seven-dimension model, we described how emotional pain, negative or aversive cognitions, interpersonal disconnection, suboptimal physical habits or illness, spiritual or cultural disconnection, and maladaptive behavior patterns contribute to suicidality. Broadly speaking, excruciating psychological pain—Edwin Shneidman's dark heart of suicide—emerges as a response to stressors across these dimensions. For each client, the stressors that contribute to the dark heart of suicide are unique.

Context—The Seventh Dimension

This chapter is about broader or larger contexts or ecology as contributing factors to death by suicide. Although the six preceding dimensions are also contextual, the seventh dimension is unique in that it includes broader sociological, global, and environmental contexts. The seventh dimension is also unique because broader contexts, such as global pandemics, socioeconomic crises, systemic racism, environmental toxicity, meteorological events, and other macrolevel factors that are completely and palpably external to the individual, still contribute to suicide attempts and death by suicide (Moore et al., 2018).

Prior to this chapter, we sought to depathologize suicide and externalize problems that trigger suicidality. You may recall Elijah from Chapter 6 (the interpersonal dimension). Elijah experienced cyberbullying. His mental health provider deftly located the problem outside of Elijah, focusing on external systemic factors that activated Elijah's suicidality. The provider then recommended social skills training for Elijah but did so as an empowerment strategy, making certain that Elijah did not feel blamed for being bullied.

The purpose of depathologizing suicide and externalizing suicide-related problems is not to relieve individuals of personal responsibility. Instead, depathologizing and externalizing are social constructionist tools used to alleviate shame; these tools also allow clients to gain enough psychological distance from their problems or symptoms to view them as workable. When depathologizing and externalizing work well, clients feel uplifted and inspired to participate even harder in the battle against the internal and external stressors contributing to their suicidal state.

It seems odd that we would need to mention that contextual factors that drive suicide can originate outside of the self. However, society tends to blame individuals for their oppressive living conditions or stressful life circumstances. Surely, the narrative goes, people living in poverty or drinking lead-laced water in Flint, Michigan, must be lazy, criminal, or somehow defective; otherwise they would lift themselves up by their bootstraps and profit from the American dream. Of course, this narrative is false. In fact, as we think about the depth and breadth of contextual factors that contribute to suicide, we recall the words of Cassius in Shakespeare's (1623/1992) *Julius Caesar*: "The fault, dear Brutus, is not in our stars / But in ourselves" (Act I, Scene II, lines 140–141). As we look at the seventh dimension, this message is flipped: "The fault, dear Brutus, is not in ourselves, but in our stars" (or systemic socioeconomic disparity, racial inequality, or oppression).

Context and Suicide: A Glimpse at the Scientific Literature

Humans exist within a complex web of political, environmental, sociological, economic, and other ecological forces. People are constantly inundated with information and images, cajoled to make purchases, and prompted to engage in social comparison. Opportunities and threats are constant. Climate change, viral pandemics, racial injustice, war, scarcity, wage inequities, natural disasters, unemployment, and many other natural and human-made events and contexts affect individuals. Making the preceding list of larger contextual factors that might contribute to suicide was easy, but the contextual factors we list in this paragraph are mostly speculative.

Rather than relying on speculation, the scientific literature offers information about larger ecological dynamics that increase suicide risk. The following bulleted list provides a quick glimpse at the literature on context and suicide:

- *Poverty*. In a sample of 558,147 older South Koreans (ages 60–119 years), poverty increased suicide risk. Males living in poverty were significantly more likely to die by suicide than males not living in poverty (J. W. Choi et al., 2019). In rural China, along with interpersonal factors (e.g., being disappointed in love), family poverty and loss of face were associated with suicide attempts among 1,200 previous suicide attempters (Bao-Peng et al., 2019). Over a 7-year span, financial problems were linked to death by suicide among farm and agricultural workers in the state of Georgia in the United States (Scheyett et al., 2019).
- *Poverty amelioration*. In Brazil, socioeconomically disadvantaged residents from 5,507 different municipalities were provided with direct financial assistance. The authors concluded that "the results provide evidence that the conditional cash [program] . . . may reduce suicide in Brazilian municipalities . . ." (Alves et al., 2019, p. 599).
- *Poverty plus lack of health care providers*. In a study of suicide rates by region, high-risk clusters of suicide were identified. The authors concluded that "socio-economic deprivation and lower provider densities" were linked to suicide (Fontanella et al., 2018, p. 177).
- *Poverty and suicide modeling*. In a study of 5,331 Icelandic adolescents in 83 school communities, household poverty and contact "with suicidal others" were linked to suicidal behavior (Bernburg et al., 2009, p. 380).
- *Neighborhood safety*. In a sample of 13,335 adolescents in the United States, living in socioeconomically disadvantaged neighborhoods was linked to increased suicide attempts. After controlling for moderating factors, the authors concluded that exposure to violence and lack of neighborhood safety explained this contextual effect (Yildiz et al., 2019).

- *Sexual harassment.* In a U.S. military survey study of 12,567 soldiers in 180 units, "sexual harassment was associated with a fivefold increase for risk of suicide" (Griffith, 2019, p. 41). On the positive side, having unit leaders who could be trusted "was associated with a decreased suicide risk by about one-third" (p. 41).
- *Lack of teacher support.* In a study of 4,241 Israeli high schoolers, lower ratings of classroom teacher support were linked to suicidal ideation and suicidal behaviors. The authors concluded that "the school environment can play a significant role in reducing risk for suicidal ideation and behaviors" (Madjar et al., 2018, p. 185).
- *Racism.* In a community sample of 236 African American men and women, perceived racial discrimination plus low religiosity was associated with increased suicidal ideation (Walker et al., 2014).
- *Racial microaggressions.* Among 135 African American young adults, racial microaggressions were linked to being a social burden, and being a social burden was associated with higher levels of suicidal ideation (Hollingsworth et al., 2017).
- *Racial discrimination.* In a study of 3,157 Chinese elders in Chicago, individuals who reported discrimination had nearly double the odds of suicidal ideation than those who did not report discrimination (L. W. Li et al., 2018).
- *Lack of purpose in life.* In a study of 289 Asian American, Hispanic, and Black emerging adults, greater purpose in life decreased the impact of perceived racial discrimination on suicidal ideation (Hong et al., 2018).

The studies reviewed here highlight several larger environmental factors with empirical links to suicidal ideation, suicide attempts, or suicide itself. Consistent with Bronfenbrenner's (1979) ecological model, these research studies (and many more) imply that stressful, debilitating global, national, regional, and local factors—largely outside of the individual client's control—contribute to suicidality. Alternatively, the presence of social forces that reduce stress and support individuals can decrease incidents of suicide.

Uncontrollable Aversive Events and Toxic Stress

As we write these words, a global pandemic has mandated social distancing and other health precautions. At the same time, the deaths of George Floyd and other Black Americans have triggered protests and rallies against racial injustice. These stressors have been added to preexisting anxieties about increasing reports of floods, fires, hurricanes, and earthquakes—all of which contribute to the existential angst of living in the 21st century.

Counselors should be aware of toxic stress and be prepared to help clients who are suicidal develop resilience in the face of external stressors. *Toxic stress* is defined as chronic and excessive activation or arousal of the sympathetic nervous system. Toxic stress in general and adverse childhood experiences in particular predict a variety of health and behavioral problems across the life span (Joos et al., 2019). Although not specific causal factors in death by suicide, external, uncontrollable, and aversive stressors accumulate and can contribute to suicidality. Uncontrollable aversive events are particularly malignant stressors (Job, 2002).

Externalizing the External
At age 82, in an interview with the *Los Angeles Times* (Stein, 1986), B. F. Skinner said, "I have to tell people that they are not responsible for their behavior. They're not creating it; they're not initiating anything. It's all found somewhere else" ("Major Changes," para. 2).

We find Skinner's words reassuring. All humans are influenced—to some extent—by factors outside themselves. This is not to say that people are helpless victims of their environments; there are methods for coping with external stressors. But the first step, even though the stressor is obviously external, is to re-externalize it, because all too often it is all too easy to internalize the external.

Strategies for Coping With Toxic or Malignant Stressors

When clients are exposed to larger sociological and uncontrollable stressors, they can experience frustration, helplessness, and hopelessness. As a counselor, you are mostly unable to change the unchangeable for your clients. Within the counseling relationship, you can express both empathy for your client's situation and indignation that society can be so painful and difficult to change. Depending on the counseling goals, you can provide empathy, commiseration, assistance in discerning achievable goals, learning opportunities, and advocacy or support for activism.

Empathic Commiseration
News events pertaining to racism, climate change, global pandemics, and other topics activate and agitate some clients (and counselors). When this happens, providing empathic commiseration is a good

first step. Empathy from you can universalize client emotional reactions and help clients feel more normal. Simple statements like "I agree. It's so hard to watch the news" can facilitate recognition that excessive exposure to media heightens feelings of helplessness and depression.

Other scenarios in which clients are exposed to environmental toxicity but are unable to extricate themselves from the situation can be especially demoralizing. In such cases, brainstorming about how to mobilize community resources, how to gain access to safe spaces, and how to engage in self-advocacy can be important and empowering. As with goal setting in other dimensions, helping clients evaluate their own behaviors and the factors over which they have control may mitigate frustration. Having you show empathy with their frustration and show compassion is crucial.

Discernment and Goal Setting

People associated with Alcoholics Anonymous are familiar with Reinhold Niebuhr's (1987) Serenity Prayer: "God, grant me the serenity to accept the things I cannot change, courage to change the things I can, and wisdom to know the difference." Similar guidance comes from Shantideva, an eighth-century Indian Buddhist scholar, who put it this way: "If there's a remedy when trouble strikes, what reason is there for dejection? And if there is no help for it, what use is there in being glum?" (Shantideva, 2006, p. 130). Clients who are religious or spiritually oriented may find particular comfort and insight in the words of Niebuhr or Shantideva.

Yet another version of the Serenity Prayer comes from the 20th-century philosopher W. W. Bartley. Bartley (1990) took a break from writing about philosophical rationalism to put the message of the Serenity Prayer into a Mother Goose nursery rhyme format:

> *For every ailment under the sun*
> *There is a remedy, or there is none;*
> *If there be one, try to find it;*
> *If there be none, never mind it.* (p. 35)

When it comes to helping clients deal with complex contextual difficulties, these prayers or philosophies can be a good place to start, both for professionals and for clients. Recognizing and accepting that some problems in life are unchangeable can bring solace. Trying to change that which is unchangeable generally fuels unhappiness.

The developers of mindfulness-based cognitive therapy (Segal et al., 2013) put their own brain-based 21st-century spin on the Serenity Prayer. They say that the brain has two basic modes of functioning. The first mode is problem-solving. The brain is quite good at problem-solving. However, some problems are unsolvable. When faced with unsolvable problems, rather than letting go of the problem-solving process, the brain naturally persists, relentlessly continuing to problem solve, ruminate, and chew on old ideas and failures. Anxiety and fear escalate. If the brain gets hooked on unsolvable problems, it can take clients down into bottomless rabbit holes and exacerbate emotional discomfort.

What about that second basic brain modality? Mindfulness practitioners say that engaging the second mode can unhitch our brains from the out-of-control problem-solving train. The second brain modality operates on a less natural principle: the principle of acceptance. Mindfulness-based cognitive therapists emphasize shifting into noticing, or nonjudgmental acceptance. Although the brain is capable of intermittent nonjudgmental acceptance, shifting into that modality is tough. Most clients cannot make that switch in the moment. Accepting one's failure to switch into nonjudgmental mindfulness is part of mindful acceptance. Coaching clients to make efforts at mindfulness and then to accept their failings and inadequacies might facilitate client self-acceptance and grow mindful parts of the brain, like the insula (Haase et al., 2016). Nonjudgmental acceptance requires regular practice. No one ever gets it right all the time.

Opportunity Ameliorates

James Garbarino (2001) wrote, "Stress accumulates; opportunity ameliorates" (p. 361). Within the trauma literature, it is clear that toxic stress increases illness (Shern et al., 2016); it is also clear that providing traumatized youth and adults with physical, social, and academic opportunities mitigates trauma and increases health. In part, your role with clients who have experienced trauma and who are chronically reactivated by sociopolitical events is to assist them in finding and participating in local resources and opportunities.

Clients who are suicidal and in the midst of toxic and uncontrollable contextual factors often feel that they do not have the time or energy for new opportunities. Like Katie from Chapter 5, they may need support, assistance, and resources to step outside of their survival mode. Practical problems like child care, transportation, and inaccessible community organizations can loom large. In such situations, you may need to engage in advocacy or activism to help your clients get connected to the resources and opportunities they need.

The Role of Activism

Throughout this book, we have emphasized a positive, strengths-based approach to helping clients who are suicidal. Our view is that even across the first six dimensions, clients who are suicidal are not well served when mental health professionals pathologize them for their problems. However, in the seventh dimension, clients sometimes face massive inequities and social problems that will not change without advocacy, activism, and wisdom. Social justice, climate change, community tragedies—these and many other areas of society need professional involvement. The American Counseling Association (ACA) has increasingly pointed mental health professionals toward advocacy (e.g., Lee, 2007). ACA also has a thoughtful set of advocacy competencies for counselors (see Ratts et al., 2010).

Counselors frequently witness the painful damage done by contextual stressors and adverse events. Helping clients heal, grow, and overcome is an important way to contribute to the world, but social justice and advocacy for systemic change are also needed. In fact, trying to bring about social change can be a healthy way to vent emotions that have built up as you have worked nonjudgmentally and empathically with clients who have been wounded and chronically exposed to oppressive systems. A suggested healthy activity called forest bathing follows in Wellness Practice 10.1.

Concluding Comments: In the End

Overall, our goal with this book was to provide counseling practitioners with a practical and strengths-based model for working effectively with clients and students who are suicidal. In this effort, we have pummeled you with information and ideas on how to assess, treatment plan, and intervene with clients who are suicidal. When possible, we have tried to keep the discourse light, but we have also dipped deep into suicidal pain and angst. If all of this has been too much, we apologize. We hope you took the advice in Chapter 1 to take care of yourself and to take breaks from reading.

Wellness Practice 10.1
Forest Bathing

In 2018, happiness researcher Dr. Qing Li wrote a book called *Forest Bathing*, which includes this guidance:

> In Japan, we practice something called forest bathing, or *shinrin-yoku. Shinrin* in Japanese means "forest," and *yoku* means "bath." So *shinrin-yoku* means bathing in the forest atmosphere, or taking in the forest through our senses.
>
> This is not exercise, or hiking, or jogging. It is simply being in nature, connecting with it through our senses of sight, hearing, taste, smell and touch. Shinrin-yoku is like a bridge. By opening our senses, it bridges the gap between us and the natural world.
>
> First, find a spot. Make sure you have left your phone and camera behind. You are going to be walking aimlessly and slowly. You don't need any devices. Let your body be your guide. Listen to where it wants to take you. Follow your nose. And take your time. It doesn't matter if you don't get anywhere. You are not going anywhere. You are savoring the sounds, smells and sights of nature and letting the forest in.
>
> The key to unlocking the power of the forest is in the five senses. Let nature enter through your ears, eyes, nose, mouth, hands and feet. Listen to the birds singing and the breeze rustling in the leaves of the trees. Look at the different greens of the trees and the sunlight filtering through the branches. Smell the fragrance of the forest and breathe in the natural aromatherapy of phytoncides. Taste the freshness of the air as you take deep breaths. Place your hands on the trunk of a tree. Dip your fingers or toes in a stream. Lie on the ground. Drink in the flavor of the forest and release your sense of joy and calm. This is your sixth sense, a state of mind. Now you have connected with nature. You have crossed the bridge to happiness.

Dr. Li is an impressive researcher. Forest bathing can be a great habit to establish and maintain (Li, 2018).

Like the uncontrollable aversive and disturbing events that happen in the world, whether your clients or students die by suicide or choose to live long and prosperous lives is not completely within your control. However, this should not deter you from using your remarkable skills and strengths to intervene and, when possible, save lives. In the end, like most humans, you will probably remember your failures. Too often your clients will forget to say, "Thank you so much for sharing yourself with me and for lending me your strength and skills." We hope they do not forget, but in case they do, we would like to say it for them. Thank you for being the kind of person and professional who is dedicated to making the world a better place. You may not realize it, but you are amazing, and you are needed.

Practitioner Guidance and Key Points to Remember

This chapter only skimmed the surface of the many different larger contextual or sociological factors that contribute to suicide. The main factors discussed included (a) poverty; (b) lack of health care providers; (c), neighborhood safety; (d) sexual harassment; (e) lack of teacher support; (f) racism, discrimination, and microaggressions; and (g) lack of purpose in life. Interventions in the contextual dimension include the following:

- Help clients identify uncontrollable aversive events, toxic stress, and other oppressive contextual factors that exist outside of the self.
- Teach coping strategies for dealing with toxic or malignant stressors.
- Use empathic commiseration.
- Help clients set achievable goals and recognize situations over which they have little or no power and control.
- Connect clients with school, community, and other opportunities.
- As appropriate, learn about and engage in activist and advocacy roles.
- When possible, spend time in healthy outdoor environments, and encourage your clients to do so as well.

References

Adames, H. Y., Chavez-Dueñas, N. Y., Sharma, S., & La Roche, M. J. (2018). Intersectionality in psychotherapy: The experiences of an AfroLatinx queer immigrant. *Psychotherapy, 55*(1), 73–79. https://doi.org/10.1037/pst0000152

Adler, A. (1938). *Social interest: A challenge to mankind* (J. Linton & R. Vaughn, Trans.). Faber and Faber.

Adler, A. (1958). *What life should mean to you.* Capricorn. (Original work published 1931)

Ahuja, A., Webster, C., Gibson, N., Brewer, A., Toledo, S., & Russell, S. (2015). Bullying and suicide: The mental health crisis of LGBTQ youth and how you can help. *Journal of Gay & Lesbian Mental Health, 19*(2), 125–144. https://doi.org/10.1080/19359705.2015.1007417

Ainsworth, M. D. S., Blehar, M. C., Waters, E., & Wall, S. (1978). *Patterns of attachment: A psychological study of the strange situation.* Erlbaum.

Ali, S., & Lee, C. C. (2019). Using creativity to explore intersectionality in counseling. *Journal of Creativity in Mental Health, 14*(4), 510–518. https://doi.org/10.1080/15401383.2019.1632767

Alves, F. J. O., Machado, D. B., & Barreto, M. L. (2019). Effect of the Brazilian cash transfer programme on suicide rates: A longitudinal analysis of the Brazilian municipalities. *Social Psychiatry and Psychiatric Epidemiology, 54*(5), 599–606. https://doi.org/10.1007/s00127-018-1627-6

American Academy of Child and Adolescent Psychiatry. (2001). Practice parameter for the assessment and treatment of children and adolescents with suicidal behavior. *Journal of the American Academy of Child & Adolescent Psychiatry, 40*(7), 24S–51S. https://doi.org/10.1097/00004583-200107001-00003

American Association of Suicidology. (2010). *Core competencies for the assessment and management of individuals at risk for suicide.* https://suicidology.org/wp-content/uploads/2019/06/RRSR_Core_Competencies.pdf

American Counseling Association. (2014). *ACA code of ethics.* https://www.counseling.org/resources/aca-code-of-ethics.pdf

American Foundation for Suicide Prevention. (2020). *Suicide statistics.* https://afsp.org/about-suicide/suicide-statistics/

American Psychiatric Association. (2013). *Diagnostic and statistical manual of mental disorders* (5th ed.).

American Psychological Association. (2010). *Ethical principles for psychologists and code of conduct.*

American Psychological Association. (2017). *Clinical practice guideline for the treatment of posttraumatic stress disorder (PTSD) in adults.*

American School Counselor Association. (2020). *The school counselor and suicide risk assessment.* https://www.schoolcounselor.org/asca/media/asca/PositionStatements/PS_Suicide-Risk-Assessment.pdf

Anestis, M. D., & Houtsma, C. (2018). The association between gun ownership and statewide overall suicide rates. *Suicide and Life-Threatening Behavior, 48*(2), 204–217. https://doi.org/10.1111/sltb.12346

Angelakis, I., Austin, J. L., & Gooding, P. (2020). Association of childhood maltreatment with suicide behaviors among young people: A systematic review and meta-analysis. *Journal of the American Medical Association, 3*(8), e2012563. https://doi.org/10.1001/jamanetworkopen.2020.12563

Ansbacher, H. L. (1968). The concept of social interest. *Journal of Individual Psychology, 24*(2), 131–149. https://doi.org/10.1037/0022-3514.47.1.164

Asher, J. (2007). *13 reasons why.* Razorbill.

Azulay, J., Smart, C. M., Mott, T., & Cicerone, K. D. (2013). A pilot study examining the effect of mindfulness-based stress reduction on symptoms of chronic mild traumatic brain injury/postconcussive syndrome. *Journal of Head Trauma Rehabilitation, 28*(4), 323–331. https://doi.org/10.1097/HTR.0b013e318250ebda

Babyak, M., Blumenthal, J. A., Herman, S., Khatri, P., Doraiswamy, M., Moore, K., Craighead, E. W., Baldewicz, T. T., & Krishnan, R. K. (2000). Exercise treatment for major depression: Maintenance of therapeutic benefit at 10 months. *Psychosomatic Medicine, 62*(5), 633–638. https://doi.org/10.1097/00006842-200009000-00006

Bao-Peng, L., Jie, Z., Jie, C., Hui-Min, Q., Cun-Xian, J., & Hennessy, D. A. (2019, June). Negative life events as triggers on suicide attempt in rural China: A case-crossover study. *Psychiatry Research, 276*, 100–106. https://doi.org/10.1016/j.psychres.2019.04.008

Bartley, W. W. (1990). *The retreat to commitment* (New ed.). Open Court.

Baumeister, R. F. (1990). Suicide as escape from self. *Psychological Review, 97*(1), 90–113. https://doi.org/10.1037/0033-295x.97.1.90

Beck, A. T. (1976). *Cognitive therapy and the emotional disorders*. International Universities Press.

Beck, A. T. (2009). Introduction. In A. Wenzel, G. Brown, & A. T. Beck, *Cognitive therapy for suicidal patients: Scientific and clinical applications* (pp. iii–vi). American Psychological Association.

Beck, A. T., Kovacs, M., & Weissman, A. (1979). Assessment of suicide ideation: The Scale for Suicide Ideation. *Journal of Consulting and Clinical Psychology, 47*(2), 343–352. https://doi.org/10.1037/0022-006X.47.2.343

Beck, A. T., Rush, A., Shaw, B., & Emery, G. (1979). *Cognitive therapy of depression*. Guilford Press.

Beck, A. T., & Steer, R. A. (1988). *Manual for the Beck Hopelessness Scale*. Psychological Corporation.

Beck, J. S. (2011). *Cognitive therapy: Basics and beyond* (2nd ed.). Guilford Press.

Bedrosian, R. C., & Beck, A. T. (1979). Cognitive aspects of suicidal behavior. *Suicide and Life-Threatening Behavior, 9*(2), 87–96. https://doi.org/10.1111/j.1943-278X.1979.tb00433.x

Belsher, B. E., Smolenski, D. J., Pruitt, L. D., Bush, N. E., Beech, E. H., Workman, D. E., Morgan, R. L., Evatt, D. P., Tucker, J., & Skopp, N. A. (2019). Prediction models for suicide attempts and deaths: A systematic review and simulation. *JAMA Psychiatry, 76*(6), 642–651. https://doi.org/10.1001/jamapsychiatry.2019.0174

Berg, I. K., & Dolan, Y. (2001). *Tales of solutions: A collection of hope-inspiring stories*. Norton.

Berk, M. S., Starace, N. K., Black, V. P., & Avina, C. (2019). Implementation of dialectical behavior therapy with suicidal and self-harming adolescents in a community clinic. *Archives of Suicide Research*, 24(1), 64–81. https://doi.org/10.1080/13811118.2018.1509750

Bernburg, J. G., Thorlindsson, T., & Sigfusdottir, I. D. (2009). The spreading of suicidal behavior: The contextual effect of community household poverty on adolescent suicidal behavior and the mediating role of suicide suggestion. *Social Science & Medicine*, 68(2), 380–389. https://doi.org/10.1016/j.socscimed.2008.10.020

Bernert, R. A., Turvey, C. L., Conwell, Y., & Joiner, T. E., Jr. (2014). Association of poor subjective sleep quality with risk for death by suicide during a 10-year period: A longitudinal, population-based study of late life. *JAMA Psychiatry*, 71(10), 1129–1137. https://doi.org/10.1001/jamapsychiatry.2014.112

Bigner, J. B., & Wetchler, J. L. (2012). *Handbook of LGBT-affirmative couple and family therapy*. Routledge.

Binkley, E. E., & Leibert, T. W. (2015). Prepracticum counseling students' perceived preparedness for suicide response. *Counselor Education and Supervision*, 54(2), 98–108. https://doi.org/10.1002/ceas.12007

Bittner, M. D., Rigby, B. R., Silliman-French, L., Nichols, D. L., & Dillon, S. R. (2017, August 1). Use of technology to facilitate physical activity in children with autism spectrum disorders: A pilot study. *Physiology & Behavior*, 177, 242–246. https://doi.org/10.1016/j.physbeh.2017.05.012

Black, J., Belicki, K., Emberley-Ralph, J., & McCann, A. (2020). Internalized versus externalized continuing bonds: Relations to grief, trauma, attachment, openness to experience, and posttraumatic growth. *Death Studies*. Advance online publication. https://doi.org/10.1080/07481187.2020.1737274

Boisvert, D., Wells, J., Armstrong, T. A., & Lewis, R. H. (2018, May/June). Serotonin and self-control: A genetically moderated stress sensitization effect. *Journal of Criminal Justice*, 56, 98–106. https://doi.org/10.1016/j.jcrimjus.2017.07.008

Bolton, J. M., Pagura, J., Enns, M. W., Grant, B., & Sareen, J. (2010). A population-based longitudinal study of risk factors for suicide attempts in major depressive disorder. *Journal of Psychiatric Research*, 44(13), 817–826. https://doi.org/10.1016/j.jpsychires.2010.01.003

Bolton, J. M., Spiwak, R., & Sareen, J. (2012). Predicting suicide attempts with the SAD PERSONS scale: A longitudinal analysis. *Journal of Clinical Psychiatry*, 73(6), e735–e741. https://doi.org/10.4088/JCP.11m07362

Bongar, B., Sullivan, G., & James, L. (Eds.). (2017). *Handbook of military and veteran suicide: Assessment, treatment, and prevention.* Oxford University Press.

Bono, T. (2018). *When likes aren't enough: A crash course in the science of happiness.* Hachette Book Group.

Bordin, E. S. (1979). The generalizability of the psychoanalytic concept of the working alliance. *Psychotherapy, 16*(3), 252–260. https://doi.org/10.1037/h0085885

Bostik, K. E., & Everall, R. D. (2007). Healing from suicide: Adolescent perceptions of attachment relationships. *British Journal of Guidance & Counselling, 35*(1), 79–96. https://doi.org/10.1080/03069880601106815

Brehm, S. S., & Brehm, J. W. (1981). *Psychological reactance: A theory of freedom and control.* Wiley.

Brent, D. A., Bridge, J., Johnson, B. A., & Connolly, J. (1996). Suicidal behavior runs in families: A controlled family study of adolescent suicide victims. *Archives of General Psychiatry, 53*(12), 1145–1152. https://doi.org/10.1001/archpsyc.1996.01830120085015

Brezo, J., Klempan, T., & Turecki, G. (2008). The genetics of suicide: A critical review of molecular studies. *Psychiatric Clinics of North America, 31*(2), 179–203. https://doi.org/10.1016/j.psc.2008.01.008

Britton, P. C., Bryan, C. J., & Valenstein, M. (2016). Motivational interviewing for means restriction counseling with patients at risk for suicide. *Cognitive and Behavioral Practice, 23*(1), 51–61. https://doi.org/10.1016/j.cbpra.2014.09.004

Bronfenbrenner, U. (1979). *The ecology of human development.* Harvard University Press.

Brown, L. A., Boudreaux, E. D., Arias, S. A., Miller, I. W., May, A. M., Camargo, C. A., Jr., Bryan, C. J., & Armey, M. F. (2020). C-SSRS performance in emergency department patients at high risk for suicide. *Suicide and Life-Threatening Behavior.* Advance online publication. https://doi.org/10.1111/sltb.12657

Bryan, C. J., Bryan, A. O., & Baker, J. C. (2020). Associations among state-level physical distancing measures and suicidal thoughts and behaviors among U.S. adults during the early COVID-19 pandemic. *Suicide and Life Threatening Behavior.* Advance online publication. https://doi.org/10.1111/sltb.12653

Bryan, C. J., Bryan, A. O., Roberge, E., Leifker, F. R., & Rozek, D. C. (2018). Moral injury, posttraumatic stress disorder, and suicidal behavior among National Guard personnel. *Psychological Trauma: Theory, Research, Practice, and Policy, 10*(1), 36–45. https://doi.org/10.1037/tra0000290

Bryan, C. J., & Rudd, M. D. (2018). *Brief cognitive-behavioral therapy for suicide prevention.* Guilford Press.

Bryan, C. J., Stone, S. L., & Rudd, M. D. (2011). A practical, evidence-based approach for means-restriction counseling with suicidal patients. *Professional Psychology: Research and Practice, 42*(5), 339-346. http://doi.org/10.1037/a0025051

Camus, A. (1955). *The myth of Sisyphus and other essays.* Knopf.

Capuzzi, D., & Stauffer, M. D. (2016). *Counseling and psychotherapy: Theories and interventions* (6th ed.). American Counseling Association.

Cashwell, C. S., & Young, J. S. (2020). *Integrating spirituality and religion into counseling: A guide to competent practice* (3rd ed.). American Counseling Association.

Cassidy, F. (2011). Risk factors of attempted suicide in bipolar disorder. *Suicide and Life-Threatening Behavior, 41*(1), 6–11. https://doi.org/10.1111/j.1943-278X.2010.00007.x

Castro, A., Gili, M., Ricci-Cabello, I., Roca, M., Gilbody, S., Perez-Ara, M., Seguí, A., & McMillan, D. (2020, January 1). Effectiveness and adherence of telephone-administered psychotherapy for depression: A systematic review and meta-analysis. *Journal of Affective Disorders, 260*, 514–526. https://doi.org/10.1016/j.jad.2019.09.023

Centers for Disease Control and Prevention. (2020, July 10). *Leading causes of death and injury.* https://www.cdc.gov/injury/wisqars/LeadingCauses.html

Chaouloff, F. (1997). Effects of acute physical exercise on central serotonergic systems. *Medicine & Science in Sports & Exercise, 29*(1), 58–62. https://doi.org/10.1097/00005768-199701000-00009

Chaouloff, F., Berton, O., & Mormède, P. (1999). Serotonin and stress. *Neuropsychopharmacology, 21*(2S), 29S–32S. https://doi.org/10.1016/s0893-133x(99)00008-1

Chapman, D. P., Dube, S. R., & Anda, R. F. (2007). Adverse childhood events as risk factors for negative mental health outcomes. *Psychiatric Annals, 37*(5), 359–364. https://doi.org/10.1016/j.chiabu.2017.03.016

Choi, J. W., Kim, T. H., Shin, J., & Han, E. (2019). Poverty and suicide risk in older adults: A retrospective longitudinal cohort study. *International Journal of Geriatric Psychiatry, 34*(11), 1565–1571. https://doi.org/10.1002/gps.5166

Choi, K. W., Zheutlin, A. B., Karlson, R. A., Wang, M., Dunn, E. C., Stein, M. B., Karlson, E. W., & Smoller, J. W. (2019). Physical activity offsets genetic risk for incident depression assessed via electronic health records in a biobank cohort study. *Depression and Anxiety, 37*(2), 106–114. https://doi.org/10.1002/da.22967

Chow, T. S., & Wan, H. Y. (2017, December 1). Is there any "Facebook depression"? Exploring the moderating roles of neuroticism, Facebook social comparison and envy. *Personality and Individual Differences, 119,* 277–282. https://doi.org/10.1016/j.paid.2017.07.032

Chu, J., Khoury, O., Ma, J., Bahn, F., Bongar, B., & Goldblum, P. (2017). An empirical model and ethnic differences in cultural meanings via motives for suicide. *Journal of Clinical Psychology, 73*(10), 1343–1359. https://doi.org/10.1002/jclp.22425

Chung, D. T., Ryan, C. J., & Large, M. M. (2016). Adverse experiences in psychiatric hospitals might be the cause of some postdischarge suicides. *Bulletin of the Menninger Clinic, 80*(4), 371–375. https://doi.org/10.1521/bumc.2016.80.4.371

Cipriani, A., Hawton, K., Stockton, S., & Geddes, J. R. (2013). Lithium in the prevention of suicide in mood disorders: Updated systematic review and meta-analysis. *The BMJ, 346,* 13. https://doi.org/10.1136/bmj.f3646

Cohen, J. A., Mannarino, A. P., Kliethermes, M., & Murray, L. A. (2012). Trauma-focused CBT for youth with complex trauma. *Child Abuse & Neglect, 36*(6), 528–541. https://doi.org/10.1016/j.chiabu.2012.03.007

Collins, J. (2003). *Sanity and grace: A journey of suicide, survival, and strength.* Penguin.

Conner, A., Azrael, D., & Miller, M. (2019). Suicide case-fatality rates in the United States, 2007 to 2014: A nationwide population-based study. *Annals of Internal Medicine, 171*(12), 885–895. https://doi.org/10.7326/m19-1324

Cooper, B., & Widdows, N. (2008). *The social success workbook for teens.* New Harbinger.

Copelan, R. (2020, March 18). Mental health effects of COVID-19 pandemic: A ripple or a wave. *MedPage Today.* https://www.medpagetoday.com/blogs/suicide-watch/85484

Corey, G. (2020). *Personal reflections on counseling.* American Counseling Association.

Corey, G., Muratori, M., Austin, J. T., & Austin, J. A. (2018). *Counselor self-care.* American Counseling Association.

Corona, C. D., Van Orden, K. A., Wisco, B. E., & Pietrzak, R. H. (2019). Meaning in life moderates the association between morally injurious experiences and suicide ideation among U.S. combat veterans: Results from the National Health and Resilience in Veterans Study. *Psychological Trauma: Theory, Research, Practice, and Policy, 11*(6), 614–620. https://doi.org/10.1037/tra0000475

Council for Accreditation of Counseling and Related Educational Programs. (2016). *2016 CACREP standards.* http://www.cacrep.org/for-programs/2016-cacrep-standards/

Cramer, R. J., Johnson, S. M., McLaughlin, J., Rausch, E. M., & Conroy, M. A. (2013). Suicide risk assessment training for psychology doctoral programs: Core competencies and a framework for training. *Training and Education in Professional Psychology, 7*(1), 1–11. https://doi.org/10.1037/a0031836

Crenshaw, K. (1989). Demarginalizing the intersection of race and sex: A Black feminist critique of antidiscrimination doctrine, feminist theory and antiracist politics. *University of Chicago Legal Forum, 1989*, Article 8. https://chicagounbound.uchicago.edu/uclf/vol1989/iss1/8

Crenshaw, K. (1991). Mapping the margins: Intersectionality, identity politics, and violence against women of color. *Stanford Law Review, 43*(6), 1241–1299. https://doi.org/10.2307/1229039

Cunningham, J. E. A., & Shapiro, C. M. (2018, March). Cognitive behavioural therapy for insomnia (CBT-I) to treat depression: A systematic review. *Journal of Psychosomatic Research, 106,* 1–12. https://doi.org/10.1016/j.jpsychores.2017.12.012

Cureton, J. L., & Clemens, E. V. (2015). Affective constellations for countertransference awareness following a client's suicide attempt. *Journal of Counseling & Development, 93*(3), 352–360. https://doi.org/10.1002/jcad.12033

Cureton, J. L., & Fink, M. (2019). Shores: A practical mnemonic for suicide protective factors. *Journal of Counseling & Development, 97*(3), 325–335. https://doi.org/10.1002/jcad.12272

Curry, O. S., Rowland, L. A., Van Lissa, C. J., Zlotowitz, S., McAlaney, J., & Whitehouse, H. (2018, May). Happy to help? A systematic review and meta-analysis of the effects of performing acts of kindness on the well-being of the actor. *Journal of Experimental Social Psychology, 76,* 320–329. https://doi.org/10.1016/j.jesp.2018.02.014

Curtin, S. C., & Hedegaard, H. (2019). *Suicide rates for females and males by race and ethnicity: United States, 1999 and 2017.* https://www.cdc.gov/nchs/data/hestat/suicide/rates_1999_2017.pdf

Dahlem, N. W., Zimet, G. D., & Walker, R. R. (1991). The Multidimensional Scale of Perceived Social Support: A confirmation study. *Journal of Clinical Psychology, 47*(6), 756–761. https://doi.org/10.1002/1097-4679(199111)47:6%3C756::AID-JCLP2270470605%3E3.0.CO;2-L

Davidson, C. L., Babson, K. A., Bonn-Miller, M. O., Souter, T., & Vannoy, S. (2013). The impact of exercise on suicide risk: Examining pathways through depression, PTSD, and sleep in an inpatient sample of veterans. *Suicide and Life-Threatening Behavior, 43*(3), 279–289. https://doi.org/10.1111/sltb.12014

Davidson, P. R., & Parker, K. C. H. (2001). Eye movement desensitization and reprocessing (EMDR): A meta-analysis. *Journal of Consulting and Clinical Psychology, 69*(2), 305–316. https://doi.org/10.1037//0022-006x.69.2.305

de Beurs, D. P., Ghoncheh, R., Geraedts, A. S., & Kerkhof, A. J. F. M. (2016). Psychological distress because of asking about suicidal thoughts: A randomized controlled trial among students. *Archives of Suicide Research, 20*(2), 153–159. https://doi.org/10.1080/13811118.2015.1004475

Dobson, D., & Dobson, K. S. (2017). *Evidence-based practice of cognitive-behavioral therapy*. Guilford Press.

Drye, R. C., Goulding, R. L., & Goulding, M. E. (1973). No-suicide decisions: Patient monitoring of suicidal risk. *American Journal of Psychiatry, 130*(2), 171–174. https://doi.org/10.1176/ajp.130.2.171

Eliot, T. S. (1943). *Four quartets*. Houghton Mifflin Harcourt.

Elliott, R., Bohart, A. C., Watson, J. C., & Murphy, D. (2018). Therapist empathy and client outcome: An updated meta-analysis. *Psychotherapy, 55*(4), 399–410. https://doi.org/10.1037/pst0000175

Ellis, A. (1962). *Reason and emotion in psychotherapy*. Lyle Stuart.

Enright, R. D. (2019). *Forgiveness is a choice: A step-by-step process for resolving anger and restoring hope*. American Psychological Association.

Enright, R. D., & Fitzgibbons, R. P. (2015). *Forgiveness therapy: An empirical guide for resolving anger and restoring hope*. American Psychological Association. https://doi.org/10.1037/14526-000

Erbacher, T. A., Singer, J. B., & Poland, S. (2015). *Suicide in the schools: A practitioner's guide to multi-level prevention, assessment, intervention, and postvention*. Routledge.

Erford, B. T., Jackson, J., Bardhoshi, G., Duncan, K., & Atalay, Z. (2018). Selecting suicide ideation assessment instruments: A meta-analytic review. *Measurement and Evaluation in Counseling and Development, 51*(1), 42–59. https://doi.org/10.1080/07481756.2017.1358062

Erikson, E. H., & Erikson, J. M. (1998). *The life cycle completed: Extended version*. Norton.

Erlich, M. D., Rolin, S. A., Dixon, L. B., Adler, D. A., Oslin, D. W., Levine, B., Berlant, J. L., Goldman, B., Koh, S., First, M. B., Pabbati, C., & Siris, S. G. (2017). Why we need to enhance suicide postvention: Evaluating a survey of psychiatrists' behaviors after the suicide of a patient. *Journal of Nervous and Mental Disease*, 205(7), 507–511. https://doi.org/10.1097/NMD.0000000000000682

Fawcett, J., Clark, D. C., & Busch, K. A. (1993). Assessing and treating the patient at risk for suicide. *Psychiatric Annals*, 23(5), 244–255. https://doi.org/10.3928/0048-5713-19930501-05

Felitti, V. J., Anda, R. F., Nordenberg, D., Williamson, D. F., Spitz, A. M., Edwards, V., Koss, M. P., & Marks, J. S. (1998). Relationship of childhood abuse and household dysfunction to many of the leading causes of death in adults: The Adverse Childhood Experiences (ACE) study. *American Journal of Preventive Medicine*, 14, 245–258. https://doi.org/10.1016/S0749-3797(98)00017-8

Field, T. A., & Ghoston, M. R. (2020). *Neuroscience-informed counseling with children and adolescents*. American Counseling Association.

Finn, S. E., Handler, L., & Fischer, C. T. (2012). *Collaborative/therapeutic assessment: A casebook and guide*. Wiley.

Fischer, C. T. (1969). Rapport as mutual respect. *Personnel and Guidance Journal*, 48(3), 201–204.

Fischer, C. T. (1970). The testee as co-evaluator. *Journal of Counseling Psychology*, 17(1), 70–76.

Fischer, C. T. (1985). *Individualizing psychological assessment*. Erlbaum.

Flemons, D., & Gralnik, L. M. (2013). *Relational suicide assessment: Risks, resources, and possibilities for safety*. Norton.

Flentje, A., Heck, N. C., Brennan, J. M., & Meyer, I. H. (2019). The relationship between minority stress and biological outcomes: A systematic review. *Journal of Behavioral Medicine*. Advance online publication. https://doi.org/10.1007/s10865-019-00120-6

Flückiger, C., Del Re, A. C., Wampold, B. E., & Horvath, A. O. (2018). The alliance in adult psychotherapy: A meta-analytic synthesis. *Psychotherapy*, 55(4), 316–340. https://doi.org/10.1037/pst0000172

Foa, E. B., Hembree, E. A., & Rothbaum, B. O. (2007). *Prolonged exposure therapy for PTSD: Emotional processing of traumatic experiences*. Oxford University Press.

Fogg, B. J. (2019, December 30). Better control of your emotions will help you create better habits. *Time*. https://time.com/5756833/better-control-emotions-better-habits/

Fontanella, C. A., Saman, D. M., Campo, J. V., Hiance-Steelesmith, D., Bridge, J. A., Sweeney, H. A., & Root, E. D. (2018, January). Mapping suicide mortality in Ohio: A spatial epidemiological analysis of suicide clusters and area level correlates. *Preventive Medicine, 106*, 177–184. https://doi.org/10.1016/j.ypmed.2017.10.033

Forcano, L., Álvarez, E., Santamaría, J. J., Jimenez-Murcia, S., Granero, R., Penelo, E., Alonso, P., Sanchez, I., Mehchon, M. J., Ulman, F., Bulik, C. M., & Fernández-Arand, F. (2011). Suicide attempts in anorexia nervosa subtypes. *Comprehensive Psychiatry, 52*(4), 352–358. https://doi.org/10.1016/j.comppsych.2010.09.003

Foreman, T. (2018). Wellness, exposure to trauma, and vicarious traumatization: A pilot study. *Journal of Mental Health Counseling, 40*(2), 142–155. https://doi.org/10.17744/mehc.40.2.04

Fowler, J. C. (2012). Suicide risk assessment in clinical practice: Pragmatic guidelines for imperfect assessments. *Psychotherapy, 49*(1), 81–90. https://doi.org/10.1037/a0026148

Frances, A. (2014). *Saving normal: An insider's revolt against out-of-control psychiatric diagnosis, DSM-5, big pharma, and the medicalization of ordinary life*. HarperCollins.

Frances, A. (2016, July 1). Yes, benzos are bad for you: So easy to start, so hard to stop. *Psychology Today*. https://www.psychologytoday.com/us/blog/saving-normal/201607/yes-benzos-are-bad-you

Frankl, V. (1962). *Man's search for meaning; An introduction to logotherapy*. Beacon Press.

Frankl, V. (1967). *Psychotherapy and existentialism: Selected papers on logotherapy*. Clarion.

Franklin, J. C., Ribeiro, J. D., Fox, K. R., Bentley, K. H., Kleiman, E. M., Huang, X., Musacchio, M. K., Jaroszewski, A. C., Chang, B. P., & Nock, M. K. (2017). Risk factors for suicidal thoughts and behaviors: A meta-analysis of 50 years of research. *Psychological Bulletin, 143*(2), 187–232. https://doi.org/10.1037/bul0000084

Freedenthal, S. (2018). *Helping the suicidal person: Tips and techniques for professionals*. Routledge.

Ganzini, L., Denneson, L. M., Press, N., Bair, M. J., Helmer, D. A., Poat, J., & Dobscha, S. K. (2013). Trust is the basis for effective suicide risk screening and assessment in veterans. *Journal of General Internal Medicine, 28*(9), 1215–1221. https://doi.org/10.1007/s11606-013-2412-6

Garbarino, J. (2001). An ecological perspective on the effects of violence on children. *Journal of Community Psychology, 29*(3), 361–378. https://doi.org/10.1002/jcop.1022

Gilbert, E. (2009). *Eat, pray, love*. Bloomsbury.

Ginicola, M. M., Filmore, J. M., Smith, C., & Abdullah, J. (2017). Physical and mental health challenges found in the LGBTQI+ population. In M. M. Ginicola, C. Smith, & J. M. Filmore (Eds.), *Affirmative counseling with LGBTQI+ people* (pp. 75–85). American Counseling Association.

Glasser, W. (1998). *Choice theory: A new psychology of personal freedom*. HarperCollins.

Granello, D. H. (2010a). The process of suicide risk assessment: Twelve core principles. *Journal of Counseling & Development, 88*(3), 363–371. https://doi.org/10.1002/j.1556-6678.2010.tb00034.x

Granello, D. H. (2010b). A suicide crisis intervention model with 25 practical strategies for implementation. *Journal of Mental Health Counseling, 32*(3), 218–235. https://doi.org/10.17744/mehc.32.3.n6371355496t4704

Gray, M. J., Nash, W. P., & Litz, B. T. (2017). When self-blame is rational and appropriate: The limited utility of Socratic questioning in the context of moral injury: Commentary on Wachen et al. (2016). *Cognitive and Behavioral Practice, 24*(4), 383–387. https://doi.org/10.1016/j.cbpra.2017.03.001

Griffith, J. (2019). The sexual harassment–suicide connection in the U.S. military: Contextual effects of hostile work environment and trusted unit leaders. *Suicide and Life-Threatening Behavior, 49*(1), 41–53. https://doi.org/10.1111/sltb.12401

Gunn, J. F., Lester, D., & McSwain, S. (2011). Testing the warning signs of suicidal behavior among suicide ideators using the 2009 National Survey on Drug Abuse and Health. *International Journal of Emergency Mental Health, 13*(3), 147–154. https://pubmed.ncbi.nlm.nih.gov/22708144/

Haase, L., Thom, N. J., Shukla, A., Davenport, P. W., Simmons, A. N., Stanley, E. A., Paulus, M. P., & Johnson, D. C. (2016). Mindfulness-based training attenuates insula response to an aversive interoceptive challenge. *Social Cognitive and Affective Neuroscience, 11*(1), 182–190. https://doi.org/10.1093/scan/nsu042

Hagan, C. R., Podlogar, M. C., Chu, C., & Joiner, T. E. (2015). Testing the interpersonal theory of suicide: The moderating role of hopelessness. *International Journal of Cognitive Therapy, 8*(2), 99–113. https://doi.org/10.1521/ijct.2015.8.2.99

Hahn, W. K., & Marks, L. I. (1996). Client receptiveness to the routine assessment of past suicide attempts. *Professional Psychology: Research and Practice, 27*(6), 592–594. https://doi.org/10.1037/0735-7028.27.6.592

Hanley, T., & Reynolds, D. J. (2009). Counselling psychology and the internet: A review of the quantitative research into online outcomes and alliances within text-based therapy. *Counselling Psychology Review, 24*(2), 4–13.

Hansen, J. T. (2015). The relevance of postmodernism to counselors and counseling practice. *Journal of Mental Health Counseling, 37*(4), 355–363. https://doi.org/10.17744/mehc.37.4.06

Harris, K. M., & Goh, M. T. (2017). Is suicide assessment harmful to participants? Findings from a randomized controlled trial. *International Journal of Mental Health Nursing, 26*(2), 181–190. https://doi.org/10.1111/inm.12223

Hayes, S. C. (2004). Acceptance and commitment therapy, relational frame theory, and the third wave of behavioral and cognitive therapies. *Behavior Therapy, 35*(4), 639–665. https://doi.org/10.1016/S0005-7894(04)80013-3

Hayes, S. C. (2016). Acceptance and commitment therapy, relational frame theory, and the third wave of behavioral and cognitive therapies. *Behavior Therapy, 47*(6), 869–885. https://doi.org/10.1016/j.beth.2016.11.006 (Reprinted from "Acceptance and commitment therapy, relational frame theory, and the third wave of behavioral and cognitive therapies," 2004, *Behavior Therapy, 35*[4], 639–665, https://doi.org/10.1016/S0005-7894(04)80013-3)

Hayes, S. C., Strosahl, K. D., & Wilson, K. G. (1999). *Acceptance and commitment therapy: An experiential approach to behavior change.* Guilford Press.

Hays, P. A. (2014). *Creating well-being: Four steps to a happier, healthier life.* American Psychological Association.

Healy, D. (2009). Are selective serotonin reuptake inhibitors a risk factor for adolescent suicide? *The Canadian Journal of Psychiatry/La Revue Canadienne De Psychiatrie, 54*(2), 69–71. https://doi.org/10.1177/070674370905400201

Hedegaard, H., Curtin, S. C., & Warner, M. (2020, April). *Increase in suicide mortality in the United States, 1999–2018* (NCHS Data Brief No. 362). https://www.cdc.gov/nchs/products/databriefs/db362.htm

Herbert, A., & Pavel, M. P. (1982). *Random kindness and senseless acts of beauty.* New Village Press.

Hindman, R. (2018, February 21). *Behavioral activation tip.* https://beckinstitute.org/behavioral-activation-tip/

Hoffman, B. M., Babyak, M. A., Sherwood, A., Hill, E. E., Patidar, S. M., Doraiswamy, P. M., & Blumenthal, J. A. (2009). Effects of aerobic exercise on sexual functioning in depressed adults. *Mental Health and Physical Activity, 2*(1), 23–28. https://doi.org/10.1016/j.mhpa.2008.12.001

Hoffmann, J. A., Farrell, C. A., & Monuteaux, M. C. (2020). Association of pediatric suicide with county-level poverty in the United States, 2007-2016. *JAMA Pediatrics, 174*(3), 287–294. https://doi.org/10.1001/jamapediatrics.2019.5678

Hofmann, S. G. (2020). *The anxiety skills workbook: Simple CBT and mindfulness strategies for overcoming anxiety, fear, and worry.* New Harbinger.

Hollenbaugh, K. M., & Lenz, A. S. (2018). An examination of the effectiveness of dialectical behavior therapy skills groups. *Journal of Counseling & Development, 96*(3), 233–242. https://doi.org/10.1002/jcad.12198

Hollingsworth, D. W., Cole, A. B., O'Keefe, V. M., Tucker, R. P., Story, C. R., & Wingate, L. R. (2017). Experiencing racial microaggressions influences suicide ideation through perceived burdensomeness in African Americans. *Journal of Counseling Psychology, 64*(1), 104–111. https://doi.org/10.1037/cou0000177

Holt-Lunstad, J., Smith, T. B., & Layton, J. B. (2010). Social relationships and mortality risk: A meta-analytic review. *PLoS Medicine, 7*(7), e1000316. https://doi.org/10.1371/journal.pmed.1000316

Hong, J. H., Talavera, D. C., Odafe, M. O., Barr, C. D., & Walker, R. L. (2018). Does purpose in life or ethnic identity moderate the association for racial discrimination and suicide ideation in racial/ethnic minority emerging adults? *Cultural Diversity and Ethnic Minority Psychology.* Advance online publication. https://doi.org/10.1037/cdp0000245

Hor, K., & Taylor, M. (2010). Suicide and schizophrenia: A systematic review of rates and risk factors. *Journal of Psychopharmacology, 24*(4), 81–90. https://doi.org/10.1177/1359786810385490

Houtsma, C., Butterworth, S. E., & Anestis, M. D. (2018, August). Firearm suicide: Pathways to risk and methods of prevention. *Current Opinion in Psychology, 22,* 7–11. https://doi.org/10.1016/j.copsyc.2017.07.002

Hughes, C. W., Barnes, S., Barnes, C., DeFina, L. F., Nakonezny, P., & Emslie, G. J. (2013). Depressed Adolescents Treated with Exercise (DATE): A pilot randomized controlled trial to test feasibility and establish preliminary effect sizes. *Mental Health and Physical Activity, 6*(2), 119–131. https://doi.org/10.1016/j.mhpa.2013.06.006

Ilgen, M. A., Bohnert, A. S. B., Ganoczy, D., Bair, M. J., McCarthy, J. F., & Blow, F. C. (2016). Opioid dose and risk of suicide. *Pain*, *157*(5), 1079–1084. https://doi.org/10.1097/j.pain.0000000000000484

Incaprera, J. (Producer). (2017). *13 reasons why* [Television series]. Netflix.

Indian Health Service. (2019, October). *Disparities*. https://www.ihs.gov/newsroom/factsheets/disparities/

Jacobson, E. (1938). *Progressive relaxation*. University of Chicago Press.

Jacobson, N. S., Dobson, K. S., Truax, P. A., Addis, M. E., Koerner, K., Gollan, J. K., Gortner, E., & Prince, S. E. (1996). A component analysis of cognitive-behavioral treatment for depression. *Journal of Consulting and Clinical Psychology*, *64*(2), 295–304. https://doi.org/10.1037//0022-006x.64.2.295

Jia, C., Wang, L., Xu, A., Dai, A., & Qin, P. (2014). Physical illness and suicide risk in rural residents of contemporary China: A psychological autopsy case-control study. *Crisis*, *35*(5), 330–337. https://doi.org/10.1027/0227-5910/a000271

Job, R. F. S. (2002). The effects of uncontrollable, unpredictable aversive and appetitive events: Similar effects warrant similar, but not identical, explanations? *Integrative Physiological & Behavioral Science*, *37*(1), 59–81. https://doi.org/10.1007/BF02688806

Jobes, D. A. (2016). *Managing suicidal risk: A collaborative approach* (2nd ed.). Guilford Press.

Jobes, D. A., Jacoby, A. M., Cimbolic, P., & Hustead, L. A. T. (1997). Assessment and treatment of suicidal clients in a university counseling center. *Journal of Counseling Psychology*, *44*(4), 368–377. https://doi.org/10.1037/0022-0167.44.4.368

Jobes, D. A., Moore, M. M., & O'Connor, S. S. (2007). Working with suicidal clients using the Collaborative Assessment and Management of Suicidality (CAMS). *Journal of Mental Health Counseling*, *29*(4), 283–300. https://doi.org/10.17744/mehc.29.4.k881k101v0u79rqp

Jobes, D. A., & O'Connor, S. S. (2009). The duty to protect suicidal clients: Ethical, legal, and professional considerations. In J. L. Werth, Jr., E. R. Welfel, & G. A. H. Benjamin (Eds.), *The duty to protect: Ethical, legal, and professional considerations for mental health professionals* (pp. 163–180). American Psychological Association.

Johnson, R. (2013). *Spirituality in counseling and psychotherapy: An integrative approach that empowers clients*. Wiley.

Joiner, T. (2005). *Why people die by suicide*. Harvard University Press.

Jones, M. C. (1924a). The elimination of children's fears. *Journal of Experimental Psychology*, *7*(5), 382–390. https://doi.org/10.1037/h0072283

Jones, M. C. (1924b). A laboratory study of fear: The case of Peter. *Pediatric Seminars*, *31*(4), 308–316.

Joos, C. M., McDonald, A., & Wadsworth, M. E. (2019, September). Extending the toxic stress model into adolescence: Profiles of cortisol reactivity. *Psychoneuroendocrinology*, *107*, 46–58. https://doi.org/10.1016/j.psyneuen.2019.05.002

Kabat-Zinn, J. (1990). *Full catastrophe living*. Bantam Books.

Kaniuka, A., Pugh, K. C., Jordan, M., Brooks, B., Dodd, J., Mann, A. K., Williams, S. L., & Hirsch, J. K. (2019). Stigma and suicide risk among the LGBTQ population: Are anxiety and depression to blame and can connectedness to the LGBTQ community help? *Journal of Gay & Lesbian Mental Health*, *23*(2), 205–220. https://doi.org/10.1080/19359705.2018.1560385

Katz, C., Randall, J. R., Leong, C., Sareen, J., & Bolton, J. M. (2018, March/April). Psychotropic medication use before and after suicidal presentations to the emergency department: A longitudinal analysis. *General Hospital Psychiatry*, *63*, 68–75. https://doi.org/10.1016/j.genhosppsych.2018.10.003

Khatri, P., Blumenthal, J. A., Babyak, M. A., Craighead, W. E., Herman, S., Baldewicz, T., Madden, D. J., Doraiswamy, M., Waugh, R., & Krishnan, K. R. (2001). Effects of exercise training on cognitive functioning among depressed older men and women. *Journal of Aging and Physical Activity*, *9*(1), 43–57. https://doi.org/10.1123/japa.9.1.43

King, C. A., Gipson, P. Y., Horwitz, A. G., & Opperman, K. J. (2015). Teen options for change: An intervention for young emergency patients who screen positive for suicide risk. *Psychiatric Services*, *66*(1), 97–100. https://doi.org/10.1176/appi.ps.201300347

Kistler, D., Thöni, C., & Welzel, C. (2017). Survey response and observed behavior: Emancipative and secular values predict prosocial behaviors. *Journal of Cross-Cultural Psychology*, *48*(4), 461–489. https://doi.org/10.1177/0022022117696799

Kleespies, P. M., Hough, S., & Romeo, A. M. (2009). Suicide risk in people with medical and terminal illness. In P. M. Kleespies (Ed.), *Behavioral emergencies: An evidence-based resource for evaluating and managing risk of suicide, violence, and victimization* (pp. 103–121). American Psychological Association.

Klonsky, E. D., Kotov, R., Bakst, S., Rabinowitz, J., & Bromet, E. J. (2012). Hopelessness as a predictor of attempted suicide among first admission patients with psychosis: A 10-year cohort study. *Suicide and Life-Threatening Behavior*, *42*(1), 1–10. https://doi.org/10.1111/j.1943-278X.2011.00066.x

Klonsky, E. D., & May, A. M. (2014). Differentiating suicide attempters from suicide ideators: A critical frontier for suicidology research. *Suicide and Life Threatening Behavior, 44*(1), 1–5. http://doi.org/10.1111/sltb.12068

Klonsky, E. D., & May, A. M. (2015). The three-step theory (3ST): A new theory of suicide rooted in the "ideation-to-action" framework. *International Journal of Cognitive Therapy, 8*(2), 114–129. https://doi.org/10.1521/ijct.2015.8.2.114

Kocet, M. M., & Herlihy, B. J. (2014). Addressing value-based conflicts within the counseling relationship: A decision-making model. *Journal of Counseling & Development, 92*(2), 180–186. https://doi.org/10.1002/j.1556-6676.2014.00146.x

Krakow, B., & Zadra, A. (2010). Imagery rehearsal therapy: Principles and practice. *Sleep Medicine Clinics, 5*(2), 289–298. https://doi.org/10.1016/j.jsmc.2010.01.004

Kress, V. E., & Hoffman, R. M. (2008). Non-suicidal self-injury and motivational interviewing: Enhancing readiness for change. *Journal of Mental Health Counseling, 30*(4), 311–329. https://doi.org/10.17744/mehc.30.4.n2136170r5732u6h

Lagacé, M. (2020, September 1). *360 death quotes that will bring you instant calm.* https://wisdomquotes.com/death-quotes/

Lake, A. M., & Gould, M. S. (2014). Suicide clusters and suicide contagion. In S. H. Koslow, P. Ruiz, & C. B. Nemeroff (Eds.), *A concise guide to understanding suicide: Epidemiology, pathophysiology, and prevention* (pp. 52–61). Cambridge University Press. https://doi.org/10.1017/CBO9781139519502.008

Lantz, J. E. (1981). Depression and social interest tasks. *Journal of Individual Psychology, 37*(1), 113–116.

Large, M. M., & Kapur, N. (2018). Psychiatric hospitalisation and the risk of suicide. *British Journal of Psychiatry, 212*(5), 269–273. https://doi.org/10.1192/bjp.2018.22

Lau, M. A., Haigh, E. A. P., Christensen, B. K., Segal, Z. V., & Taube-Schiff, M. (2012). Evaluating the mood state dependence of automatic thoughts and dysfunctional attitudes in remitted versus never-depressed individuals. *Journal of Cognitive Psychotherapy, 26*(4), 381–389. https://doi.org/10.1891/0889-8391.26.4.381

Lawrence, R. E., Brent, D., Mann, J. J., Burke, A. K., Grunebaum, M. F., Galfalvy, H. C., & Oquendo, M. A. (2016). Religion as a risk factor for suicide attempt and suicide ideation among depressed patients. *Journal of Nervous and Mental Disease, 204*(11), 845–850. https://doi.org/10.1097/NMD.0000000000000484

Layous, K., Nelson, S. K., & Lyubomirsky, S. (2013). What is the optimal way to deliver a positive activity intervention? The case of writing about one's best possible selves. *Journal of Happiness Studies, 14*(2), 635–654. https://doi.org/10.1007/s10902-012-9346-2

Lazarus, A. A. (2006). *Brief but comprehensive psychotherapy: The multimodal way.* Springer.

Lee, C. C. (2007). Social justice: A moral imperative for counselors. *Professional Counseling Digest.* https://www.counseling.org/resources/library/ACA%20Digests/ACAPCD-07.pdf

Lenes, E., Swank, J. M., Hart, K. A., Machado, M. M., Darilus, S., Ardelt, M., Smith-Adcock, S., Rockwood Lane, M., & Puig, A. (2020). Color-conscious multicultural mindfulness training in the counseling field. *Journal of Counseling & Development, 98*(2), 147–158. https://doi.org/10.1002/jcad.12309

Lester, D., McSwain, S., & Gunn, J. F. (2011). A test of the validity of the IS PATH WARM warning signs for suicide. *Psychological Reports, 108*(2), 402–404. https://doi.org/10.2466/09.12.13.PR0.108.2.402-404

Levine, P. A. (2010). *In an unspoken voice: How the body releases trauma and restores goodness.* North Atlantic Books.

Levy-Hint, J., London, M. (Producers), & Hardwicke, C. (Writer/Director). (2003). *Thirteen* [Motion picture]. Working Title Films.

Li, L. W., Gee, G. C., & Dong, X. (2018). Association of self-reported discrimination and suicide ideation in older Chinese Americans. *American Journal of Geriatric Psychiatry, 26*(1), 42–51. https://doi.org/10.1016/j.jagp.2017.08.006

Li, Q. (2018, May 1). 'Forest bathing' is great for your health. Here's how to do it. *Time.* https://time.com/5259602/japanese-forest-bathing/

Lilienfeld, S. O., Schwartz, S. J., Meca, A., Sauvigné, K. C., & Satel, S. (2015). Neurocentrism: Implications for psychotherapy practice and research. *The Behavior Therapist, 38*(7), 173–181. www.abct.org/docs/PastIssue/38n7.pdf

Linehan, M. (1993). *Cognitive behavioral therapy of borderline personality disorder.* Guilford Press.

Linehan, M. (2015). *DBT® skills training manual* (2nd ed.). Guilford Press.

Linehan, M. M., Comtois, K. A., & Ward-Ciesielski, E. F. (2012). Assessing and managing risk with suicidal individuals. *Cognitive and Behavioral Practice, 19*(2), 218–232. https://doi.org/10.1016/j.cbpra.2010.11.008

Linehan, M. M., Goodstein, J. L., Nielsen, S. L., & Chiles, J. A. (1983). Reasons for staying alive when you are thinking of killing yourself: The Reasons for Living Inventory. *Journal of Consulting and Clinical Psychology, 51*(2), 276–286. https://doi.org/10.1037/0022-006X.51.2.276

Litz, B. T., Stein, N., Delaney, E., Lebowitz, L., Nash, W. P., Silva, C., & Maguen, S. (2009). Moral injury and moral repair in war veterans: A preliminary model and intervention strategy. *Clinical Psychology Review*, 29(8), 695–706. https://doi.org/10.1016/j.cpr.2009.07.003

López-Goñi, J. J., Fernández-Montalvo, J., Arteaga, A., & Haro, B. (2018, November). Suicidal ideation and attempts in patients who seek treatment for substance use disorder. *Psychiatry Research*, 269, 542–548. https://doi.org/10.1016/j.psychres.2018.08.100

Luke, C. (2020). *Neuroscience for counselors and therapists*. Cognella.

Luke, M., Harper, A. J., Goodrich, K. M., & Singh, A. A. (2017). LGBTQI+ youth development. In M. M. Ginicola, C. Smith, & J. M. Filmore (Eds.), *Affirmative counseling with LGBTQI+ people* (pp. 41–48). American Counseling Association.

Lund, E. M., Schultz, J. C., Nadorff, M. R., Galbraith, K., & Thomas, K. B. (2017). Experience, knowledge, and perceived comfort and clinical competency in working with suicidal clients among vocational rehabilitation counselors. *Rehabilitation Counseling Bulletin*, 61(1), 54–63. https://doi.org/10.1177%2F0034355217695776

Lyddon, W. J. (1995). Cognitive therapy and theories of knowing: A social constructionist view. *Journal of Counseling & Development*, 73(6), 579–585. https://doi.org/10.1002/j.1556-6676.1995.tb01799.x

Lyubomirsky, S. (2007). *The how of happiness: A scientific approach to getting the life you want*. Penguin Press.

Lyubomirsky, S. (2013). *The myths of happiness*. Penguin Press.

Madjar, N., Walsh, S. D., & Harel-Fisch, Y. (2018, November). Suicidal ideation and behaviors within the school context: Perceived teacher, peer and parental support. *Psychiatry Research*, 269, 185–190. https://doi.org/10.1016/j.psychres.2018.08.045

Maffei, C., Cavicchioli, M., Movalli, M., Cavallaro, R., & Fossati, A. (2018). Dialectical behavior therapy skills training in alcohol dependence treatment: Findings based on an open trial. *Substance Use & Misuse*, 53(14), 2368–2385. https://doi.org/10.1080/10826084.2018.1480035

Mandal, E., & Zalewska, K. (2012). Childhood violence, experience of loss and hurt in close relationships at adulthood and emotional rejection as risk factors of suicide attempts among women. *Archives of Psychiatry and Psychotherapy*, 14(3), 45–50. www.archivespp.pl/uploads/images/2012_14_3/Mandal45_ArchivesPP_3_2012.pdf

Maple, M., Poštuvan, V., & McDonnell, S. (2019). Progress in postvention: A call to a focused future to support those exposed to suicide. *Crisis*, 40(6), 379–382. https://doi.org/10.1027/0227-5910/a000620

Marco, J. H., Cañabate, M., Llorca, G., & Pérez, S. (2019). Meaning in life moderates hopelessness, suicide ideation, and borderline psychopathology in participants with eating disorders: A longitudinal study. *Clinical Psychology & Psychotherapy, 27*(2), 146–158. https://doi.org/10.1002/cpp.2414

Maris, R. W. (2019). *Suicidology: A comprehensive biopsychosocial perspective*. Guilford Press.

Martin, E. H. (2020). Psychological assessment as treatment: Collaborative therapeutic assessment. In M. Sellbom & J. Suhr (Eds.), *Cambridge handbook of clinical assessment and diagnosis* (pp. 90–100). Cambridge University Press.

Martinčeková, L., & Klatt, J. (2017). Mothers' grief, forgiveness, and posttraumatic growth after the loss of a child. *Omega, 75*(3), 248–265. https://doi.org/10.1177/0030222816652803

Marvasti, J. A., & Wank, A. A. (2013). Suicide in U.S. veterans. *American Journal of Forensic Psychology, 31*(4), 27–54.

May, R. (1983). *The discovery of being: Writings in existential psychology*. Norton.

Mazaheri, M., Gharraee, B., Shabani, A., & Lotfi, M. (2019, May). Studying the predictive factors of suicide attempts in patients with type 1 bipolar disorder. *Psychiatry Research, 275,* 373–378. https://doi.org/10.1016/j.psychres.2019.04.012

McGlothlin, J. (2008). *Developing clinical skills in suicide assessment, prevention and treatment*. American Counseling Association.

McHugh, C. M., Corderoy, A., Ryan, C. J., Hickie, I. B., & Large, M. (2019). Association between suicidal ideation and suicide: Meta-analyses of odds ratios, sensitivity, specificity and positive predictive value. *BJPsych Open*, e24. https://doi.org/10.1192/bjo.2018.88

Meichenbaum, D. (2006). *Trauma and suicide: A constructive narrative perspective*. American Psychological Association.

Melhem, N. M., Porta, G., Oquendo, M. A., Zelazny, J., Keilp, J. G., Iyengar, S., Burke, A., Birmaher, B., Stanley, B., John Mann, J., & Brent, D. A. (2019). Severity and variability of depression symptoms predicting suicide attempt in high-risk individuals. *JAMA Psychiatry, 76*(6), 603–613. https://doi.org/10.1001/jamapsychiatry.2018.4513

Michel, K., & Jobes, D. A. (2010). *Building a therapeutic alliance with the suicidal patient*. American Psychological Association.

Miller, M. (1985). *Information center: Training workshop manual*. The Information Center.

Miller, W. R. (1978). Behavioral treatment of problem drinkers: A comparative outcome study of three controlled drinking therapies. *Journal of Consulting & Clinical Psychology, 46*(1), 74–86. https://doi.org/10.1037//0022-006x.46.1.74

Miller, W. R., & Rollnick, S. (2013). *Motivational interviewing: Preparing people for change* (3rd ed.). Guilford Press.

Millon, E. M., & Shors, T. J. (2019, December 30). Taking neurogenesis out of the lab and into the world with MAP Train My Brain. *Behavioural Brain Research, 376*, 1–10. https://doi.org/10.1016/j.bbr.2019.112154

Minois, G. (1999). *History of suicide: Voluntary death in western culture* (L. G. Cochrane, Trans.). Johns Hopkins University Press.

Molnar, B. E., Berkman, L. F., & Buka, S. L. (2001). Psychopathology, childhood sexual abuse and other childhood adversities: Relative links to subsequent suicidal behaviour in the US. *Psychological Medicine, 31*(6), 965–977. https://doi.org/10.1017/S0033291701004329

Moore, F. R., Bell, M., Macleod, M., Smith, E., Beaumont, J., Graham, L., & Harley, T. A. (2018, December). Season, weather, and suicide: Further evidence for ecological complexity. *Neurology, Psychiatry and Brain Research, 30*, 110–116. https://doi.org/10.1016/j.npbr.2018.08.002

Morris, C. A. W., & Minton, C. A. B. (2012). Crisis in the curriculum? New counselors' crisis preparation, experiences, and self-efficacy. *Counselor Education and Supervision, 51*(4), 256–269. https://doi.org/10.1002/j.1556-6978.2012.00019.x

Mosak, H. H. (1985). Interrupting a depression: The pushbutton technique. *Individual Psychology, 41*(2), 210–214.

Murphy, J. J. (2015). *Solution-focused counseling in middle and high schools* (3rd ed.). American Counseling Association.

Myers, J. E. (1991). Wellness as a paradigm for counseling and development: The possible future. *Counselor Education and Supervision, 30*(3), 183–193. https://doi.org/10.1002/j.1556-6978.1991.tb01199.x

Na, P. J., Yaramala, S. R., Kim, J. A., Kim, H., Goes, F. S., Zandi, P. P., Vande Voort, J. L., Sutor, B., Croarkin, P., & Bobo, W. V. (2018, May). The PHQ-9 Item 9 based screening for suicide risk: A validation study of the Patient Health Questionnaire (PHQ)–9 Item 9 with the Columbia Suicide Severity Rating Scale (C-SSRS). *Journal of Affective Disorders, 232*, 34–40. https://doi.org/10.1016/j.jad.2018.02.045

Nasstasia, Y., Baker, A. L., Lewin, T. J., Halpin, S. A., Hides, L., Kelly, B. J., & Callister, R. (2019, December). Differential treatment effects of an integrated motivational interviewing and exercise intervention on depressive symptom profiles and associated factors: A randomised controlled cross-over trial among youth with major depression. *Journal of Affective Disorders, 259*, 413–423. https://doi.org/10.1016/j.jad.2019.08.035

National Association of Social Workers. (2017). *Code of ethics of the National Association of Social Workers.*

Nelson, J. R., Hall, B. S., Anderson, J. L., Birtles, C., & Hemming, L. (2018). Self-compassion as self-care: A simple and effective tool for counselor educators and counseling students. *Journal of Creativity in Mental Health*, 13(1), 121–133. https://doi.org/10.1080/15401383.2017.1328292

Nelson, K. M., Hagedorn, W. B., & Lambie, G. W. (2019). Influence of attachment style on sexual abuse survivors' posttraumatic growth. *Journal of Counseling & Development*, 97(3), 227–237. https://doi.org/10.1002/jcad.12263

Nezu, A. M., Nezu, C. M., & D'Zurilla, T. J. (2013). *Problem-solving therapy: A treatment manual*. Springer.

Niebuhr, R. (1987). *The essential Reinhold Niebuhr: Selected essays and addresses* (R. M. Brown, Ed.). Yale University Press.

Nielssen, O., Wallace, D., & Large, M. (2017). Pokorny's complaint: The insoluble problem of the overwhelming number of false positives generated by suicide risk assessment. *BJPsych Bulletin*, 41(1), 18–20. https://www.ncbi.nlm.nih.gov/pmc/articles/PMC5288088/pdf/pbrcpsych_41_1_005.pdf

Nobles, C. J., Valentine, S. E., Borba, C. P. C., Gerber, M. W., Shtasel, D. L., & Marques, L. (2016, June). Black-White disparities in the association between posttraumatic stress disorder and chronic illness. *Journal of Psychosomatic Research*, 85, 19–25. https://doi.org/10.1016/j.jpsychores.2016.03.126

Norcross, J., & Lambert, M. (2018). Psychotherapy relationships that work III. *Psychotherapy*, 55(4), 303–315. https://doi.org/10.1037/pst0000193

Norcross, J. C., & Vandenbos, G. (2018). *Leaving it at the office: A guide to psychotherapist self-care* (2nd ed.). Guilford Press.

O'Connor, R. C. (2011). The integrated motivational-volitional model of suicidal behavior. *Crisis*, 32(6), 295–298. https://doi.org/10.1027/0227-5910/a000120

Oliva, E. M., Bowe, T., Manhapra, A., Kertesz, S., Hah, J. M., Henderson, P., Robinson, A., Paik, M., Sandbrink, F., Gordon, A. J., & Trafton, J. A. (2020). Associations between stopping prescriptions for opioids, length of opioid treatment, and overdose or suicide deaths in US veterans: Observational evaluation. *The BMJ*, 368, 10. https://doi.org/10.1136/bmj.m283

Ozen, L. J., Dubois, S., Gibbons, C., Short, M. M., Maxwell, H., & Bédard, M. (2016). Mindfulness interventions improve depression symptoms after traumatic brain injury: Are individual changes clinically significant? *Mindfulness*, 7(6), 1356–1364. https://doi.org/10.1007/s12671-016-0577-x

Özkan, S. A., Kücükkelepce, D. S., Korkmaz, B., Yılmaz, G., & Bozkurt, M. A. (2020). The effectiveness of an exercise intervention in reducing the severity of postpartum depression: A randomized controlled trial. *Perspectives in Psychiatric Care*. Advance online publication. https://doi.org/10.1111/ppc.12500

Parrow, K. K., Sommers-Flanagan, J., Sky Cova, J., & Lungu, H. (2019). Evidence based relationship factors: A new focus for mental health counseling research, practice, and training. *Journal of Mental Health Counseling, 41*(4), 327–342. https://doi.org/10.17744/mehc.41.4.04

Patterson, W. M., Dohn, H. H., Bird, J., & Patterson, G. A. (1983). Evaluation of suicidal patients: The SAD PERSONS scale. *Psychosomatics, 24*(4), 343–349. https://doi.org/10.1016/s0033-3182(83)73213-5

Penney, A., Mazmanian, D., Jamieson, J., & Black, N. (2012). Factors associated with recent suicide attempts in clients presenting for addiction treatment. *International Journal of Mental Health and Addiction, 10*(1), 132–140. https://doi.org/10.1007/s11469-010-9307-0

Peterson, C., Sussell, A., Li, J., Schumacher, P. K., Yeoman, K., & Stone, D. M. (2020). Suicide rates by industry and occupation: National Violent Death Reporting System, 32 states, 2016. *Morbidity and Mortality Weekly Report, 69*(3), 57–62. https://doi.org/10.15585/mmwr.mm6903a1

Pfeffer, C. R. (2006). Suicide in children and adolescents. In D. J. Stein, D. J. Kupfer, & A. F. Schatzberg (Eds.), *The American Psychiatric Publishing textbook of mood disorders* (pp. 497–507). American Psychiatric Publishing.

Plöderl, M., Kunrath, S., & Fartacek, C. (2020). God bless you? The association of religion and spirituality with reduction of suicide ideation and length of hospital stay among psychiatric patients at risk for suicide. *Suicide and Life-Threatening Behavior, 50*(1), 95–110. https://doi.org/10.1111/sltb.12582

Posner, K., Brown, G. K., Stanley, B., Brent, D. A., Yershova, K. V., Oquendo, M. A., Currier, G. W., Melvin, G. A., Greenhill, L., Shen, S., & Mann, J. J. (2011). The Columbia-Suicide Severity Rating Scale: Initial validity and internal consistency findings from three multisite studies with adolescents and adults. *American Journal of Psychiatry, 168*(12), 1266–1277. https://doi.org/10.1176/appi.ajp.2011.10111704

Puetz, T. W., Flowers, S. S., & O'Connor, P. J. (2008). A randomized controlled trial of the effect of aerobic exercise training on feelings of energy and fatigue in sedentary young adults with persistent fatigue. *Psychotherapy and Psychosomatics, 77*(3), 167–174. https://doi.org/10.1159/000116610

Quinn, J. M., Pascoe, A., Wood, W., & Neal, D. T. (2010). Can't control yourself? Monitor those bad habits. *Personality and Social Psychology Bulletin, 36*(4), 499–511. https://doi.org/10.1177/0146167209360665

Rashid, T., & Seligman, M. E. P. (2018). *Positive psychotherapy: Clinician manual*. Oxford University Press.

Ratts, M. J., Singh, A. A., Nassar-McMillan, S., Butler, S. K., & McCullough, J. R. (2016). Multicultural and social justice counseling competencies: Guidelines for the counseling profession. *Journal of Multicultural Counseling and Development, 44*(1), 28–48. https://doi.org/10.1002/jmcd.12035

Ratts, M. J., Toporek, R., & Lewis, J. A. (2010). *ACA advocacy competencies*. American Counseling Association.

Read, J., Agar, K., Barker-Collo, S., Davies, E., & Moskowitz, A. (2001). Assessing suicidality in adults: Integrating childhood trauma as a major risk factor. *Professional Psychology: Research and Practice, 32*(4), 367–372. https://doi.org/10.1037/0735-7028.32.4.367

Recommendations for reporting on suicide. (n.d.). https://www.datocms-assets.com/12810/1577098761-recommendations.pdf

Reed, K. P., Nugent, W., & Cooper, R. L. (2015, August). Testing a path model of relationships between gender, age, and bullying victimization and violent behavior, substance abuse, depression, suicidal ideation, and suicide attempts in adolescents. *Children and Youth Services Review, 55*, 128–137. https://doi.org/10.1016/j.childyouth.2015.05.016

Reinecke, M. A. (2006). Problem solving: A conceptual approach to suicidality and psychotherapy. In T. E. Ellis (Ed.), *Cognition and suicide: Theory, research, and therapy* (pp. 237–260). American Psychological Association.

Resick, P. A., Monson, C. M., & Chard, K. M. (2017). *Cognitive processing therapy for PTSD: A comprehensive manual*. Guilford Press.

Ribeiro, J. D., Pease, J. L., Gutierrez, P. M., Silva, C., Bernert, R. A., Rudd, M. D., & Joiner, T. E. (2012). Sleep problems outperform depression and hopelessness as cross-sectional and longitudinal predictors of suicidal ideation and behavior in young adults in the military. *Journal of Affective Disorders, 136*(3), 743–750. https://doi.org/10.1016/j.jad.2011.09.049

Ribeiro, J. D., Silva, C., & Joiner, T. E. (2014). Overarousal interacts with a sense of fearlessness about death to predict suicide risk in a sample of clinical outpatients. *Psychiatry Research, 218*(1–2), 106–112. https://doi.org/10.1016/j.psychres.2014.03.036

Rogers, C. R. (1957). The necessary and sufficient conditions of therapeutic personality change. *Journal of Consulting Psychology, 21*(2), 95–103. https://doi.org/10.1037/h0045357

Rogers, C. R. (1961). *On becoming a person.* Houghton Mifflin.

Rosenberg, J. I. (1999). Suicide prevention: An integrated training model using affective and action-based interventions. *Professional Psychology: Research and Practice, 30*(1), 83–87. https://doi.org/10.1037/0735-7028.30.1.83

Roush, J. F., Brown, S. L., Jahn, D. R., Mitchell, S. M., Taylor, N. J., Quinnett, P., & Ries, R. (2018). Mental health professionals' suicide risk assessment and management practices: The impact of fear of suicide-related outcomes and comfort working with suicidal individuals. *Crisis, 39*(1), 55–64. https://doi.org/10.1027/0227-5910/a000478

Rowland, L., & Curry, O. S. (2019). A range of kindness activities boost happiness. *Journal of Social Psychology, 159*(3), 340–343. https://doi.org/10.1080/00224545.2018.1469461

Rubin, S. S. (2012). Tracking through bereavement: A framework for intervention. In R. A. Neimeyer (Ed.), *Techniques of grief therapy: Creative practices for counseling the bereaved* (pp. 20–24). Routledge.

Rudd, M. D. (2006). *Assessment and management of suicidality.* Professional Resource Press.

Rudd, M. D. (2014). Core competencies, warning signs, and a framework for suicide risk assessment in clinical practice. In M. Nock (Ed.), *Oxford handbook of suicide and self-injury* (pp. 323–336). Oxford University Press.

Rudd, M. D., Mandrusiak, M., & Joiner, T. E. (2006). The case against no-suicide contracts: The commitment to treatment statement as a practice alternative. *Journal of Clinical Psychology, 62*(2), 243–251. https://doi.org/10.1002/jclp.20227

Rummell, C. M., & Joyce, N. R. (2010). "So wat do u want to wrk on 2day?": The ethical implications of online counseling. *Ethics & Behavior, 20*(6), 482–496. https://doi.org/10.1080/10508422.2010.521450

Runyan, C. W., Brown, T. L., & Brooks-Russell, A. (2015). Preventing the invisible plague of firearm suicide. *American Journal of Orthopsychiatry, 85*(3), 221–224. https://doi.org/10.1037/ort0000065

Safran, J. D., & Kraus, J. (2014). Alliance ruptures, impasses, and enactments: A relational perspective. *Psychotherapy, 51*(3), 381–387. https://doi.org/10.1037/a0036815

Sands, D. C., Jordan, J. R., & Neimeyer, R. A. (2011). The meanings of suicide: A narrative approach to healing. In J. R. Jordan & J. L. McIntosh (Eds.), *Grief after suicide: Understanding the consequences and caring for the survivors* (pp. 249–282). Routledge.

Sansone, R. A., Kelley, A. R., & Forbis, J. S. (2013). The relationship between forgiveness and history of suicide attempt. *Mental Health, Religion & Culture, 16*(1), 31–37. https://doi.org/10.1080/13674676.2011.643860

Scarf, M. (1987). *Intimate partners: Patterns in love and marriage.* Ballantine.

Schauer, M., Neuner, F., & Elbert, T. (2011). *Narrative exposure therapy: A short term treatment for traumatic stress disorders* (2nd ed.). Hogrefe.

Scheyett, A., Bayakly, R., & Whitaker, M. (2019). Characteristics and contextual stressors in farmer and agricultural worker suicides in Georgia from 2008–2015. *Journal of Rural Mental Health, 43*(2–3), 61–72. https://doi.org/10.1037/rmh0000114

Schudson, Z. C., Beischel, W. J., & van Anders, S. M. (2019). Individual variation in gender/sex category definitions. *Psychology of Sexual Orientation and Gender Diversity, 6*(4), 448–460. https://doi.org/10.1037/sgd0000346

Segal, Z. V., Williams, J. M. G., & Teasdale, J. D. (2013). *Mindfulness-based cognitive therapy for depression* (2nd ed.). Guilford Press.

Seligman, M. E. P. (2002). *Authentic happiness.* Free Press.

Seligman, M. E. P. (2018). *The hope circuit: A psychologist's journey from hopelessness to optimism.* Hachette Book Group.

Seligman, M. E. P., Rashid, T., & Parks, A. C. (2006). Positive psychotherapy. *American Psychologist, 61*(8), 774–788. https://doi.org/10.1037/0003-066X.61.8.774

Shakespeare, W. (1992). *Julius Caesar* (B. A. Mowat & P. Werstine, Eds.). Washington Square Press. (Original work published 1623)

Shannonhouse, L., Hill, M., & Hightower, J. (2020). Trauma exposure, suicidality, and reporting in college students. *Journal of American College Health.* Advance online publication. https://doi.org/10.1080/07448481.2020.1752695

Shantideva. (2006). *The way of the Bodhisattva* (Padmakara Translation Group, Trans.; 2nd ed.). Shambhala.

Shapiro, F. (2001). *Eye movement desensitization and reprocessing: Basic principles, protocols, and procedures* (2nd ed.). Guilford Press.

Shea, S. C. (2011). *The practical art of suicide assessment: A guide for mental health professionals and substance abuse counselors* (2nd ed.). Wiley.

Shearer, A., Russon, J., Herres, J., Wong, A., Jacobs, C., Diamond, G. M., & Diamond, G. S. (2018). Religion, sexual orientation, and suicide attempts among a sample of suicidal adolescents. *Suicide and Life-Threatening Behavior, 48*(4), 431–437. https://doi.org/10.1111/sltb.12372

Shern, D. L., Blanch, A. K., & Steverman, S. M. (2016). Toxic stress, behavioral health, and the next major era in public health. *American Journal of Orthopsychiatry, 86*(2), 109–123. https://doi.org/10.1037/ort0000120

Shneidman, E. S. (1980). Psychotherapy with suicidal patients. In T. B. Karasu & A. S. Bellack (Eds.), *Specialized techniques in individual psychotherapy* (pp. 306–328). Brunner/Mazel.

Shneidman, E. S. (1993). *Suicide as psychache: A clinical approach to self-destructive behavior*. Jason Aronson.

Shneidman, E. S. (1996). *The suicidal mind*. Oxford University Press.

Shneidman, E. S. (2001). *Comprehending suicide: Landmarks in 20th century suicidology*. American Psychological Association.

Shneidman, E. S. (2004). *Autopsy of a suicidal mind*. Oxford University Press.

Shors, T. J., Olson, R. L., Bates, M. E., Selby, E. A., & Alderman, B. L. (2014). Mental and physical (MAP) training: A neurogenesis-inspired intervention that enhances health in humans. *Neurobiology of Learning and Memory, 115,* 3–9. https://doi.org/10.1016/j.nlm.2014.08.012

Simoneau, H., Ménard, J., & Blanchette-Martin, N. (2017). Addiction severity and suicidal behaviors among persons entering treatment. *Archives of Suicide Research, 21*(2), 341–353. https://doi.org/10.1080/13811118.2016.1182093

Sommers-Flanagan, J. (2015a, December 5). *Constructivism vs. social constructionism: What's the difference?* https://johnsommersflanagan.com/2015/12/05/constructivism-vs-social-constructionism-whats-the-difference/

Sommers-Flanagan, J. (2015b). Evidence-based relationship practice: Enhancing counselor competence. *Journal of Mental Health Counseling, 37*(2), 95–108. https://doi.org/10.17744/mehc.37.2.g13472044600588r

Sommers-Flanagan, J. (2018a). Conversations about suicide: Strategies for detecting and assessing suicide risk. *Journal of Health Service Psychology, 44*(1), 33–45. https://doi.org/10.1007/BF03544661

Sommers-Flanagan, J. (2018b). *Suicide assessment and intervention with suicidal clients* [Video]. Psychotherapy.net.

Sommers-Flanagan, J., & Campbell, D. G. (2009). Psychotherapy and (or) medications for depression in youth? An evidence-based review with recommendations for treatment. *Journal of Contemporary Psychotherapy, 39*(2), 111–120. https://doi.org/10.1007/s10879-008-9106-0

Sommers-Flanagan, J., Johnson, V. I., & Rides At The Door, M. (2020). Clinical interviewing. In M. Sellbom & J. A. Suhr (Eds.), *Cambridge handbook of clinical assessment and diagnosis* (pp. 113–122). Cambridge University Press.

Sommers-Flanagan, J., & Shaw, S. L. (2017). Suicide risk assessment: What psychologists should know. *Professional Psychology: Research and Practice, 48*(2), 98–106. https://doi.org/10.1037/pro0000106

Sommers-Flanagan, J., & Sommers-Flanagan, R. (2007). *Tough kids, cool counseling: User-friendly approaches with challenging youth* (2nd ed.). American Counseling Association.

Sommers-Flanagan, J., & Sommers-Flanagan, R. (2017). *Clinical interviewing* (6th ed.). Wiley.

Sommers-Flanagan, J., & Sommers-Flanagan, R. (2018). *Counseling and psychotherapy theories in context and practice: Skills, strategies, and techniques* (3rd ed.). Wiley.

Sommers-Flanagan, R., Elliott, D., & Sommers-Flanagan, J. (1998). Exploring the edges: Boundaries and breaks. *Ethics & Behavior, 8*(1), 37–48. https://doi.org/10.1207/s15327019eb0801_3

Stanley, B., & Brown, G. K. (2012). Safety planning intervention: A brief intervention to mitigate suicide risk. *Cognitive and Behavioral Practice, 19*(2), 256–264. https://doi.org/10.1016/j.cbpra.2011.01.001

Stargell, N. A., Zoldan, C. A., Kress, V. E., Walker-Andrews, L., & Whisenhunt, J. L. (2017). Student non-suicidal self-injury: A protocol for school counselors. *Professional School Counseling, 21*(1), 10. https://doi.org/10.5330/1096-2409-21.1.37

Stefansson, J., Nordström, P., & Jokinen, J. (2012). Suicide intent scale in the prediction of suicide. *Journal of Affective Disorders, 136*(1–2), 167–171. https://doi.org/10.1016/j.jad.2010.11.016

Stein, R. (1986, August 17). B. F. Skinner, at 82, grows pessimistic that world will accept his ideas. *Los Angeles Times*. https://www.latimes.com/archives/la-xpm-1986-08-17-mn-16533-story.html

Stoll, J., Müller, J. A., & Trachsel, M. (2020). Ethical issues in online psychotherapy: A narrative review. *Frontiers in Psychiatry, 10*, 16. https://doi.org/10.3389/fpsyt.2019.00993

Stone, C. (2018, July 1). Suicide and child abuse reporting. *ASCA School Counselor*. https://schoolcounselor.org/magazine/blogs/july-august-2018/suicide-and-child-abuse-reporting

Substance Abuse and Mental Health Services Administration. (2019). *Civil commitment and the mental health care continuum: Historical trends and principles for law and practice.* https://www.samhsa.gov/sites/default/files/civil-commitment-continuum-of-care.pdf

Sue, D. W., Sue, D., Neville, H. A., & Smith, L. (2019). *Counseling the culturally diverse: Theory and practice* (8th ed.). Wiley.

Sullivan, G. R., & Bongar, B. (2009). Assessing suicide risk in the adult patient. In P. M. Kleespies (Ed.), *Behavioral emergencies: An evidence-based resource for evaluating and managing risk of suicide, violence, and victimization* (pp. 59–78). American Psychological Association.

Sytine, A. I., Britt, T. W., Sawhney, G., Wilson, C. A., & Keith, M. (2019). Savoring as a moderator of the daily demands and psychological capital relationship: A daily diary study. *Journal of Positive Psychology, 14*(5), 641–648. https://doi.org/10.1080/17439760.2018.1519590

Szkody, E., & McKinney, C. (2019). Stress-buffering effects of social support on depressive problems: Perceived vs. received support and moderation by parental depression. *Journal of Child and Family Studies, 28*(8), 2209–2219. https://doi.org/10.1007/s10826-019-01437-1

Szuhany, K. L., & Otto, M. W. (2019). Efficacy evaluation of exercise as an augmentation strategy to brief behavioral activation treatment for depression: A randomized pilot trial. *Cognitive Behaviour Therapy, 49*(3), 228–241. https://doi.org/10.1080/16506073.2019.1641145

Szumilas, M., & Kutcher, S. (2011). Post-suicide intervention programs: A systematic review. *Canadian Journal of Public Health, 102*(1), 8–29. https://doi.org/10.1007/BF03404872

Tarasoff v. Regents of the University of California, 131 Cal. Rptr. 14 (Cal. 1976).

Tarrier, N., Taylor, K., & Gooding, P. (2008). Cognitive-behavioral interventions to reduce suicide behavior: A systematic review and meta-analysis. *Behavior Modification, 32*(1), 77–108. https://doi.org/10.1177/0145445507304728

Tran, A. G. T. T., Lam, C. K., & Legg, E. (2018). Financial stress, social supports, gender, and anxiety during college: A stress-buffering perspective. *The Counseling Psychologist, 46*(7), 846–869. https://doi.org/10.1177/0011000018806687

Trippany, R. L., Kress, V. E. W., & Wilcoxon, S. A. (2004). Preventing vicarious trauma: What counselors should know when working with trauma survivors. *Journal of Counseling & Development, 82*(1), 31–37. https://doi.org/10.1002/j.1556-6678.2004.tb00283.x

Tromholt, M. (2016). The Facebook experiment: Quitting Facebook leads to higher levels of well-being. *Cyberpsychology, Behavior, and Social Networking, 19*(11), 661–666. https://doi.org/10.1089/cyber.2016.0259

Tryon, G. S., Birch, S. E., & Verkuilen, J. (2018). Meta-analyses of the relation of goal consensus and collaboration to psychotherapy outcome. *Psychotherapy, 55*(4), 372–383. https://doi.org/10.1037/pst0000170

U.S. Department of Veterans Affairs. (2019). *2019 national veteran suicide prevention annual report.* https://www.mentalhealth.va.gov/docs/data-sheets/2019/2019_National_Veteran_Suicide_Prevention_Annual_Report_508.pdf

U.S. Food and Drug Administration. (2007). *FDA proposes new warnings about suicidal thinking, behavior in young adults who take antidepressant medications.* https://www.fda.gov/media/77404/download

UM News Service. (2011, October 18). *What makes life worth living? (Part 1)* [Video]. YouTube. https://www.youtube.com/watch?v=DRiIAqGXLKA

VA/DoD Clinical Practice Guideline Working Group. (2017). *VA/DoD clinical practice guideline for the management of posttraumatic stress disorder and acute stress disorder.* VA Office of Quality and Performance.

van der Kolk, B. (2014). *The body keeps the score: Brain, mind, and body in the healing of trauma.* Penguin.

van der Kolk, B. A., Spinazzola, J., Blaustein, M. E., Hopper, J. W., Hopper, E. K., Korn, D. L., & Simpson, W. B. (2007). A randomized clinical trial of eye movement desensitization and reprocessing (EMDR), fluoxetine, and pill placebo in the treatment of posttraumatic stress disorder: Treatment effects and long-term maintenance. *Journal of Clinical Psychiatry, 68*(1), 37–46. https://doi.org/10.4088/jcp.v68n0105

Van Orden, K. A., Witte, T. K., Cukrowicz, K. C., Braithwaite, S. R., Selby, E. A., & Joiner, T. E. (2010). The interpersonal theory of suicide. *Psychological Review, 117*(2), 575–600. https://doi.org/10.1037/a0018697

Vander Stoep, A., Adrian, M., McCauley, E., Crowell, S. E., Stone, A., & Flynn, C. (2011). Risk for suicidal ideation and suicide attempts associated with co-occurring depression and conduct problems in early adolescence. *Suicide and Life-Threatening Behavior, 41*(3), 316–329. https://doi.org/10.1111/j.1943-278X.2011.00031.x

Walker, R. L., Salami, T. K., Carter, S. E., & Flowers, K. (2014). Perceived racism and suicide ideation: Mediating role of depression but moderating role of religiosity among African American adults. *Suicide and Life-Threatening Behavior, 44*(5), 548–559. https://doi.org/10.1111/sltb.12089

Warden, S., Spiwak, R., Sareen, J., & Bolton, J. M. (2014). The SAD PERSONS scale for suicide risk assessment. A systematic review. *Archives of Suicide Research, 18*(4), 313–326. https://doi.org/10.1080/13811118.2013.824829

Watkins, L. E., Sprang, K. R., & Rothbaum, B. O. (2018). Treating PTSD: A review of evidence-based psychotherapy interventions. *Frontiers in Behavioral Neuroscience, 12,* 1–9. https://doi.org/10.3389/fnbeh.2018.00258

Webb, J. R., Hirsch, J. K., & Toussaint, L. (2015). Forgiveness as a positive psychotherapy for addiction and suicide: Theory, research, and practice. *Spirituality in Clinical Practice, 2*(1), 48–60. https://doi.org/10.1037/scp0000054

Wenzel, A., Brown, G. K., & Beck, A. T. (2009). *Cognitive therapy for suicidal patients: Scientific and clinical applications.* American Psychological Association.

Werth, J. L., Jr., Burke, C., & Bardash, R. J. (2002). Confidentiality in end-of-life and after-death situations. *Ethics & Behavior, 12*(3), 205–222. https://doi.org/10.1207/S15327019EB1203_1

Wheeler, A. M. N., & Bertram, B. (2019). *The counselor and the law* (8th ed.). American Counseling Association.

Wikipedia. (2020). *Random act of kindness.* https://en.wikipedia.org/wiki/Random_act_of_kindness

Wilcox, H. C., & Fawcett, J. (2012). Stress, trauma, and risk for attempted and completed suicide. *Psychiatric Annals, 42*(3), 85–87. https://doi.org/10.3928/00485713-20120217-04

Witmer, J. M., & Sweeney, T. J. (1992). A holistic model for wellness and prevention over the life span. *Journal of Counseling & Development, 71*(2), 140–148. https://doi.org/10.1002/j.1556-6676.1992.tb02189.x

Wollersheim, J. P. (1974). The assessment of suicide potential via interview methods. *Psychotherapy: Theory, Research & Practice, 11*(3), 222–225. https://doi.org/10.1037/h0086344

Wong, Y. J. (2015). The psychology of encouragement: Theory, research, and applications. *The Counseling Psychologist, 43*(2), 178–216. https://doi.org/10.1177/0011000014545091

Wortmann, J. H., Eisen, E., Hundert, C., Jordan, A. H., Smith, M. W., Nash, W. P., & Litz, B. T. (2017). Spiritual features of war-related moral injury: A primer for clinicians. *Spirituality in Clinical Practice, 4*(4), 249–261. https://doi.org/10.1037/scp0000140

Wubbolding, R. E. (2000). *Reality therapy for the 21st century.* Accelerated Development.

Wygant, D. B., Burchett, D., & Harp, J. P. (2020). Assessment of noncredible reporting and responding. In M. Sellbom & J. Suhr (Eds.), *Cambridge handbook of clinical assessment and diagnosis* (pp. 63–79). Cambridge University Press.

Yalom, I. D. (1980). *Existential psychotherapy*. Basic Books.
Yalom, I. D. (1989). *Love's executioner*. Basic Books.
Yalom, I. (Expert), & Yalom, V. (Producer). (2019). *Irvin Yalom in session: Eugenia* [Video]. Psychotherapy.net.
Ybarra, M. (2015, July 29). Self-harm websites and teens who visit them. *Psychology Today*. https://www.psychologytoday.com/us/blog/connected/201507/self-harm-websites-and-teens-who-visit-them
Yildiz, M., Demirhan, E., & Gurbuz, S. (2019). Contextual socioeconomic disadvantage and adolescent suicide attempts: A multilevel investigation. *Journal of Youth and Adolescence, 48*(4), 802–814. https://doi.org/10.1007/s10964-018-0961-z
Young, J. E., Klosko, J. S., & Weishaar, M. E. (2003). *Schema therapy: A practitioner's guide*. Guilford Press.
Yu, C. C. W., Wong, S. W. L., Lo, F. S. F., So, R. C. H., & Chan, D. F. Y. (2018). Study protocol: A randomized controlled trial study on the effect of a game-based exercise training program on promoting physical fitness and mental health in children with autism spectrum disorder. *BMC Psychiatry, 18*(1), 1–10. https://doi.org/10.1186/s12888-018-1635-9
Zahl, D. L., & Hawton, K. (2004). Repetition of deliberate self-harm and subsequent suicide risk: Long-term follow-up study of 11 583 patients. *British Journal of Psychiatry, 185*(1), 70–75. https://doi.org/10.1192/bjp.185.1.70
Zalsman, G., Netanel, R., Fischel, T., Freudenstein, O., Landau, E., Orbach, I., Weizman, A., Pfeffer, C. R., & Apter, A. (2000). Human figure drawings in the evaluation of severe adolescent suicidal behavior. *Journal of the American Academy of Child & Adolescent Psychiatry, 39*(8), 1024–1031. https://doi.org/10.1097/00004583-200008000-00018
Zimet, G. D., Dahlem, N. W., Zimet, S. G., & Farley, G. K. (1988). The Multidimensional Scale of Perceived Social Support. *Journal of Personality Assessment, 52*(1), 30–41. https://doi.org/10.1207/s15327752jpa5201_2

Index

References to figures and tables are indicated by "f" and "t" following the page numbers.

A

AAS (American Association of Suicidology), 24, 60
Abuse
 child abuse, 23, 36, 38, 170–171, 176
 LGBTQ+ clients and, 58
 reporting requirements for, 23, 38
 self-hatred resulting from, 136
 sexual, 170–171, 176
ACA. *See* American Counseling Association
ACA Code of Ethics, 23
Acceptance
 in addiction treatment, 220
 in distress tolerance, 105–106
 empathetic, 88, 93, 190, 193
 in motivational interviewing, 99
 nonjudgmental, 241
 of suicidal impulses, 11
Acceptance and commitment therapy, 114
Acculturative stress, 191–192
Acquired capability, 215
Active-constructive responses, 160
Active listening skills, 65, 69
Activism, 242
Activity scheduling, 125, 218
Addictions treatment, 219–220. *See also* Substance use
Adler, Alfred, 111–112, 171, 210

Adolescents. *See* Children and adolescents
Adverse Childhood Experiences Study, 171
Advocacy, 192, 194, 242
African Americans
 discrimination against, 191, 238
 protests against racial injustice, 238–239
 suicide deaths among, 54*f*, 55
After-hours contact, 38–39
Age, suicide rates by, 54, 55*f*, 207
Agitation
 assessment of, 31, 62, 75
 depression and, 81
 inability to collaborate and, 29
 in physical dimension, 169–170, 184
 sleep disturbances and, 171
 toxic relationships and, 146
Akathisia, 75, 166
Alcohol. *See* Substance use
Alcoholics Anonymous, 220, 240
Ali, S., 194
Alternatives to suicide intervention, 121–126, 140
Ambivalence, 77, 98–99, 102, 143
American Academy of Child and Adolescent Psychiatry, 23
American Association of Suicidology (AAS), 24, 60

• 277

American Counseling Association (ACA)
  ACA Code of Ethics, 23
  advocacy competencies from, 242
  distance counseling guidelines from, 41
American Indians. *See* Native Americans
American Psychological Association, 23, 41, 184
American School Counselor Association, 23, 34–36
Anger
  agitation and, 81
  in cultural-spiritual dimension, 205
  in emotional dimension, 88–90, 107, 108
  in mental health professionals, 44
  as warning sign, 60
Anorexia nervosa, 56
Antidepressants, 17, 56–57, 75, 166–169, 168f, 196
Antipsychotics, 177
Anxiety
  exercise for, 172–174
  genetic risk of suicide as cause of, 165–166
  management of, 177–179
  of mental health professionals, 1–2, 4, 18, 22, 50, 126
  in physical dimension, 170, 177–179
  social, 149, 152
  unsolvable problems and, 241
Aristotle, 141
Arousal, 75, 169–170, 184, 239
Asian Americans
  cultural disconnection and dislocation of, 191
  discrimination against, 238
  questioning strategies for, 202
Assessment. *See* Suicide assessment
Astronomical conditions, 58
Attitudes
  of acceptance, 99, 114
  ethical bracketing of, 11–13, 19
  positive, 84
  self-awareness of, 24–25
Autism spectrum disorder, 172–174

B

Bartley, W. W., 240
Beauvoir, Simone de, 188
Beck, Aaron, 62, 68, 111–112, 114, 133, 218
Beck Depression Scale, 68
Beck Hopelessness Scale, 62, 68
Beck Scale for Suicide Ideation, 50
Beck Suicide Intent Scale, 79
Behavioral activation, 124–125, 140, 218
Behavioral dimension, 213–233
  access to lethal means in, 216
  addictions treatment in, 219–220
  behavioral activation in, 218
  case examples, 220–223, 225–230
  clinical application of, 17–18
  directive approach in, 230–231
  impulsivity in, 215–216
  lethal means restriction in, 219–225, 228–229
  overview, 15, 16t
  practitioner guidance, 232–233
  Reasons for Living inventory in, 216–218
  safety planning in, 219, 224–230
  strengths-based approach in, 214
  suicide desensitization in, 215, 218–219
  suicide planning and intent in, 214–215
  working in, 213–216
Beliefs. *See also* Cultural-spiritual dimension
  core, 89, 113–115, 133, 135–136, 144, 159
  ethical bracketing of, 11–13, 19
  self-awareness of, 24–25
Belsher, B. E., 26, 27
Benzodiazepines, 170
Biases. *See* Discrimination
Biogenetics and medical treatments, 165–166
Bipolar disorder, 56, 216
Bisexual clients. *See* LGBTQ+ clients
Black Americans. *See* African Americans
Boisvert, D., 164
Bono, T., 167, 168
Borderline personality disorder, 56, 90–91, 106, 216
Bordin, E. S., 108–110
Boundary setting, 39, 41–44, 228
Bronfenbrenner, U., 238
Brown, G. K., 29, 71, 224
Bryan, C. J., 14, 29, 133–135, 221–223
Bullying, 43, 58, 74, 152–155, 207–209, 236

C

CACREP (Council for Accreditation of Counseling and Related Educational Programs), 22–23
Camus, A., 187
CBT. *See* Cognitive behavior therapy
Centers for Disease Control and Prevention (CDC), 61
Challenging Questions Worksheet, 133–134
Child protective services, 23, 35–36, 38
Children and adolescents
　abuse and neglect of, 23, 36, 38, 170–171, 176
　bullying of, 43, 74, 152–155, 207–209
　depression in, 67, 174
　medication consultations for, 175–177
　mood rating procedure for, 63–65, 153
　motivational interviewing with, 100–101, 120
　neighborhood safety for, 59, 237
　reporting responsibilities for, 34–36
　suicide rates among, 54, 55f
　suicide risk factors for, 58, 59
　teacher support for, 238
　therapeutic relationships with, 97, 115
Choi, K. W., 168–169
Civil commitment. *See* Involuntary hospitalization
Clients. *See also* Therapeutic relationships
　collaboration with, 27–30, 62–67
　eliciting risk and protective factors from, 26–27
　high-risk, 28, 126, 196, 215, 237
　LGBTQ+. *See* LGBTQ+ clients
　matching language of, 129–130
　resistance of. *See* Resistance
　self-control of, 31, 72, 73, 75, 164
　terminally ill, 37, 200
　transference reactions in, 193
Clinical decision-making, 22, 47, 81–82
Cognitive behavior therapy (CBT), 77, 113–114, 133–136, 184
Cognitive dimension, 111–137
　alternatives to suicide intervention in, 121–126, 140
　behavioral activation in, 124–125, 140
　case examples, 116, 118–126, 121t
　clinical application of, 17

　cognitive behavior therapy in, 113–114, 133–136
　collaborative problem-solving in, 113, 117–120, 128
　core beliefs in, 113–115, 133, 135–136
　decision-making dilemmas in, 126–127
　empathy in, 115–116, 128
　hopelessness in, 112–113, 118, 127–133, 135
　maladaptive thinking in, 112–114
　motivational interviewing in, 120–121
　overview, 15, 16t
　practitioner guidance, 137
　problem-solving impairments in, 113
　psychoeducation in, 123–125
　self-hatred in, 114–115, 136
　strengths-based approach in, 115, 131
　working in, 112–115
Cognitive distortions, 123–124, 127–128, 131, 133, 135
Cognitive processing therapy, 77, 184, 196, 226
Cognitive reappraisal, 133–135, 134f
Collaboration. *See also* Collaborative safety planning
　on counseling goals, 108
　in decision-making, 80
　on framing strategies, 104
　invitations for, 64, 95, 96
　in motivational interviewing, 99
　in problem-solving, 51, 80, 113, 117–120, 128
　resistance to, 29
　in therapeutic assessment, 49–50
Collaborative empiricism, 114, 115, 133, 135
Collaborative safety planning
　failure of, 230
　firearms in, 18, 31, 81, 221–223
　risk and protective factor considerations in, 27
　skill development for, 22
Collateral informants, 28, 51, 82
Collectivist orientation, 155–159, 188, 191
Collins, Judy, 15, 16
Columbia-Suicide Severity Rating Scale (C-SSRS), 61
Coming Together to Care (postvention toolkit), 46

Command hallucinations, 56, 81
Commiseration, 239–240
Commitment to intervention. *See* Safety planning
Communication. *See also* Listening skills; Questions
  anger management and, 108
  interprofessional, 197
  with prescribers, 166
  on safety planning, 95
  training in, 149, 152
Compassion
  boundary setting and, 41
  empathic commiseration and, 240
  expression of, 22
  in motivational interviewing, 99
  self-compassion, 89, 102
  in suicide assessment, 62
  in therapeutic assessment, 49
  in therapeutic relationship, 108, 121, 190
Competencies. *See also* Suicide competencies
  advocacy, 242
  multicultural, 194
Conduct disorder, 56
Confidentiality, 28–30, 36–40, 82
Consent. *See* Informed consent
Constructionism, ix, 15, 188
Consultations
  on boundary setting, 42
  documentation of, 30, 31
  importance of, 44
  on legal issues, 32
  medication, 175–177
  for risk level determination, 28
  spiritual, 198
  in suicide assessment, 51, 82
Contextual dimension, 235–244
  activism in, 242
  clinical application of, 18
  coping strategies in, 239–242
  discernment and goal setting in, 240–241
  empathic commiseration in, 239–240
  literature review, 236–238
  overview, 15, 16*t*, 235–236
  practitioner guidance, 244
  toxic stress in, 239, 241
  uncontrollable aversive events in, 238–239, 243
Contextual risk factors, 57–59

Coping strategies
  in behavioral dimension, 215
  in cognitive dimension, 119, 120
  in contextual dimension, 239–242
  development of, ix, 74
  in distress tolerance, 106
  in emotional dimension, 97
  for mental health professionals, 6–8
  orientation to reasons for dying, 77
  positive psychology and, 8
  in safety planning, 224, 226–227
  self-regulation, 154, 198
  for veterans, 197
Core beliefs, 89, 113–115, 133, 135–136, 144, 159
Coronavirus. *See* COVID-19 pandemic
Council for Accreditation of Counseling and Related Educational Programs (CACREP), 22–23
Counterconditioning, 177–179
Countertransference, 50, 103
COVID-19 pandemic, 3, 10, 39, 227, 238
Cramer, R. J., 24, 26, 47
Crisis response planning. *See* Safety planning
Crisis Text Line, 39
C-SSRS (Columbia-Suicide Severity Rating Scale), 61
Cultural competency, 194
Cultural disconnection and dislocation, 191–192
Cultural-spiritual dimension, 187–211
  acculturative stress in, 191–192
  case examples, 196–205, 202*t*, 207–209
  clinical application of, 17
  collectivist orientation in, 188, 191
  cultural disconnection and dislocation in, 191–192
  discussions of religion and spirituality in, 192–193
  empathy in, 190, 192, 193
  excommunication and exile in, 197–198
  exploring, framing, and enhancing meaning in, 201–203
  forgiveness in, 202, 206, 208
  intersectionality in, 191, 193–195, 195*f*
  meaninglessness and meaning fulfillment in, 190–191, 201–203, 209
  moral injury in, 195–197
  overview, 15, 16*t*, 187–188
  passive suicidal ideation in, 198, 200–201, 209

practitioner guidance, 211
reconstructing community
connections in, 206
religious/spiritual disconnection
and connection in, 189–190
seeking higher causes in, 207–209
strengths-based approach in, 193,
196
working in, 188–192
Cutting. *See* Self-mutilation
Cyberbullying, 152–155, 236

D

DBT. *See* Dialectical behavior therapy
Debriefings, 33, 197
Decision-making
on breaching confidentiality, 82
clinical, 22, 47, 81–82
collaborative, 80
complexities of, 34
dilemmas related to, 126–127
documentation of, 22, 30–32, 47, 51
ethical, 22
facilitation of, 190
Demographic risk factors, 53–55, 54–55f
Depression. *See also* Antidepressants
adverse childhood experiences
and, 171
assessment of, 68, 100
behavioral theory of, 216
in children and adolescents, 67, 174
empathetic reactions to, 22
exercise for, 167–169, 168f, 172–174
framing strategies for, 103
genetic predispositions for, 168–169
hopelessness and, 127, 128
irritability and, 67
in LGBTQ+ clients, 58
mindfulness-based approaches for, 179
postpartum, 167
psychiatric model of, 14
sadness and, 90
screening for, 62
social media use and, 144
suicide risk and, 2, 55, 81
Three Good Things activity and, 9
Desensitization, 51, 56, 72, 170, 215, 218–219
Dialectical behavior therapy (DBT), 104–106, 114, 177, 206, 216, 230

Discrimination
in contextual dimension, 18, 238
racism, 143, 193, 238, 239
systemic, 191–192
Disease as factor in suicide risk, 57
Disinhibition, 72
Dispositional pain insensitivity, 215
Distance counseling, 39–41
Distress tolerance, 17, 77, 97, 105–106
Diversity. *See* Cultural-spiritual dimension; Race and ethnicity
Dobson, D. and K. S., 136
Documentation
of consultations, 30, 31
of decision-making, 22, 30–32, 47, 51
of informed consent, 30, 31, 36
modifications to, 44
recommendations for, 30–32
of safety planning, 31
in suicide assessment, 51, 82–83
Drugs. *See* Substance use
Duty to protect, 32, 34
Dysfunctional relationship patterns, 145

E

Eating disorders, 56
Education and training
on communication skills, 149, 152
for mental health professionals, 22–23
psychoeducation, 123–125, 180–181, 229
on self-regulation skills, 198
on social skills, 151–155, 236
teacher support in, 238
Ego integrity vs. despair, 207
Eliot, T. S., 205
Ellis, Albert, 128, 135
EMDR. *See* Eye-movement desensitization and reprocessing
Emergency procedures, 39, 40, 224, 228
Emotional change trick, 106–108
Emotional dimension, 87–110
anger in, 88–90, 107, 108
case examples, 94–97, 98t, 100–102
clinical application of, 17
dialectical behavior therapy in, 104–106
emotional dysregulation in, 81, 90–91, 106
empathy in, 88, 91, 93–98

(continued)

Emotional dimension *(continued)*
  excruciating distress in, 88–90, 104
  framing strategies in, 101–104
  motivational interviewing in, 98–101
  overview, 15, 16*t*
  practitioner guidance, 109–110
  problem-solving in, 97–98
  sadness in, 90, 107
  shame and guilt in, 89, 107
  strengths-based approach in, 87, 91, 95
  three-step emotional change trick, 106–108
  working in, 88–91
Emotional dysregulation, 81, 90–91, 106
Emotional regulation, 17, 91, 106, 177
Empathic commiseration, 239–240
Empathy
  barriers to, 13
  in client interactions, 22, 25–26, 115, 128–130
  in cognitive dimension, 115–116, 128
  in contextual dimension, 239–240
  in cultural-spiritual dimension, 190, 192, 193
  in emotional dimension, 88, 91, 93–98
  listening skills and, 28
  in physical dimension, 180
  in strengths-based approach, viii
  in suicide assessment, 49, 50, 66, 83
Empty chair technique, 151
Encouragement, 111–112, 174, 203
Environmental influences on mood management, 78
Epigenetics, 168
Erikson, Erik and Joan, 207
Ethical issues, 33–47
  ACA Code of Ethics, 23
  boundary setting, 39, 41–44, 228
  case example, 33–34
  confidentiality, 28–30, 36–40, 82
  decision-making, 22
  in distance counseling, 39–41
  duty to protect, 32, 34
  ethical bracketing, 11–13, 19
  informed consent, 28–31, 36–41, 82, 228
  postvention, 46–47
  reporting responsibilities, 34–36
  values-based conflicts, 12–13, 19
Ethnicity. *See* Race and ethnicity

Evocation, 99
Excommunication and exile, 197–198
Excruciating distress, 88–90, 104, 114, 117–118, 169
Exercise, 163, 167–169, 168*f*, 171–174
Existential nihilism, 15, 190
Eye-movement desensitization and reprocessing (EMDR), 77, 136, 171–172, 183, 184, 226

F

Facebook, 144
Failed belongingness, 139, 140, 143, 144, 149
Family counseling, 83, 94, 97, 172
Family tree of strengths, 160
Felitti, V. J., 171
Females. *See* Women
Finn, Stephen, 49
Firearms
  access to, 18, 57, 58, 216, 220, 229
  in collaborative safety planning, 18, 31, 81, 221–223
  lethality of suicide attempts involving, 71
  suicide risk and, 58, 216, 220
Fischer, Constance, 49
Flemons, D., 50
Floyd, George, 238–239
Fogg, B. J., 174–175
Forest bathing (*shinrin-yoku*), 243
Forgiveness, 90, 160, 202, 206, 208, 220
Forgiveness letters, 160
Framing strategies
  in emotional dimension, 101–104
  failure of, 103–104
  hospitalization and, 230–231
  normalizing frame, 63, 65–66, 70, 72, 193
Frankl, Viktor, 103, 188, 216
Free association, 112, 159
Fromm-Reichmann, Frieda, 166
Functional model, 14, 15, 19
Functional relationship patterns, 159–160

G

Garbarino, James, 241
Gay clients. *See* LGBTQ+ clients
Gemeinschaftsgefühl (social interest), 141–142, 151

Gender differences
  in poverty, 237
  sexually abused as children, 170
  suicide rates among, 54, 54f, 207
Genetic predispositions, 165–166, 168–169
Gentle assumption strategy, 63
Geographic conditions, 58
Gestalt therapy, 151
Gilbert, Elizabeth M., 136
Goal setting, 146, 151, 155–157, 159, 175, 240–241
Goh, M. T., 50
Gralnik, L. M., 50
Granello, D. H., 24, 26, 27
Gratitude letters, 160, 232
Grief, 144, 198, 200
Guilt
  in emotional dimension, 89, 107
  in mental health professionals, 32, 44
  substance use and, 21
Guns. *See* Firearms

H

Habit formation, 174–175
Hahn, W. K., 62
Hallucinations, 56, 81, 177
Happy places, 78
Harassment, sexual, 238
Harris, K. M., 50
Health Insurance Portability and Accountability Act of 1996, 40, 225
Herbert, Anne, 141
Herlihy, B. J., 12–13, 19
High-risk clients, 28, 126, 196, 215, 237
Hindman, R., 218
Hispanic Americans
  discrimination against, 238
  suicide deaths among, 54, 54f
Homosexual clients. *See* LGBTQ+ clients
Hopelessness
  assessment of, 51, 68–69, 73
  Beck on, 62, 68, 111
  bottom-up approach to, 130–133
  in cognitive dimension, 112–113, 118, 127–133, 135
  empathetic reactions to, 22, 25, 115, 128–130
  indications of, 17, 77
  integrating solutions to, 128–129
  in LGBTQ+ clients, 58
  resonating with, 127–128

Hospitalization
  of children, 176
  framing of, 230–231
  involuntary, 28, 80, 231
  post-hospital discharge, 56
  safety planning vs., 127
  safety watch during, 215
Hostility, 50, 67, 84, 88, 93

I

IBH (integrated behavioral health) model, 196–197
Illness as factor in suicide risk, 57
Imagery rehearsal therapy, 182–184
Impulsivity
  from arousal and agitation, 170
  assessment of, 72, 73, 75
  conduct disorder and, 56
  disinhibition and, 72
  inability to collaborate and, 29
  trait impulsivity, 215
  treatments for, 216
Indigenous peoples. *See* Native Americans
Informed consent, 28–31, 36–41, 82, 228
Insomnia, 56, 171, 179–181, 183, 184
Inspiring events, witnessing of, 117
Instagram, 144
Integrated behavioral health (IBH) model, 196–197
Intentional kindness, 141–142
Interpersonal dimension, 139–161
  case examples, 146–159, 149t
  clinical application of, 17
  collectivist orientation in, 155–159
  dysfunctional relationship patterns in, 145
  failed belongingness in, 139, 140, 143, 144, 149
  functional relationship patterns in, 159–160
  loss and grief in, 144
  overview, 15, 16t
  perceived burdengness in, 139, 140, 144
  practitioner guidance, 161
  romantic relationship breakups in, 143, 144, 149–151
  social disconnection in, 141–143
  social skills deficits in, 144–145
  social skills training in, 151–155, 236
  (continued)

Interpersonal dimension *(continued)*
  social universe activity in, 145–149
  strengths-based approach in, 159–160
  toxic relationships in, 146–149
  working in, 140–145
Intersectionality, 191, 193–195, 195*f*
Involuntary hospitalization, 28, 80, 231
Irritability, 22, 51, 67–68, 84, 90, 127
Isolation. *See* Social isolation
IS PATH WARM warning signs, 60, 81

J

Jacobson, Edmund, 178
Jacobson, N. S., 218
Jobes, D. A., 26, 32, 62, 76, 77
Joiner, Thomas, 4, 139, 140, 143, 144, 165–166, 215
Jones, Mary Cover, 177, 178

K

Kindness, 141–142
King, Laura, 210
Klonsky, E. D., 213
Knowledge acquisition, 22
Kocet, M. M., 12–13, 19

L

Latinos/Latinas. *See* Hispanic Americans
Lee, C. C., 194
Legal policies and procedures, 32
Lethal means restriction, 71, 219–225, 228–229
LGBTQ+ clients
  cyberbullying and, 152–155
  discrimination against, 191
  rejection experienced by, 146
  religious condemnation of, 198
  suicide risk among, 58
  therapeutic relationship with, 199
Li, Qing, 243
Linehan, M. M., 29, 77, 90–91, 104, 216–217, 230
Listening skills, 28, 64–65, 67–69, 108, 145, 193
Lithium, 216
Losses
  emotional distress over, 140
  existential nihilism triggered by, 190
  grief associated with, 144, 198

mental health professionals and, 6
replacement of, 204
as suicide risk factor, 57
Lyubomirsky, Sonja, 92

M

Macroaggressions, 17, 191
Major depression. *See* Depression
Maladaptive thinking, 112–114
Males. *See* Men
Marks, L. I., 62
May, A. M., 213
Meaningfulness and meaninglessness, 190–191, 201–203, 209
Medication consultations, 175–177
Meditation, 8, 178, 197, 220
Meichenbaum, Donald, 170
Men
  in poverty, 237
  sexually abused as children, 170
  suicide rates among, 54, 54*f*, 207
Mental constriction, 73, 113, 118, 119, 121, 125
Mental disorder risk factors, 55–57. *See also specific disorders*
Mental health professionals
  anxiety of, 1–2, 4, 18, 22, 50, 126
  competencies. *See* Competencies
  consultation groups for, 44
  coping strategies for, 6–8
  counseling for, 10–11
  countertransference and, 50, 103
  education and training for, 22–23
  emotional responses to suicide, 6, 24, 44
  guilt in, 32, 44
  relationship with clients. *See* Clients; Therapeutic relationships
  self-care for, vii, 6–11, 18, 33, 89
  self-doubt in, 2, 18, 44, 47, 126
MI. *See* Motivational interviewing
Microaggressions, 17, 191, 238, 244
Military veterans. *See* Veterans
Miller, M., 70
Miller, W. R., 98, 99
Mindfulness
  in addictions treatment, 220
  for anger management, 108
  for depression treatment, 179
  in dialectical behavior therapy, 104–105, 177
  emotional regulation and, 106
  for veterans, 179, 197

Mindfulness-based cognitive therapy, 114, 241
Minorities. See Race and ethnicity
Minors. See Children and adolescents
Miracle question, 131
Mood management strategies, 45, 78
Mood rating procedure, 63–65, 153
Moral injury, 171, 195–197
Motivational interviewing (MI)
  amplification in, 128, 129
  in cognitive dimension, 120–121
  in emotional dimension, 98–101
  firearms safety and, 223
  nondirective, 12, 13
  principles of, 98–99
Multicultural and Social Justice Counseling Competencies, 194
Multiculturalism. See Cultural-spiritual dimension; Race and ethnicity
Multidimensional Scale of Perceived Social Support, 145
Murphy, J. J., 129
Music, 45
Mutual reminiscence, 92, 220

N

Narcotics Anonymous, 220
Narrative therapies, 136, 153, 184
National Association of Social Workers, 23, 41
National Board for Certified Counselors, 41
National Comorbidity Survey, 170–171
National Institute of Mental Health, 61
National Suicide Prevention Lifeline, 39, 224
Native Americans
  cultural disconnection and dislocation of, 191
  discrimination against, 191
  dreams in tribal culture of, 184
  suicide as viewed by, 203, 205
  suicide deaths among, 54, 54–55f
  sweat lodges and, 197
Negative core beliefs, 114–115, 136
Negative predictions, 135
Neglect, 23, 35–36, 38
Neighborhood safety, 59, 237
Niebuhr, Reinhold, 240
Nietzsche, Friedrich, 190
Nightmares, 171, 179, 181–184
Nondirective listening skills, 193
Nonjudgmental acceptance, 241

Nonsuicidal self-injury. See Self-mutilation
Norcross, J. C., 7
Normalizing frame, 63, 65–66, 70, 72, 193
No-suicide contracts, ix, 80

O

Occupation as factor in suicide risk, 58–59
O'Connor, S. S., 32, 215
One-mindfully process, 105
"One thing" question, 51, 76–77
Online counseling, 39–41
Open-ended questions, 66, 223
Opioids, 56

P

Pandemic. See COVID-19 pandemic
Passive suicidal ideation, 61, 83, 152, 198, 200–201, 209
Pastoral counselors, 42–43
Patient Health Questionnaire–9, 62, 69, 100
Perceived burdensomeness, 139, 140, 144
Personality disorders, 56, 90–91, 106, 216
Personal loss as factor in suicide risk, 57
Person-first language, ix
Peterson, Christopher, 142–143
Physical activity. See Exercise
Physical dimension, 163–185
  agitation and arousal in, 169–170, 184
  anxiety and anxiety management in, 170, 177–179
  biogenetics and medical treatments in, 165–166
  case examples, 172–174, 176–177, 179–184, 185t
  clinical application of, 17
  empathy in, 180
  exercise in, 163, 167–169, 168f, 171–174
  medication consultations in, 175–177
  overview, 15, 16t
  practitioner guidance, 185
  psychoeducation in, 180–181
  self-regulation in, 177–179
  sleep disturbances in, 171, 179–184
  trauma in, 169–171, 182–184
  working in, 163–171

Physical illness as factor in suicide risk, 57
Pit of despair metaphor, 115, 116
PMR (progressive muscle relaxation), 178
Pomodoro technique, 7
Positive mood questions, 69–70
Positive psychology. *See also* Wellness practices
    in cognitive dimension, 112
    coping strategies and, 8
    in cultural-spiritual dimension, 190
    defined, x
    in emotional dimension, 90
    in interpersonal dimension, 143, 159–160
    suicide assessment and, 70
Post-hospital discharge, 56
Postpartum depression, 167
Posttraumatic stress disorder (PTSD)
    insomnia and, 171
    psychiatric model of, 14
    substance use and, 156
    suicide risk and, 56, 57
    in veterans, 156, 195–197
Postvention, 46–47
Poverty, 59, 191, 236, 237
Prejudice. *See* Discrimination
Privacy. *See* Confidentiality
Problem-solving
    collaborative, 51, 80, 113, 117–120, 128
    competency in, 26
    in emotional dimension, 97–98
    impairments in, 73, 113, 169, 171
    relational, 160
    unsolvable problems, 241
    in values-based conflicts, 12
Progressive muscle relaxation (PMR), 178
Prolonged exposure, 184
Protective factors
    assessment of, 59, 81
    clinician knowledge of, 26–27, 51–53, 59
    defined, 51–52
    eliciting from clients, 26–27
    general, 59
    inaccuracy of, 14
    religious/spiritual, 189
    specific, 59
Proximity of social support networks, 71–72
Psychache. *See* Excruciating distress
Psychiatric model, 14
Psychodynamic approaches, 159
Psychoeducation, 123–125, 180–181, 229
Psychological reactance, 25, 88, 89
Psychotropic medications, 166, 177. *See also* Antidepressants
PTSD. *See* Posttraumatic stress disorder

Q

Queer or questioning clients. *See* LGBTQ+ clients
Questions
    cultural considerations, 202
    miracle, 131
    "one thing," 51, 76–77
    open-ended, 66, 223
    positive mood, 69–70
    reflective, 148
    6-months-to-live, 200–201, 203
    Socratic, 128, 131, 134, 223
    solution-focused, 73, 129, 131, 201
    "what's helping now?," 75–76

R

Race and ethnicity. *See also specific racial and ethnic groups*
    discrimination based on, 191–192, 238
    protests against racial injustice, 238–239
    suicide deaths by, 54–55, 54–55f, 192
Racism, 143, 193, 238, 239
Rashid, T., 160
Reality therapy, 76
Reasons for Living (RFL) inventory, 61, 77, 216–218
Recordkeeping. *See* Documentation
Reflective listening, 64, 67–68
Reflective questions, 148
Reframing strategies. *See* Framing strategies
Reinecke, M. A., 117
Religion. *See* Cultural-spiritual dimension
Reporting responsibilities, 34–36
Resistance
    activation of, 11, 25, 93
    to collaboration, 29
    to family counseling, 94
    motivational interviewing and, 120
    psychological reactance, 25, 88, 89
    to rational rebuttals, 128
    to social support networks, 30

Revenge fantasies, 90
RFL (Reasons for Living) inventory, 61, 77, 216–218
Rinpoche, Sogyal, 203
Risk categorization, 28–29, 80–82
Risk factor model, 14
Risk factors
　assessment of, 51–59, 80–81
　clinician knowledge of, 26–27, 51–59
　contextual, 57–59
　defined, 51
　demographic, 53–55, 54–55f
　eliciting from clients, 26–27
　genetic, 165–166
　inaccuracy of, 14, 26
　mental disorders and psychiatric treatment, 55–57
　personal and behavioral, 57–59
　previous suicide attempts, 26, 57, 80
　social isolation, 2, 15, 30, 57, 170
Rogers, Carl, 93, 116
Rollnick, S., 98, 99
Romantic relationship breakups, 143, 144, 149–151
Rosenberg, J. I., 101–102
Rudd, M. D., 14, 29, 75, 133–135, 221, 223

S

Sadness
　cultural considerations, 157
　in emotional dimension, 90, 107
　hopelessness and, 111
　in mental health professionals, 44
　music as trigger for, 45
Safety planning. *See also* Collaborative safety planning
　assessment of, 51
　communication on, 95
　coping strategies in, 224, 226–227
　documentation of, 31
　emergency procedures in, 224, 228
　in emotional dimension, 97
　for high-risk clients, 28
　hospitalization vs., 127
　lethal means restriction in, 224–225, 228–229
　short-term, 29
　social support networks in, 30, 119, 224, 227–228
　suicide desensitization and, 219
　warning signs in, 224–226

SAMHSA (Substance Abuse and Mental Health Services Administration), 231
Savoring positive moments, 91–92
Schemas. *See* Core beliefs
Schema therapy, 136
Schizophrenia, 56, 102, 176–177
School counselors, 23, 34–37, 43–44, 67, 82
Selective serotonin reuptake inhibitors (SSRIs), 56–57, 75, 166, 169, 196
Self-awareness, 2, 22, 24–25, 194
Self-care, vii, 6–11, 18, 33, 89, 102–103
Self-control, 31, 72, 73, 75, 164
Self-doubt, 2, 18, 44, 47, 126, 146
Self-hatred, 114–115, 136, 146
Self-mutilation, 3, 17, 52–53, 57, 72, 215
Self-regulation, 5, 154, 177–179, 198
Self-soothing behaviors, 10, 18
Self-talk, 175
Seligman, Martin, 9, 160
Serenity Prayer, 240–241
Sertraline (Zoloft), 167–168, 168f
Seven-dimension model
　behavior in. *See* Behavioral dimension
　clinical application of, 17–18
　cognitions in. *See* Cognitive dimension
　context in. *See* Contextual dimension
　culture and spirituality in. *See* Cultural-spiritual dimension
　dimension overview, 15, 16t, 19
　emotions in. *See* Emotional dimension
　interpersonal issues in. *See* Interpersonal dimension
　physical body in. *See* Physical dimension
　as strengths-based approach, 15, 19
Sexual abuse, 170–171, 176
Sexual harassment, 238
Sexual identity. *See* LGBTQ+ clients
Shame
　in emotional dimension, 89
　impact on clients, 12
　in mental health professionals, 44
　in moral injury, 195
　normalizing frame and, 66
　strategies for alleviating, 236
　triggering of, 157, 159, 189–190, 198
Shantideva (Buddhist scholar), 240
Shea, S. C., 63

Shinrin-yoku (forest bathing), 243
Shneidman, Edwin
  on alternatives to suicide
    intervention, 121
  on emotional distress, ix, 87, 88, 91,
    113, 235
  on mental constriction, 73
  on postvention, 46
  on reframing strategies, 101
Short-term goal setting, 175
Short-term safety planning, 29
6-months-to-live question, 200–201,
  203
Skill development, 22, 91
Skinner, B. F., 213, 239
SLAP assessment, 70–72, 79
Sleep disturbances, 56, 171, 179–184
Social anxiety, 149, 152
Social constructionism, ix, 15, 188, 236
Social disconnection, 141–143, 169
Social distancing, 3, 10, 39, 143, 225,
  238
Social interest (*Gemeinschaftsgefühl*),
  141–142, 151
Social isolation
  negative effects of, 151
  suicide risk and, 2, 15, 30, 57, 170
  toxic relationships and, 146
Social media, 38–39, 144, 154
Social skills deficits, 144–145
Social skills training, 151–155, 236
Social support networks, 30, 71–72,
  119, 220, 224, 227–228
Social trauma, 58
Social universe activity, 145–149
Social workers, 43
Sociopolitical conditions as factor in
  suicide risk, 58
Socratic questioning, 128, 131, 134, 223
Solution-focused questions, 73, 129,
  131, 201
Solution-focused therapy, 153
Specificity of suicide plans, 70–71
Spirituality. *See* Cultural-spiritual
  dimension
Spoiling cognitions, 123–124
SSF (Suicide Status Form), 62, 76, 77
SSRIs. *See* Selective serotonin reuptake
  inhibitors
Stanley, B., 29, 71, 224
Stimulus control, 9–10
Stone, Carolyn, 34–36
Strengths and Solutions Worksheet,
  133–134, 134*f*

Strengths-based approach. *See also*
  Positive psychology
  in behavioral dimension, 214
  in cognitive dimension, 115, 131
  in cultural-spiritual dimension,
    193, 196
  in emotional dimension, 87, 91, 95
  in interpersonal dimension,
    159–160
  language use in, ix–x
  principles of, vii–ix
  seven-dimension model as, 15, 19
  to suicide assessment, 66, 69, 73, 80
Substance Abuse and Mental Health
  Services Administration (SAMHSA),
  231
Substance use
  addictions treatment for, 219–220
  adverse childhood experiences
    and, 171
  assessment of, 17, 51
  counseling for, 21
  desensitization and, 51, 56, 72, 170,
    215
  impulsivity and, 216
  motivational interviewing and, 100
  PTSD and, 156
  self-soothing through, 10
  suicide attempts and, 1
  suicide risk and, 56
  toxic relationships and, 146
Suicidal intent, 27, 51, 78–79, 81,
  214–215
Suicide Affect-Behavior-Cognition
  scale, 50
Suicide and suicidal ideation
  assessment of. *See* Suicide assessment
  collaborative exploration of, 27–28,
    62–67
  cultural perspectives on, 203, 205
  emotional responses to, 6, 24, 44
  empathetic reactions to, 25
  laws regarding, 32
  media influences on, 3, 46–47
  passive, 61, 83, 152, 198, 200–201, 209
  prevalence of, 2–3, 53–55, 54–55*f*
  protective factors against. *See*
    Protective factors
  reporting requirements, 34–36
  risk factors for. *See* Risk factors
  treatment models, 14–15, 19. *See
    also* Seven-dimension model
  warning signs of. *See* Warning
    signs

Suicide assessment, 49–85
　of arousal/agitation, 75
　collaborative exploration of
　　suicidal ideation, 62–67
　collateral informants in, 51, 82
　consultations in, 51, 82
　core components of, 51, 84–85
　documentation in, 51, 82–83
　gathering of details in, 66
　gentle assumption strategy for, 63
　of hopelessness, 51, 68–69, 73
　of impulsivity, 72, 73, 75
　instruments and questionnaires for,
　　50, 60–62, 68, 69, 79
　of irritability and hostility, 67–68
　mood rating procedure for, 63–65,
　　153
　normalizing frame for, 63, 65–66,
　　70, 72
　"one thing" question for, 51, 76–77
　positive mood questions in, 69–70
　practitioner guidance, 84–85
　of previous suicide attempts, 72–74
　of reasons for living and dying,
　　77–78
　of risk and protective factors,
　　51–59, 80–81
　risk categorization in, 80–82
　science and art of, 49
　of self-control, 72, 73, 75
　strengths-based approach to, 66,
　　69, 73, 80
　of suicidal intent, 51, 78–79, 81
　suicide plan evaluations, 33, 51,
　　70–72
　as therapeutic assessment, 49–50,
　　53, 69, 77, 83, 145
　of trauma, 79–80, 182–183
　of warning signs, 52, 60, 81
　"what's helping now?" question
　　for, 75–76
Suicide attempts
　assessment of, 72–74
　gender differences in, 54
　LGBTQ+ clients and, 58
　prevalence of, 3
　as risk factor, 26, 57, 80
　substance use and, 1
Suicide competencies, 21–48. See also
　Ethical issues
　collaboration with clients, 29–30
　collaborative exploration of
　　suicidal ideation, 27–28, 62–67
　core competencies, 24–33, 47

　debriefings, 33, 197
　defined, 21
　documentation. See Documentation
　elements of, 4, 22
　empathy. See Empathy
　knowledge of risk and protective
　　factors, 26–27, 51–59
　legal policies and procedures, 32
　practitioner guidance, 47–48
　professional guidance on, 22–23
　risk categorization, 28–29, 80–82
　self-awareness, 2, 22, 24–25, 194
　self-care. See Self-care
　strengthening of, 5, 26
　support network recruitment, 30
Suicide contagion, 58
Suicide desensitization, 215, 218–219
Suicide plans, 33, 51, 70–72, 146, 150,
　214–215
Suicide Prevention Resource Center, 47
Suicide Status Form (SSF), 62, 76, 77
Suicide treatment models, 14–15, 19.
　See also Seven-dimension model
Sweat lodges, 197
Systemic discrimination, 191–192

T

Teacher support, 238. See also Education
　and training
Teenagers. See Children and adolescents
Teen Options for Change (TOC) inter-
　vention, 100–101
Telehealth counseling, 39–41
Terminally ill clients, 37, 200
Text-based counseling, 39–41
Therapeutic assessment, 49–50, 53, 69,
　77, 83, 145
Therapeutic relationships. See also
　Clients
　barriers to, 11, 27, 52
　boundary setting in, 39, 41–44, 228
　with children and adolescents, 97,
　　115
　compassion in, 108, 121, 190
　damage to, 30, 36, 82, 104–105
　development and maintenance of,
　　2, 22
　in distance counseling, 40
　with LGBTQ+ clients, 199
　monitoring, 143
　repairing, 104
Three Good Things activity, 9

Three-step emotional change trick, 106–108
TOC (Teen Options for Change) intervention, 100–101
Toxic relationships, 146–149
Toxic stress, 239, 241
Training. *See* Education and training
Trait impulsivity, 215
Transference, 193
Transgender clients. *See* LGBTQ+ clients
Trauma. *See also* Posttraumatic stress disorder
    assessment of, 79–80, 182–183
    evidence-based treatments for, 183–184
    manifestations of, 169–171
    self-hatred resulting from, 136
    social, 58
    vicarious, 8, 215
Trauma-focused cognitive behavior therapy, 77, 136, 184
Traumatic brain injuries, 57, 93, 115, 179
12-step programs, 220

U

Uncontrollable aversive events, 238–239, 243
Unemployment, 57

V

Validation, 65–68, 129–130, 147, 193
Values-based conflicts, 12–13, 19
Vandenbos, G., 7
Veterans
    firearms safety and, 223
    PTSD in, 156, 195–197
    suicide risk among, 57, 81, 195–196
    traumatic brain injuries in, 93, 115, 179
Vicarious traumatization, 8, 215
Video counseling, 39–41

W

Warning signs
    assessment of, 52, 60, 81
    clinician knowledge of, 27, 51–52, 60
    defined, 52
    inaccuracy of, 14
    IS PATH WARM, 60, 81
    in safety planning, 224–226
Wellness practices
    creating new habits, 174–175
    expressing gratitude, 232
    forest bathing, 243
    intentional kindness, 141–142
    mood management strategies, 45, 78
    savoring positive moments, 91–92
    Three Good Things activity, 9
    witness something inspiring, 117
    Your Best Possible Self activity, 210
"What's helping now?" question, 75–76
White Americans, suicide deaths among, 54, 54–55f, 192
Wollersheim, J. P., 70
Women. *See also* Gender differences
    self-mutilation among, 57
    sexually abused as children, 170–171
    suicide rates among, 54, 54f
Working alliances. *See* Therapeutic relationships
Wubbolding, R. E., 202

Y

Yalom, Irvin, 200–203
Yoga, 163, 169, 173, 197
Young, J. E., 136
Your Best Possible Self activity, 210
Youth. *See* Children and adolescents

Z

Zoloft (sertraline), 167–168, 168f
Zur Institute, 40–41